single le...
HOMEPLANS

MW01041055

8th edition

the **Garlinghouse** company

Copyright 2001 by The Garlinghouse Co., Inc.
Glastonbury, Connecticut. Building a house
...m a design found in this publication without
...t purchasing a set of home plans is a copy-
...nt violation. Printed in the USA.
...e photographed home may have been modi-
...d to suit individual tastes

...rary of Congress No.: 00-136079
...N: 0-938708-97-x
...vers & Interior Layouts by Debra Novitch

TABLE OF CONTENTS

Publisher
JAMES D. MCNAIR III

Editorial Director
STEVE CULPEPPER

Managing Editor
DEBRA COCHRAN

Submit all Canadian plan orders to:
The Garlinghouse Company
60 Baffin Place, Unit #5
Waterloo, Ontario N2V 1Z7

Canadians Order only: 1-800-561-4169
Fax#: 1-800-719-3291
Customer Service#: 1-519-746-4169

PLAN: 20100

WIDE-OPEN AND CONVENIENT

TOTAL LIVING AREA	1,737 SQ. FT
MAIN AREA	1,737 SQ. FT.
BASEMENT	1,727 SQ. FT.
GARAGE	484 SQ. FT.
BEDROOMS	THREE
BATHROOMS	2 FULL
FOUNDATION	BASEMENT, SLAB OR CRAWL SPACE

PHOTOGRAPHY BY JOHN EHRENCLOU

BL/ML/ZIP/RRR

Stacked windows fill the wall in the front bedroom of this one-level home, creating an attractive facade. Around the corner, two more bedrooms and two full baths complete the bedroom wing, set apart for bedtime quiet. Notice the elegant vaulted-ceiling in the master bedroom, the master tub and shower illuminated by a skylight, and a dual vanity in both baths. Active areas enjoy a spacious feeling. Look at the high, sloping ceilings in the fire-placed living room, the sliders that unite the breakfast room and kitchen with an adjoining deck and the vaulted ceilings in the formal dining room off the foyer. The photographed home may have been modified to suit individual tastes.

MAIN AREA

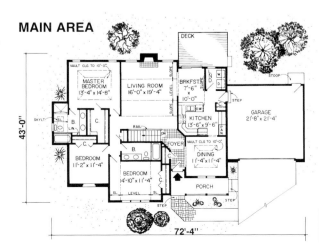

PRICE CODE B

STATELY HOME

With a traditional, elegant exterior and lively interior spaces, this three bedroom executive home makes both everyday life and entertaining a breeze. A palladian window floods the foyer with light for a dramatic entrance alluding to a surprising, open floor plan. Whip up a gourmet meal in the well-planned kitchen while chatting with family and friends in the large Great room with cathedral ceiling, fireplace and built-in cabinets. The screened porch, breakfast area and master suite access the deck with optional spa. The large master suite, located in the rear for privacy, features a luxurious skylit bath with separate shower, corner whirlpool tub and separate vanities. A skylit bonus room above the garage adds space when needed. The photographed home may have been modified to suit individual tastes.

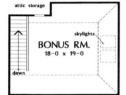

attic storage

BONUS RM.
18-0 x 19-0

skylights

down

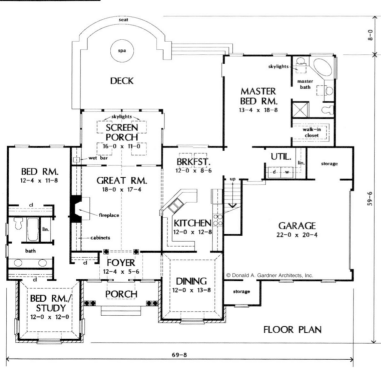

seat

spa

DECK

8-0

skylights

MASTER BED RM.
13-4 x 18-8

master bath

walk-in closet

skylights

SCREEN PORCH
16-0 x 11-0

wet bar

BRKFST.
12-0 x 8-6

UTIL.

lin.

storage

d w

59-6

BED RM.
12-4 x 11-8

GREAT RM.
18-0 x 17-4

fireplace

cl

lin.

bath

cabinets

up

KITCHEN
12-0 x 12-8

GARAGE
22-0 x 20-4

cl

d

FOYER
12-4 x 5-6

DINING
12-0 x 13-8

© Donald A. Gardner Architects, Inc.

BED RM./ STUDY
12-0 x 12-0

PORCH

storage

FLOOR PLAN

69-8

PRICE CODE E

TOTAL LIVING AREA	1,977 SQ. FT
MAIN FLOOR	1,977 SQ. FT.
BONUS AREA	430 SQ. FT.
GARAGE	610 SQ. FT.
BEDROOMS	THREE
BATHROOMS	2 FULL
FOUNDATION	CRAWL SPACE

PHOTOGRAPHY BY JON RILEY OF RILEY & RILEY PHOTOGRAPHY

BL/ML/ZIP/RRR

PLAN: 99803

PERFECT COMPACT RANCH

This Ranch home features a large sunken Great room, centralized with a cozy fireplace. The master bedroom has an unforgettable bathroom with a super skylight. The huge three-car plus garage can include a work area for the family carpenter. In the center of this home, a kitchen includes an eating nook for family gatherings. The porch at the rear of the house has easy access from the dining room. One other bedroom and a den, which can easily be converted to a bedroom, are on the opposite side of the house from the master bedroom. The photographed home may have been modified to suit individual tastes.

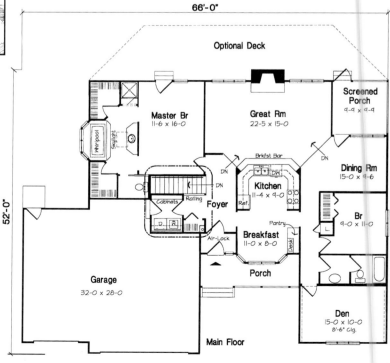

Crawl / Slab Option

66'-0"

52'-0"

Optional Deck

Master Br
11-6 x 16-0

Great Rm
22-5 x 15-0

Screened Porch
9-9 x 9-9

Whirlpool

Skylight

Brkfst Bar

Dining Rm
15-0 x 9-6

DN

DN

Kitchen
11-4 x 9-0

Cabinets

Railing

Foyer

Ref

Br
9-0 x 11-0

Pantry

Breakfast
11-0 x 8-0

Desk

Air-Lock

Garage
32-0 x 28-0

Porch

Den
15-0 x 10-0
8'-6" Clg.

Main Floor

TOTAL LIVING AREA	1,738 SQ. FT
MAIN FLOOR	1,738 SQ. FT.
BASEMENT	1,083 SQ. FT.
GARAGE	796 SQ. FT.
BEDROOMS	TWO
BATHROOMS	2 FULL
FOUNDATION	BASEMENT, SLAB OR CRAWL SPACE

PHOTOGRAPHY BY JOHN EHRENCLOU

BL/ML/ZIP/RRR

PLAN: 10839

VICTORIAN CHARM

This home combines the Victorian charm of yesteryear with a plan designed for today's families. Accented by columns, the Great room with fireplace is vaulted, while the foyer, dining room, kitchen, breakfast bay and bedroom/study boast impressive ten foot ceilings. With double door entry, the secluded master suite features a tray ceiling, walk in closet and private, skylit bath. Two additional bedrooms are located on the opposite side of the house and share a full bath with linen closet. Front and back porches extend the living space to the outdoors and the two-car garage offers storage space. The photographed home may have been modified to suit individual tastes.

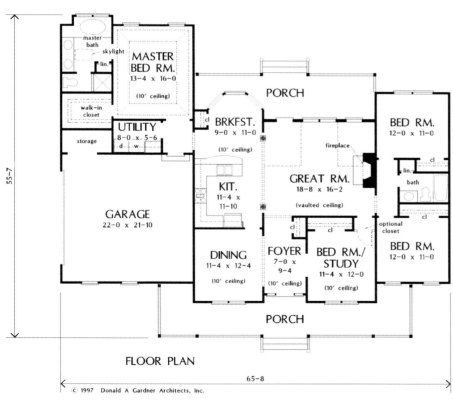

FLOOR PLAN

master bath
skylight
lin.

MASTER BED RM.
13-4 x 16-0
(10' ceiling)

walk-in closet

UTILITY
8-0 x 5-6
d · w

storage

GARAGE
22-0 x 21-10

cl

BRKFST.
9-0 x 11-0
(10' ceiling)

PORCH

KIT.
11-4 x 11-10

fireplace

GREAT RM.
18-8 x 16-2
(vaulted ceiling)

BED RM.
12-0 x 11-0

lin.
bath
cl

cl

DINING
11-4 x 12-4
(10' ceiling)

FOYER
7-0 x 9-4
(10' ceiling)

cl

BED RM./STUDY
11-4 x 12-0
(10' ceiling)

cl

optional closet

BED RM.
12-0 x 11-0

PORCH

55-7

65-8

© 1997 Donald A Gardner Architects, Inc.

TOTAL LIVING AREA	1,903 SQ. FT
MAIN FLOOR	1,903 SQ. FT.
GARAGE & STORAGE	531 SQ. FT.
BEDROOMS	FOUR
BATHROOMS	2 FULL
FOUNDATION	CRAWL SPACE

PHOTOGRAPHY BY JON RILEY OF RILEY & RILEY PHOTOGRAPHY

BL/ML/RRR

PLAN: 96405

GROWING FAMILIES

Great privacy as well as an open great room for gathering make this exciting three bedroom country home perfect for the active young family. The Great room features a fireplace, cathedral ceiling and built-in bookshelves. The kitchen is designed for efficient use with its food preparation island and pantry. The master suite with cathedral ceiling, walk-in closet and a luxurious bath provides a welcome retreat. A second floor bonus room makes a perfect study or play area. The photographed home may have been modified to suit individual tastes.

TOTAL LIVING AREA   1,787 SQ. FT
MAIN FLOOR   1,787 SQ. FT.
BONUS ROOM   326 SQ. FT.
GARAGE   521 SQ. FT.
BEDROOMS   THREE
BATHROOMS   2 FULL
FOUNDATION   CRAWL SPACE

PHOTOGRAPHY BY JON RILEY OF
RILEY & RILEY PHOTOGRAPHY

BL/ML/ZIP/RRR

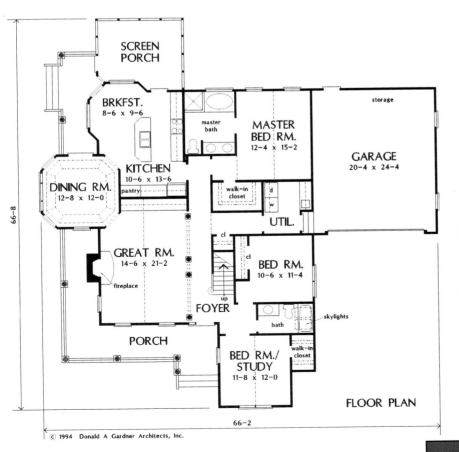

FLOOR PLAN

© 1994 Donald A Gardner Architects, Inc.

PLAN: 99805

CATHEDRAL CEILING

The clever use of interior space plus cathedral and tray ceilings gives this graceful home a feeling much larger than its 1,737 square feet. A cathedral ceiling and columns provide tremendous impact in the Great room, while the octagonal shape of the dining room provides plenty of windows for ample light. This shape is repeated in the open breakfast bay. The kitchen features a center island and a pantry. The master bedroom, with tray ceiling, is privately situated with a luxurious bath. The front bedroom with its cathedral ceiling and large circle-top window doubles as a study. Wrapping porches at front and rear of the home invite quiet relaxation. The photographed home may have been modified to suit individual taste.

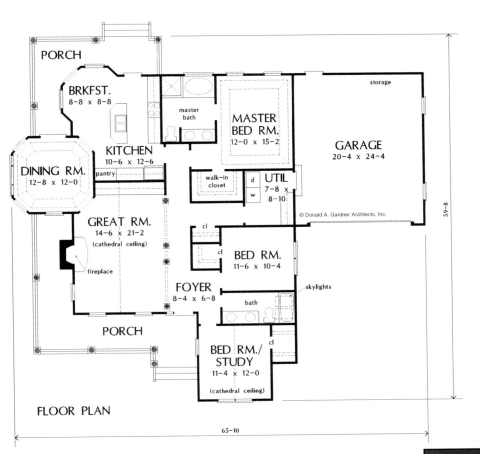

PORCH

BRKFST.
8-8 x 8-8

master
bath

storage

MASTER
BED RM.
12-0 x 15-2

GARAGE
20-4 x 24-4

KITCHEN
10-6 x 12-6

pantry

DINING RM.
12-8 x 12-0

walk-in
closet

UTIL
7-8 x
8-10

d
w

© Donald A. Gardner Architects, Inc.

GREAT RM.
14-6 x 21-2
(cathedral ceiling)

fireplace

cl

cl

BED RM.
11-6 x 10-4

FOYER
8-4 x 6-8

skylights

bath

PORCH

BED RM./
STUDY
11-4 x 12-0

cl

(cathedral ceiling)

FLOOR PLAN

59-8

65-10

TOTAL LIVING AREA	1,737 SQ. FT
MAIN FLOOR	1,737 SQ. FT.
GARAGE & STORAGE	517 SQ. FT.
BEDROOMS	THREE
BATHROOMS	2 FULL
FOUNDATION	CRAWL SPACE

PHOTOGRAPHY BY JON RILEY OF RILEY & RILEY PHOTOGRAPHY

BL/ML/RRR

PLAN: 99844

Dual porches, gables and circle-top windows give this home its special country charm. The foyer, expanded by a vaulted ceiling, introduces a formal dining room. The kitchen features columns and an island for easy entertaining. The vaulted Great room is always bright with light from the circle-top clerestory. Extra room for growth is waiting in the skylit bonus room. The front bedroom doubles as a study for versatility. A tray ceiling adds volume to the private master suite that has a bath with skylight, garden tub, dual vanity and both linen and walk-in closets. The photographed home may have been modified to suit individual tastes.

TOTAL LIVING AREA	1,832 SQ. FT
MAIN FLOOR	1,832 SQ. FT.
BONUS AREA	425 SQ. FT.
GARAGE	562 SQ. FT.
BEDROOMS	THREE
BATHROOMS	2 FULL
FOUNDATION	CRAWL SPACE

PHOTOGRAPHY BY JON RILEY OF RILEY & RILEY PHOTOGRAPHY

BL/ML/RRR/ZIP

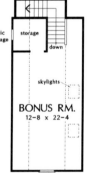

storage

down

skylights

BONUS RM.
12-8 x 22-4

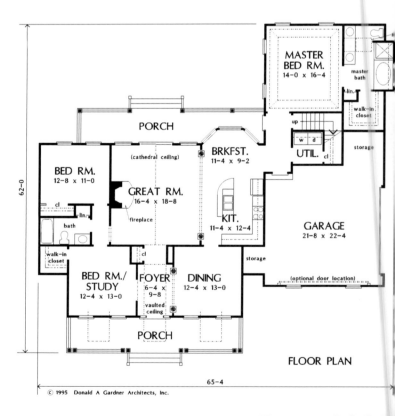

MASTER BED RM.
14-0 x 16-4

master bath

walk-in closet

PORCH

BRKFST.
11-4 x 9-2

UTIL.

storage

BED RM.
12-8 x 11-0

(cathedral ceiling)

GREAT RM.
16-4 x 18-8

fireplace

KIT.
11-4 x 12-4

GARAGE
21-8 x 22-4

bath

walk-in closet

BED RM./ STUDY
12-4 x 13-0

FOYER
6-4 x 9-8
vaulted ceiling

DINING
12-4 x 13-0

storage

(optional door location)

PORCH

62-0

65-4

FLOOR PLAN

© 1995 Donald A Gardner Architects, Inc.

PLAN: 99808

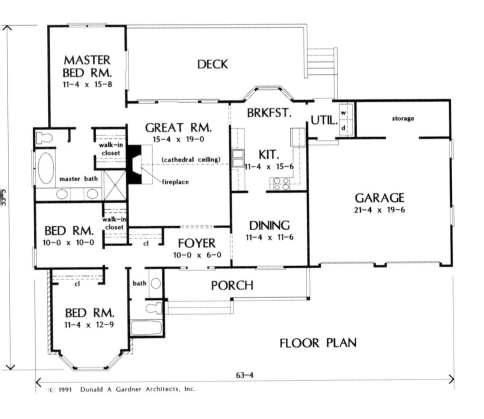

MASTER BED RM. 11-4 x 15-8

DECK

GREAT RM. 15-4 x 19-0

BRKFST.

UTIL.

w d

storage

walk-in closet

(cathedral ceiling)

KIT. 11-4 x 15-6

master bath

fireplace

GARAGE 21-4 x 19-6

BED RM. 10-0 x 10-0

walk-in closet

cl

FOYER 10-0 x 6-0

DINING 11-4 x 11-6

cl

bath

PORCH

BED RM. 11-4 x 12-9

FLOOR PLAN

63-4

© 1991 Donald A Gardner Architects, Inc.

Multi-paned bay windows, dormers, covered porch and a variety of building materials add romance to this efficient Country cottage. The foyer opens to a formal dining room and a large Great room with fireplace and cathedral ceiling. Step onto the expansive deck from the Great room or from the private master suite. Relax in the luxurious master bath with garden tub, separate shower, dual sink vanity and walk-in closet. Two family bedrooms up front share another full bath while a utility/mudroom is conveniently located off the kitchen and rear doors. The photographed home may have been modified to suit individual tastes.

TOTAL LIVING AREA	1,512 SQ. FT
MAIN FLOOR	1,512 SQ. FT.
GARAGE & STORAGE	516 SQ. FT.
BEDROOMS	THREE
BATHROOMS	2 FULL
FOUNDATION	CRAWL SPACE

PHOTOGRAPHY BY JON RILEY OF RILEY & RILEY PHOTOGRAPHY

PLAN: 96420

BL/ML/RRR

Columns and arched transoms are focal points of this ranch home elevation. The ten-foot entry has formal views of the dining room and the Great room which features a brick fireplace. The large island kitchen offers an angled range and a pantry. The sunny breakfast room has an atrium door to the backyard. The separate bedroom wing provides optimum privacy. The master suite includes a whirlpool bath with a sloped ceiling, a double vanity and a walk-in closet. This plan is available with a basement or slab foundation. Please specify when ordering. The photographed home may have been modified to suit individual tastes.

TOTAL LIVING AREA	1,806 SQ. FT
MAIN FLOOR	1,806 SQ. FT.
GARAGE	548 SQ. FT.
BEDROOMS	THREE
BATHROOMS	2 FULL
FOUNDATION	BASEMENT OR SLAB

PHOTOGRAPHY SUPPLIED BY DESIGN BASICS, INC.

BL/ML

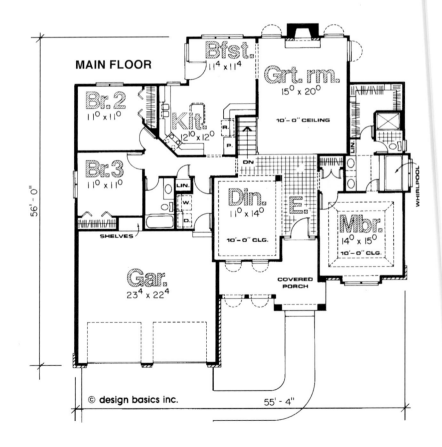

MAIN FLOOR

Bfst.
11⁴ x 11⁴

Grt. rm.
15⁰ x 20⁰

10'-0" CEILING

Br. 2
11⁰ x 11⁰

Kit.
12¹⁰ x 12⁰

Br. 3
11⁰ x 11⁰

LIN.

W.

D.

SHELVES

Din.
11⁰ x 14⁰
10'-0" CLG.

E.

Mbr.
14⁰ x 15⁰
10'-0" CLG.

WHIRLPOOL

Gar.
23⁴ x 22⁴

COVERED PORCH

© design basics inc.

56' - 0"

55' - 4"

PLAN: 9948

CLASSIC DESIGN

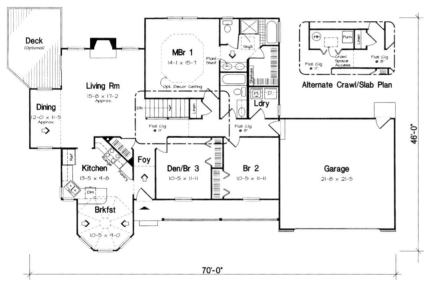

Alternate Crawl/Slab Plan

Deck (Optional)

Living Rm
15-8 x 17-2 Approx.

MBr 1
14-1 x 15-7

Dining
12-0 x 11-5 Approx.

Ldry

Kitchen
13-5 x 9-8

Foy

Den/Br 3
10-5 x 11-11

Br 2
10-5 x 11-11

Garage
21-8 x 21-5

Brkfst
10-5 x 9-0

70'-0"

46'-0"

This convenient, one-level plan is perfect for the modern family with a taste for classic design. Traditional Victorian touches in this three-bedroom beauty include a romantic, railed porch and an intriguing breakfast tower just off the kitchen. You will love the step-saving arrangement of the kitchen between the breakfast and formal dining rooms. Enjoy the wide-open living room with sliders out to a rear deck and the handsome master suite with its skylit, compartmentalized bath. Notice the convenient laundry location on the bedroom hall.

TOTAL LIVING AREA	1,583 SQ. FT
MAIN AREA	1,583 SQ. FT.
BASEMENT	1,573 SQ. FT.
GARAGE	484 SQ. FT.
BEDROOMS	THREE
BATHROOMS	2 FULL
FOUNDATION	BASEMENT, SLAB OR CRAWL SPACE

PLAN: 34043

BL/ML/ZIP/RRR

Exquisite columns, 13 foot ceiling heights and detailed ceiling treatments decorate the dining room and Great room. The gourmet kitchen with island and snack bar combine with the spacious breakfast room hearth room. The luxurious master bedroom suite with sitting area and fireplace is complemented by a deluxe dressing room with whirlpool tub, shower and dual vanities. Blueprints come with a design for a billiard room, secondary kitchen, media area, exercise area, full bath and additional bedrooms for the bonus area. The photographed home may have been modified to suit individual tastes.

TOTAL LIVING AREA	3,570 SQ. FT
MAIN FLOOR	3,570 SQ. FT.
BONUS AREA	2,367 SQ. FT.
BASEMENT	1,203 SQ. FT.
BEDROOMS	THREE
BATHROOMS	1 FULL, 1 HALF, 2 ¾
FOUNDATION	BASEMENT

PHOTOGRAPHY BY STUDER RESIDENTIAL DESIGN

BL

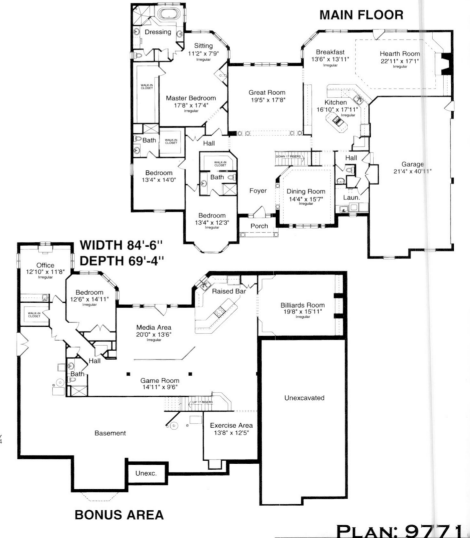

MAIN FLOOR

WIDTH 84'-6"
DEPTH 69'-4"

BONUS AREA

PLAN: 9771

SPACIOUS NEST

© Donald A. Gardner Architects, Inc.

TAL LIVING AREA	1,695 SQ. FT
IN FLOOR	1,695 SQ. FT.
RAGE & STORAGE	527 SQ. FT.
NUS ROOM	287 SQ. FT.
DROOMS	THREE
THROOMS	2 FULL
UNDATION	CRAWL SPACE

An open floor plan and an abundance of windows create horizontal spaciousness, while cathedral and tray ceilings add vertical volume to this three bedroom family home. The formal foyer, punctuated by elegant interior columns, leads to a spacious Great room with fireplace and a light filled octagonal dining room beyond. The bedroom wing hosts a master suite with double door entry, cathedral ceiling, patio access, walk-in closet and lavish bath.

BL/ML/RRR

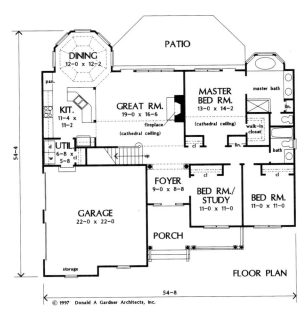

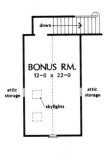

© 1997 Donald A Gardner Architects, Inc.

PLAN: 96488

© Donald A. Gardner Architects, Inc.

B. NATHAN

Comfortable family living was the motive for the design of this home which features well-planned living areas as well as a stunning brick exterior. The Great room pulls all areas of the home together, including the bedroom wing. Columns define the area set aside for formal dining and relaxed family meals are enjoyed in the sunny comfort of a bay window. Both the master suite and front bedroom boast tray ceilings. The master suite also features double doors to a rear porch, a generous walk-in closet and a lavish bath with every amenity.

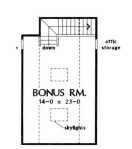

BONUS RM.
14-0 x 23-0

TOTAL LIVING AREA	1972 SQ. FT
MAIN FLOOR	1972 SQ. FT.
BONUS ROOM	398 SQ. FT.
GARAGE	600 SQ. FT.
BEDROOMS	THREE
BATHROOMS	2 FULL
FOUNDATION	CRAWL SPACE

BL/ML/RR

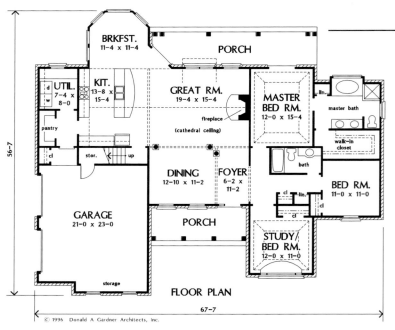

FLOOR PLAN

© 1996 Donald A Gardner Architects, Inc.

PLAN: 9982

Deck

56'-0"

Kitchen 12 x 11-4

Dining Rm 9 x 11-4

DN

pantry

W D

Ldry

MBr 1 14-2 x 14-4

32'-0"

slope

slope

ov

Living Rm 21-6 x 19-4

decor. beams

slope

slope

lin.

Br 3 12 x 12-6

Br 2 12 x 12-6

MAIN AREA

The exterior of this ranch home is all wood with interesting lines. More than an ordinary ranch home, it has an expansive feeling to drive up to. The large living area has a stone fireplace and decorative beams. The kitchen and dining room lead to an outside deck. The laundry room has a large pantry and is off the eating area. The master bedroom has a wonderful bathroom with a huge walk-in closet. In the front of the house, there are two additional bedrooms with a bathroom. This house offers one floor living and has nice big rooms.

TOTAL LIVING AREA	1,792 SQ. FT
MAIN AREA	1,792 SQ. FT.
BASEMENT	818 SQ. FT.
GARAGE	857 SQ. FT.
BEDROOMS	THREE
BATHROOMS	2 FULL, 1 THREE QUARTER
FOUNDATION	BASEMENT

PLAN: 20198

BL/ML/ZIP

This Traditional design is accented by the use of gable roofs and the blend of stucco and brick to form a truly spectacular exterior. This home has the look and feel of a much larger home. Entering the den, we find a high vaulted ceiling with built-in cabinets and a fireplace. The dining room is open to the den creating the Great room feel for this area. The U-shaped kitchen features built-in appliances. The bedrooms are designed in a split fashion. The master bedroom is located to the rear of the plan and features a private bath. This plan is available with a crawl space or slab foundation. Please specify when ordering.

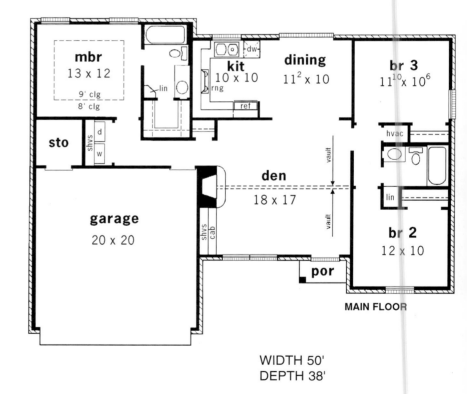

MAIN FLOOR

WIDTH 50'
DEPTH 38'

TOTAL LIVING AREA	1,237 SQ. FT
MAIN FLOUR	1,237 SQ. FT.
GARAGE	436 SQ. FT.
BEDROOMS	THREE
BATHROOMS	2 FULL
FOUNDATION	SLAB OR CRAWL SPACE

BL/ML

PLAN: 9250

BUDGET BEAUTY

Donald A. Gardner Architects, Inc.

Not only have the rear and sides of this home been squared off for easy, economical building, but other architectural elements also add a rare smoothness. Square columns with chamfered corners adorn the front porch. A partially open kitchen easily serves the generous breakfast area. The dining room, front bedroom and master suite feature tray ceilings. The master bath includes separate shower and garden tub, skylight, dual vanities and enclosed toilet.

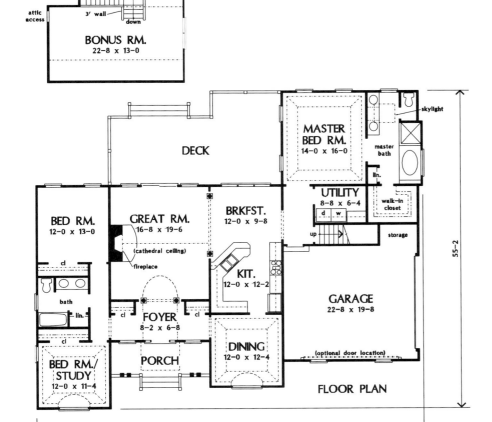

TOTAL LIVING AREA	1,959 SQ. FT.
MAIN FLOOR	1,959 SQ. FT.
BONUS ROOM	385 SQ. FT.
GARAGE	484 SQ. FT.
BEDROOMS	THREE
BATHROOMS	2 FULL
FOUNDATION	CRAWLSPACE

BL/ML/RRR

PLAN: 99813

This home features a well designed floor plan, offering convenience and style. The living room includes a two-sided fireplace shared with the dining room. An U-shaped kitchen is equipped with a peninsula counter/breakfast bar. The private master suite includes a whirlpool tub, a double vanity and a step-in shower. A large walk-in closet adds ample storage space to the suite. The secondary bedroom and the den/guest room share use of the full hall bath.

TOTAL LIVING AREA	1,625 SQ. FT
MAIN FLOOR	1,625 SQ. FT.
BASEMENT	1,625 SQ. FT.
GARAGE	455 SQ. FT.
BEDROOMS	THREE
BATHROOMS	2 FULL
FOUNDATION	BASEMENT, SLAB OR CRAWL SPACE

BL/ML/ZIP

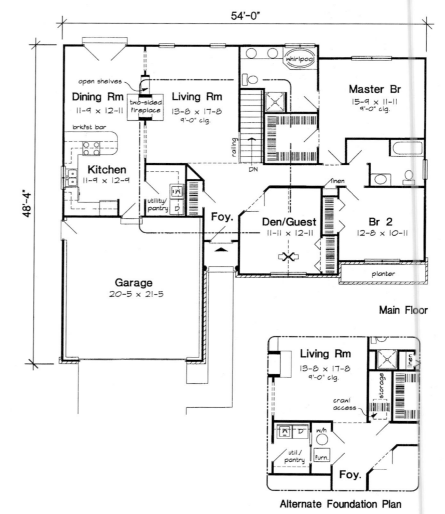

54'-0"

48'-4"

open shelves

Dining Rm
11-9 x 12-11

two-sided fireplace

Living Rm
13-8 x 17-8
9'-0" clg.

Master Br
15-9 x 11-11
9'-0" clg.

whirlpool

brk'fst bar

Kitchen
11-9 x 12-9

railing

DN

linen

utility/ pantry

Foy.

Den/Guest
11-11 x 12-11

Br 2
12-8 x 10-11

planter

Garage
20-5 x 21-5

Main Floor

Living Rm
13-8 x 17-8
9'-0" clg.

storage

linen

crawl access

util./ pantry

w/h

Furn.

Foy.

Alternate Foundation Plan

PLAN: 2470

© Donald A. Gardner Architects, Inc.

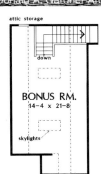

attic storage

down

BONUS RM.
14-4 x 21-8

skylights

Exciting volumes and nine-foot ceilings add elegance to this open plan. Sunlight fills the foyer from a vaulted dormer and streams through an opening into the Great room's cathedral ceiling. The dining room, delineated from the foyer by columns, features a tray ceiling. Children's bedrooms share a full bath. The front bedroom doubles as a study and is accented by a tray ceiling. The master suite is highlighted by a tray ceiling and includes a skylit bath with garden tub, private toilet, double vanity and spacious walk-in closet. A skylit bonus room provides opportunity for expansion.

skylight
lin.

MASTER BED RM.
14-0 x 17-4

master bath

walk-in closet

sto.   up

BRKFST.
11-8 x 9-0

pd. rm.

KIT.
11-8 x 12-8

UTIL.

d
w

GARAGE
23-0 x 25-8

storage

PORCH

(cathedral ceiling)

GREAT RM.
16-4 x 18-8

fireplace

opening above

opening above

DINING
14-8 x 11-8

FOYER
6-4 x 11-8

vaulted ceiling

BED RM./ STUDY
14-8 x 11-8

cl

BED RM.
12-0 x 11-0

cl

BED RM.
10-10 x 11-0

cl

lin.

bath

walk-in closet

55-8

PORCH

74-10

© 1995 Donald A Gardner Architects, Inc.

PLAN: 99838

TOTAL LIVING AREA	2,192 SQ. FT
MAIN FLOOR	2,192 SQ. FT.
GARAGE	582 SQ. FT.
BONUS ROOM	390 SQ. FT.
BEDROOMS	FOUR
BATHROOMS	2 FULL, 1 HALF
FOUNDATION	CRAWL SPACE

BL/ML/ZIP/RRR

23

You don't have to sacrifice style when buying a smaller home. Notice the palladian window with a fan light above at the front of the home. The entrance porch includes a turned post entry. Once inside, the living room is topped by an impressive vaulted ceiling. A fireplace accents the room. A decorative ceiling enhances both the master bedroom and the dining room. The kitchen includes a peninsula counter. A private bath and double closet highlight the master suite.

TOTAL LIVING AREA	1,312 SQ. FT.
MAIN AREA	1,312 SQ. FT.
BEDROOMS	THREE
BATHROOMS	2 FULL
BASEMENT	1,293 SQ. FT.
GARAGE	459 SQ. FT.
FOUNDATION	BASEMENT, SLAB OR CRAWL SPACE

BL/ML/ZIP

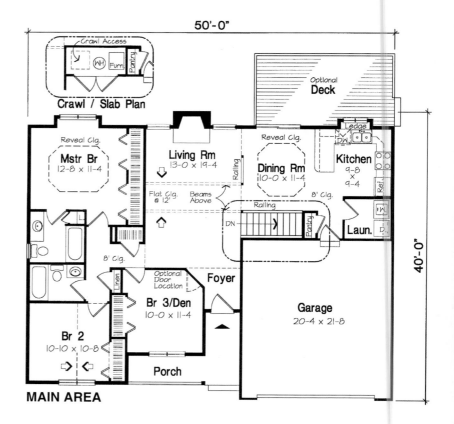

Crawl / Slab Plan

MAIN AREA

PLAN: 24700

ARCHED WINDOWS

OTAL LIVING AREA	4,328 SQ. FT
RST FLOOR	2,582 SQ. FT.
OWER FLOOR	1,746 SQ. FT.
ASEMENT	871 SQ. FT.
ECK	1,074 SQ. FT.
ORCH	80 SQ. FT.
EDROOMS	THREE
ATHROOMS	2 FULL, 1 3/4, 1 HALF
OUNDATION	BASEMENT

HOTOGRAPHY BY
TUDER RESIDENTIAL DESIGN

BL/ZIP

etailed stucco and stone ccents provide warmth and haracter to this one level ome. An arched entry invites ou to the interior where legant window styles and ramatic ceiling treatments reate an impressive showplace. n extravagant master bedroom uite and library with built-in ook shelves round out the first loor. Two additional bedrooms ith a tandem bath, a media oom, billiard room and exercise oom are created in the inished basement.

PLAN: 92657

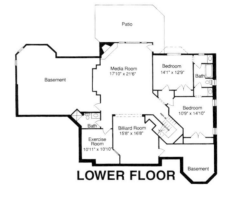

LOWER FLOOR

FIRST FLOOR

© Donald A. Gardner Architects, Inc.

This plan's wide front porch and comfortable design encourages relaxation. A center dormer lights the foyer, as columns punctuate the entry to the dining room and Great room. The spacious kitchen has an angled countertop and is open to the breakfast bay. Tray ceilings add elegance to the dining room and the master bedroom. A second master suite is located on the opposite end of the home and features an optional arrangement for the physically challenged. A skylit bonus room is located over the garage and provides room for growth.

TOTAL LIVING AREA	2,349 SQ. FT
MAIN FLOOR	2,349 SQ. FT.
GARAGE	615 SQ. FT.
BONUS ROOM	435 SQ. FT.
BEDROOMS	FOUR
BATHROOMS	3 FULL
FOUNDATION	CRAWL SPACE

BL/ML/ZIP/RRR

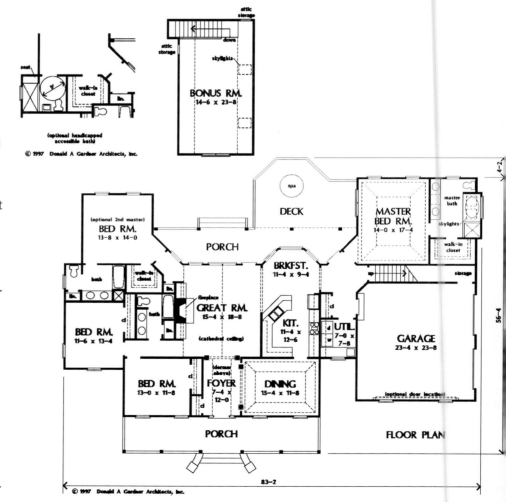

PLAN: 9641

© Donald A. Gardner Architects, Inc.

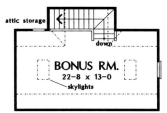

attic storage
down

BONUS RM.
22-8 x 13-0
skylights

Dormers cast light and interest into the foyer for a grand first impression that sets the tone in a home full of today's amenities. The Great room, articulated by columns, features a cathedral ceiling and is conveniently located adjacent to the breakfast room and kitchen. Tray ceilings and picture windows with circle transoms accent the front bedroom and dining room. A secluded master suite includes a bath with skylight, garden tub, separate shower, dual vanity and spacious walk-in closet.

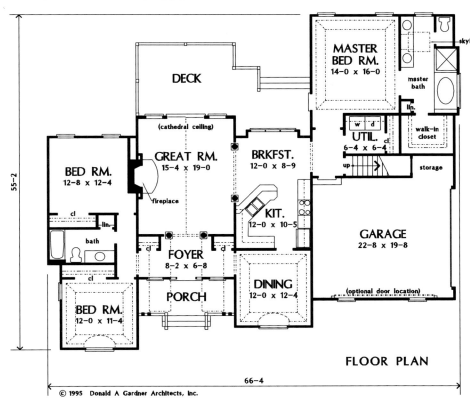

FLOOR PLAN

© 1995 Donald A Gardner Architects, Inc.

TOTAL LIVING AREA	1,879 SQ. FT
MAIN FLOOR	1,879 SQ. FT.
BONUS AREA	360 SQ. FT.
GARAGE	485 SQ. FT.
BEDROOMS	THREE
BATHROOMS	2 FULL
FOUNDATION	CRAWLSPACE

PHOTOGRAPHY BY JON RILEY, RILEY & RILEY PHOTOGRAPHY

BL/ML/ZIP/RRR

PLAN: 99807

PLAN: 99878

© 1993 Donald A. Gardner Architects, Inc.

QUAINT AND COZY COTTAGE

TOTAL LIVING AREA	1,864 SQ. FT.
MAIN FLOOR	1,864 SQ. FT.
BONUS AREA	420 SQ. FT.
GARAGE & STORAGE	614 SQ. FT.
BEDROOMS	THREE
BATHROOMS	2 FULL, 1 HAL
FOUNDATION	CRAWLSPACE

BL/ML/ZIP/RRR

With porches front and back, this country home surprises with an open floor plan featuring a large Great room with cathedral ceiling. Nine-foot ceilings add volume throughout the home. A central kitchen opens to the breakfast area and Great room for easy entertaining. A bonus room over the garage makes expanding easy.

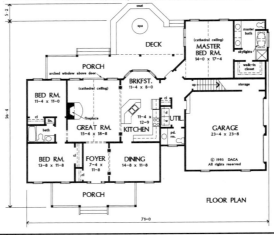

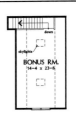

PLAN: 20161

DETAILED CHARMER

TOTAL LIVING AREA	1,307 SQ. FT.
MAIN AREA	1,307 SQ. FT.
BASEMENT	1,298 SQ. FT.
GARAGE	462 SQ. FT.
BEDROOMS	THREE
BATHROOMS	2 FULL
FOUNDATION	BASEMENT, SLAB OR CRAWL SPACE

PHOTOGRAPHY BY JOHN EHRENCLOU

BL/ML/ZIP/RRR

Walk past the charming front porch, in through the foyer and you'll be struck by the exciting, spacious living room, complete with high sloping ceilings and a beautiful fireplace. The large master bedroom has its own private bath and a decorative ceiling. The dining room provides decorative ceiling details and a full slider out to the deck. The kitchen includes a double sink and an attractive bump-out window.

MAIN AREA

Slab/Crawl Space Option

GREAT STARTER HOME

AL LIVING AREA	1,576 SQ. FT
N FLOOR	1,576 SQ. FT.
EMENT	1,454 SQ. FT.
AGE	576 SQ. FT.
ROOMS	THREE
HROOMS	2 FULL
NDATION	BASEMENT, SLAB OR CRAWL SPACE

ML/ZIP

Main Floor

Alternate Crawl/Slab Plan

This functional, all on one level home plan features a lovely country porch entry into a spacious living room that is accented by a fireplace. The efficient U-shaped kitchen has direct access to both the dining and living rooms. A screened porch is accessed directly from the kitchen. The master bedroom includes a private double vanity bath with a whirlpool tub and separate shower. The two additional bedrooms share a full double vanity bath which has the added convenience of a laundry center.

PRICE CODE B

ATTENTION GETTING DETAIL

AL LIVING AREA	2,735 SQ. FT
N FLOOR	2,735 SQ. FT.
RAGE	561 SQ. FT.
DROOMS	FOUR
THROOMS	3 FULL
UNDATION	CRAWL SPACE OR SLAB

ML

WIDTH 68'-10"
DEPTH 67'-4"

MAIN FLOOR

This spacious four bedroom home features a formal foyer leading directly into the den. The den is expansive, topped by a raised ceiling and focuses on a cozy fireplace. The kitchen uses an angled extended counter and flows into the den and eating area. The dining area includes a boxed bay window. The split bedroom plan insures privacy for the master bedroom. Crowned in a raised ceiling and pampered by a plush, whirlpool bath, the master suite is sure to please. This plan is available with a crawl space or slab foundation, Please specify when ordering.

PRICE CODE F

© Donald A. Gardner Architects, Inc.

Not only does this home live bigger than its 1,864 square feet, but it also lives easier. The space flows easily from the sunlit foyer into a generous Great room with cathedral ceiling, while interior accent columns define the open kitchen and breakfast bay. The master bedroom, located off the Great room, features a tray ceiling and back porch access, and the well-appointed master bath is separated from the bedroom by closets. A new design twist puts two more bedrooms just steps away from the bonus room, creating a great children's wing.

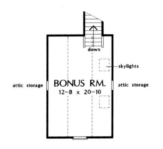

BONUS RM.
12-8 x 20-10

attic storage | attic storage

down

skylights

TOTAL LIVING AREA	1864 SQ. FT
MAIN FLOOR	1864 SQ. FT
BONUS ROOM	319 SQ. FT.
GARAGE & STORAGE	503 SQ. FT.
BEDROOMS	THREE
BATHROOMS	2 FULL,
FOUNDATION	CRAWL SPAC

BL/ML/RR

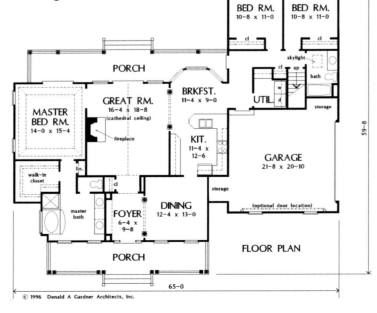

BED RM.
10-8 x 11-0

BED RM.
10-8 x 11-0

PORCH

GREAT RM.
16-4 x 18-8
(cathedral ceiling)

BRKFST.
11-4 x 9-0

UTIL.

skylight

bath

MASTER
BED RM.
14-0 x 15-4

fireplace

KIT.
11-4 x
12-6

GARAGE
21-8 x 20-10

storage

walk-in
closet

master
bath

FOYER
6-4 x
9-8

DINING
12-4 x 13-0

(optional door location)

PORCH

FLOOR PLAN

59-8

65-0

© 1996 Donald A Gardner Architects, Inc.

PLAN: 9646

OTAL LIVING AREA	1954 SQ. FT
AIN FLOOR	1954 SQ. FT.
ONUS ROOM	436 SQ. FT.
ARAGE & STORAGE	649 SQ. FT.
EDROOMS	THREE
ATHROOMS	2 FULL, 1 HALF
OUNDATION	CRAWL SPACE

L/ML/ZIP/RRR

This plan offers the best of both worlds for those torn between traditional and country style. The active family gets all the room it needs in just 1,954 square feet thanks to an open floor plan and covered porches in this three bedroom country home. Stairs to the skylit bonus room are conveniently located near the kitchen and master suite. Growing families will appreciate the extra half bath, too. Cathedral ceilings add volume to the master suite which is located at the rear for privacy. Its well-appointed skylit bath features a whirlpool tub, separate shower and dual vanities.

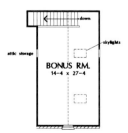

Bonus Room floor plan:
attic storage
down
skylights
BONUS RM.
14-4 x 27-4

Floor Plan:

seat
DECK
spa
PORCH
clerestory window with arched top
MASTER BED RM.
14-0 x 17-4
(cathedral ceiling)
master bath
skylights
walk-in closet
BRKFST.
11-4 x 8-8
BED RM.
11-4 x 11-0
GREAT RM.
15-4 x 18-8
(cathedral ceiling)
fireplace
KIT.
11-4 x 12-10
UTIL.
up
storage
GARAGE
23-4 x 23-8
bath
BED RM.
13-8 x 11-8
FOYER
7-4 x 11-8
DINING RM.
14-8 x 11-8
pd. rm.
62-6
71-3
PORCH
PORCH

FLOOR PLAN

PLAN: 99845

PLAN: 99856

© Donald A. Gardner Architects, Inc.

Multi-paned bay window, dormers and a covered porch give this compact country cottage visual impact. The foyer opens to a large Great room, with fireplace and cathedral ceiling. Two front bedrooms, one with bay window and the other with walk-in closet, share an ample bath. The master suite is privately located at the rear with walk-in closet and private bath with double vanity.

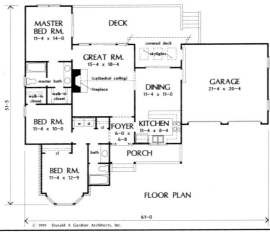

COMPACT COUNTRY COTTAGE

TOTAL LIVING AREA	1,310 SQ. FT
MAIN FLOOR	1,310 SQ. FT
GARAGE & STORAGE	455 SQ. FT.
BEDROOMS	THREE
BATHROOMS	2 FULL
FOUNDATION	CRAWL SPACE

BL/ML/RRR

PRICE CODE

PLAN: 99860

© Donald A. Gardner Architects, Inc.

We kept all the Country charm when we down-sized one of our most popular plans for home builders on a budget. Columns punctuate the open, one-level floor plan and connect the foyer and kitchen/breakfast room to the large Great room with cathedral ceiling and fireplace. Tray ceilings lift the master bedroom, dining room and bedroom/study out of the ordinary. The private master suite features a garden tub, double vanity, walk-in closet, separate shower and operable skylights.

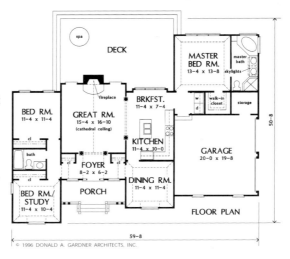

HOME BUILDERS ON A BUDGET

TOTAL LIVING AREA	1,498 SQ. FT
MAIN FLOOR	1,498 SQ. FT
GARAGE & STORAGE	427 SQ. FT.
BEDROOMS	THREE
BATHROOMS	2 FULL
FOUNDATION	CRAWL SPACE

BL/ML/ZIP/RR

PRICE CODE

WIDTH 68'-0"
DEPTH 46'-0"

MAIN FLOOR

BL/ML/ZIP

Attractive Ceiling Treatments and Open Layout

Price Code: B

■ This plan features:

— Three bedrooms

— Two full and one half baths

■ Great Room and Master Suite with step-up ceiling treatments

■ A cozy fireplace providing warm focal point in the Great Room

■ Open layout between Kitchen, Dining and Great Room lending a more spacious feeling

■ Five-piece, private Bath and walk-in closet in the pampering Master Suite

■ Two additional Bedrooms located at opposite end of home

MAIN FLOOR — 1,654 SQ. FT.
GARAGE — 480 SQ. FT.

TOTAL LIVING AREA:
1,654 SQ. FT.

BL/ML

Large Living in a Small Space

Price Code: A

■ This plan features:

— Three bedrooms

— One full bath and one three-quarter bath

■ A sheltered entrance leads into an open Living Room with a corner fireplace and a wall of windows

■ A well-equipped Kitchen features a peninsula counter with a Nook, a Laundry, a clothes closet and a built-in Pantry

■ A Master Bedroom with a private Bath

■ Two additional Bedrooms that share full hall Bath

MAIN FLOOR — 993 SQ. FT.
GARAGE — 390 SQ. FT.
BASEMENT — 987 SQ. FT.

TOTAL LIVING AREA:
993 SQ. FT.

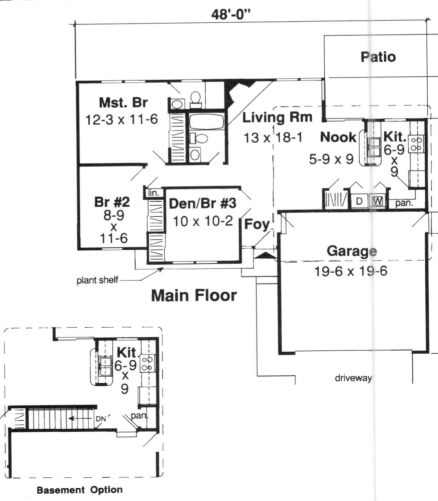

48'-0"

Patio

Mst. Br
12-3 x 11-6

Living Rm
13 x 18-1

Nook
5-9 x 9

Kit.
6-9 x 9

Br #2
8-9 x 11-6

lin.

Den/Br #3
10 x 10-2

Foy

D W pan.

Garage
19-6 x 19-6

plant shelf

Main Floor

driveway

Kit
6-9 x 9

DN

pan.

Basement Option

To order your Blueprints, call 1-800-235-5700

BL/ML/ZIP

Split Bedroom Plan

Price Code: A

■ This plan features:
— Three bedrooms
— Two full baths

■ A tray ceiling gives a decorative touch to the Master Bedroom

■ A full Bath located between the secondary Bedrooms

■ A corner fireplace and a vaulted ceiling highlight the Family Room

■ A wetbar/serving bar and a built-in Pantry add to the convenience of the Kitchen

■ An optional basement, crawl space or slab foundation — please specify when ordering

MAIN FLOOR — 1,429 SQ. FT.
BASEMENT — 1,472 SQ. FT.
GARAGE — 438 SQ. FT.

TOTAL LIVING AREA:
1,429 SQ. FT.

Floor Plan Labels

49'- 0"

53'- 0"

Master Suite 12⁰ x 15⁷
TRAY CLG.

Breakfast

PLANT SHELF ABOVE

DW.

RANGE

Kitchen

REF.

PAN.

Vaulted Family Room
SERVING BAR 16² x 17⁵
15'-3" HIGH CLG.

VAULT

FPL.

Bedroom 3 11⁰ x 10²

LIN.

Bath

Vaulted M.Bath

SHWR.

CTS.

PLANT SHELF ABOVE

W.i.c.

Laun.

W.

D.

WET BAR

Foyer 12'-0" HIGH CLG.

Dining Room 10¹ x 11¹⁰ 14'-0" HIGH CLG.

Covered Porch

Bedroom 2 11⁰ x 10¹

Storage

OPT. STAIRS TO BASEMENT

FLOOR PLAN

Garage 19⁵ x 19⁷

copyright ©1992 frank betz associates, inc.

PLAN NO. 98108

BL/ML/RRR

Finished Lower Level

Price Code: I

- This plan features:
  — Four bedrooms
  — Three full baths
- The lower level of this home features a Recreation Room, which opens onto a Patio.
- 2,105 square feet on the main level; 798 square feet on the lower level
- The Master Suite includes a bay window and separate walk-in closets and vanities.
- The bonus room adds 453 square feet.
- This home is designed with a basement foundation.

MAIN FLOOR — 2,105 SQ. FT.
GARAGE — 596 SQ. FT.

TOTAL LIVING AREA:
2,903 SQ. FT.

PLAN NO. 94219

BL

Lends itself to a Corner Lot

Price Code: G

- This plan features:
  — Three bedrooms and a study
  — Three full and one half baths
- Double doors lead to a lovely formal Living Room
- The Kitchen is open to a bright mitred glass Nook
- The Master Suite has a cozy Sitting Room and a full Bath with a garden tub
- Two Bedrooms have a walk-in closet and share a full bath
- There's plenty of storage space throughout this home

MAIN FLOOR — 2,986 SQ. FT.
GARAGE — 574 SQ. FT.

TOTAL LIVING AREA:
2,986 SQ. FT.

MAIN FLOOR

To order your Blueprints, call 1-800-235-5700

BL/ML/ZIP

Simply Cozy

Price Code: A

■ This plan features:

— Three bedrooms

— Two full baths

■ Quaint front porch sheltering Entry into the Living Area

■ Formal Dining Room accented by a bay of glass with Sun Deck access

■ Efficient, galley Kitchen with Breakfast area

■ Secluded Master Bedroom offers a roomy walk-in closet

MAIN FLOOR — 1,325 SQ. FT.
BASEMENT — 556 SQ. FT.
GARAGE — 724 SQ. FT.

TOTAL LIVING AREA:
1,325 SQ. FT.

MAIN FLOOR

Sundeck
14-0 x 10-0

© 1996, Jannis Vann & Associates, Inc.

W. D.

Brkfst.
8-2 x 8-2

Kit.
10-0 x 8-2

Dw.

Ref.

Dining
11-10 x 10-0

Bdrm.3
10-0 x 11-6

Bth.2

Built in Cab.

Cts.

M. Bath

Lin.

Master Bdrm.
10-8 x 16-10

Living Area
13-8 x 15-0
Flat Ceil. 12-9 High
Vaulted Ceil.

Dn.

Bdrm.2
13-6 x 11-2

Front Porch

52-0

BL

Low-Maintenance Facade

Price Code: A

■ This plan features:
— Three bedrooms
— Two full baths
■ The stucco exterior won't require a fresh coat of paint for years to come.
■ The Laundry Room is conveniently located near the Master Bedroom.
■ The Foyer opens to the Family Room, which features a vaulted ceiling and fireplace.
■ This home is designed with basement and crawl-space foundation options.

MAIN FLOOR — 1,361 SQ. FT.
GARAGE — 530 SQ. FT.

TOTAL LIVING AREA:
1,361 SQ. FT.

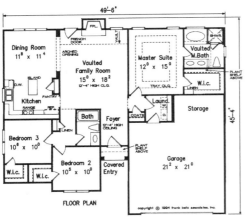

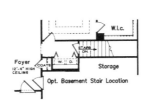

BL/ML

Spectacular Views

Price Code: F

■ This plan features:
— Four bedrooms
— Two full and one three-quarter baths
■ Creates an indoor/outdoor relationship with terrific Decks and large glass expanses
■ Family Room and Living Room enjoy highly glassed walls taking in the vistas
■ Living Room enhanced by a cathedral ceiling and a warm fireplace
■ Dining Room and Kitchen are in an open layout and a center cooktop island/snack bar highlights the Kitchen
■ Master Bedroom enhanced by floor-to-ceiling windowed area allowing natural light to filter in
■ Secondary Bedroom in close proximity to full Bath on main floor
■ Two additional Bedrooms, a three-quarter Bath and a Family Room complete the lower level

MAIN FLOOR — 1,707 SQ. FT.
LOWER FLOOR — 901 SQ. FT.

TOTAL LIVING AREA:
2,608 SQ. FT.

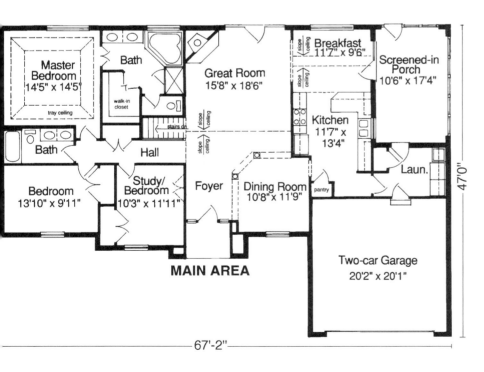

Photography by Donna & Ron Kolb — Exposures Unlimited

BL/ZIP

Charming Brick Ranch

Price Code: C

■ This plan features:

— Three bedrooms

— Two full baths

■ Sheltered entrance leads into open Foyer and Dining Room defined by columns

■ Vaulted ceiling spans Foyer, Dining Room, and Great Room which has corner fireplace and atrium door to rear yard

■ Central Kitchen has separate Laundry and Pantry areas

■ Luxurious Master Bedroom offers tray ceiling and French doors to Bath

■ No materials list is available for this plan

MAIN AREA —1,782 SQ. FT.
GARAGE — 407 SQ. FT.
BASEMENT — 1,735 SQ. FT.

TOTAL LIVING AREA:
1,782 SQ. FT.

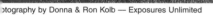

MAIN AREA

Master Bedroom 14'5" x 14'5" — tray ceiling

Bath — walk-in closet

Bath

Hall — stairs dn

Bedroom 13'10" x 9'11"

Study/ Bedroom 10'3" x 11'11"

Foyer

Great Room 15'8" x 18'6" — slope ceiling

Breakfast 11'7" x 9'6" — slope ceiling

Screened-in Porch 10'6" x 17'4"

Kitchen 11'7" x 13'4"

Dining Room 10'8" x 11'9" — pantry

Laun.

Two-car Garage 20'2" x 20'1"

67'-2"

47'0"

©1999 Donald A. Gardner, Inc.

Curved Kitchen Snack Bar

Price Code: F

- This plan features:
— Three bedrooms
— One full, one half and one three-quarter baths
- The Dining Room features a bay window that looks out onto the wraparound Porch.
- The Master Bedroom has a cathedral ceiling and separate access to the rear Porch.
- The bonus room adds 339 square feet.
- This home is designed with a crawl space foundation.

MAIN AREA — 2,078 SQ. FT.
GARAGE — 523 SQ. FT.

TOTAL LIVING AREA:
2,078 SQ. FT.

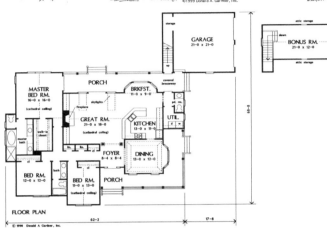

© 1996 Donald A. Gardner, Inc.

Country Convenience

Price Code: A

- This plan features:
—Three bedrooms
—Two full baths
- A cozy front Porch enhances the curb appeal of this home.
- The Kitchen/Dining Area is crowned by a vaulted ceiling.
- A covered walk connects The kitchen to the two-car Garage.
- An optional Master Bath includes a soaking tub
- This home was designed with a choice of slab or crawl space foundation.

MAIN FLOOR — 1,475 SQ. FT
GARAGE — 455 SQ. FT.

TOTAL LIVING AREA:
1,475 SQ. FT.

MAIN FLOOR

BL

Living Room Bay

Price Code: D

■ This plan features:
— Three bedrooms
— Two full and one half baths
■ Floor length windows in the formal Dining Room and Living Room help illuminate the wide Foyer.
■ The Master Suite has a tray ceiling and a luxury Bath with separate vanities and walk-in closets.
■ This home is designed with basement and crawl space foundation options.

MAIN FLOOR — 2,201 SQ. FT.
GARAGE — 452 SQ. FT.

TOTAL LIVING AREA:
2,201 SQ. FT.

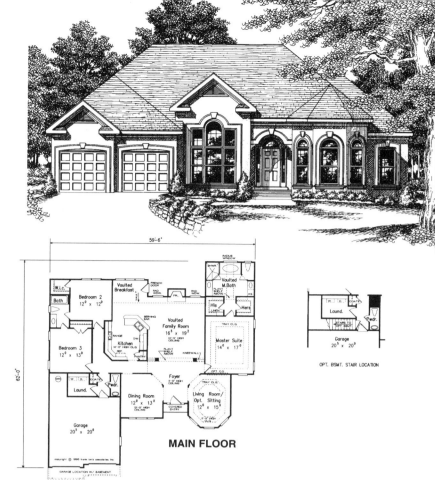

MAIN FLOOR

BL/ML/ZIP/RRR

Compact Traditional For Easy Living

Price Code: C

■ This plan features:
— Three bedrooms
— Two full baths
■ Foyer opens to Living and Dining Rooms defined by a half wall
■ Convenient Kitchen with a serving counter for Breakfast Area, Screened Porch and Family Room, and nearby Garage entry and Dining Room
■ Master Bedroom offers a walk-in closet and private Bath
■ Two front Bedrooms with ample closets, share a full Bath
■ Laundry Room located for convenience serving as a sound buffer for the bedroom wing
■ This home is designed with a basement, slab or crawl space foundation options

MAIN FLOOR — 1,786 SQ. FT.
SCREENED PORCH — 223 SQ. FT.
GARAGE — 426 SQ. FT.

TOTAL LIVING AREA:
1,786 SQ. FT.

BASEMENT / OPT.

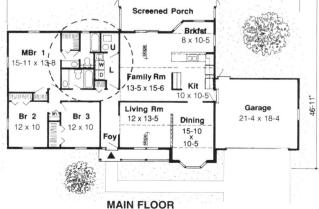

MAIN FLOOR

BL

Family Room at Heart of the Home

Price Code: F

■ This plan features:

— Four bedrooms

— Three full baths

■ The Living Room and Dining Room are to the right and left of the Foyer

■ The Dining Room with French doors opens to the Kitchen

■ The Master Bedroom is equipped with a double vanity Bath, two walk-in closets and a linear closet

■ A cozy fireplace and a decorative ceiling highlight the Family Room

■ No materials list is available for this plan

MAIN FLOOR — 2,558 SQ. FT.
GARAGE — 549 SQ. FT.

TOTAL LIVING AREA:
2,558 SQ. FT.

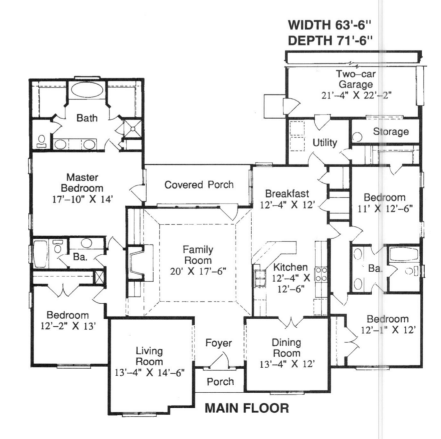

WIDTH 63'-6"
DEPTH 71'-6"

Two–car Garage 21'–4" X 22'–2"

Utility

Storage

Bath

Master Bedroom 17'–10" X 14'

Covered Porch

Breakfast 12'–4" X 12'

Bedroom 11' X 12'–6"

Ba.

Family Room 20' X 17'–6"

Kitchen 12'–4" X 12'–6"

Ba.

Bedroom 12'–2" X 13'

Bedroom 12'–1" X 12'

Living Room 13'–4" X 14'–6"

Foyer

Dining Room 13'–4" X 12'

Porch

MAIN FLOOR

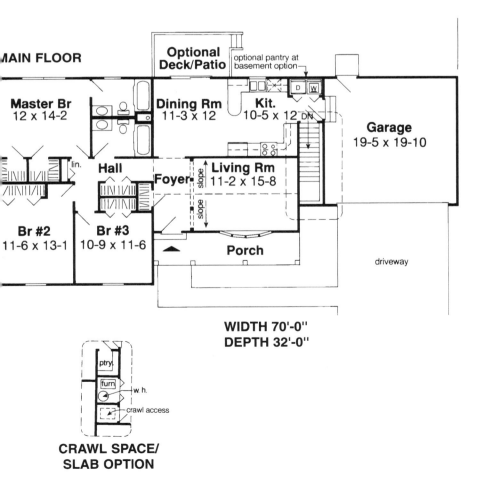

MAIN FLOOR

Master Br
12 x 14-2

Optional Deck/Patio | optional pantry at basement option

Dining Rm
11-3 x 12

Kit.
10-5 x 12 DN

D | W

Garage
19-5 x 19-10

lin.

Hall

Foyer

slope

Living Rm
11-2 x 15-8

slope

slope

Br #2
11-6 x 13-1

Br #3
10-9 x 11-6

Porch

driveway

WIDTH 70'-0"
DEPTH 32'-0"

ptry.

furn | w. h.

crawl access

CRAWL SPACE/ SLAB OPTION

BL/ML/RRR

Bow Window Adds to Curb Appeal

Price Code: A

■ This plan features:

— Three bedrooms

— Two full baths

■ Curb appeal enhanced by a beautiful bow window in the Living Room and by the front Porch

■ A Dining Room that is separated from the Kitchen by only a peninsula counter/eating bar

■ More than ample counter space, a double sink and a Laundry Center in the Kitchen

■ A Master Bedroom with a private full Bath and his and her closets

■ Two additional bedrooms that share a full hall bath

MAIN AREA — 1,373 SQ. FT.
GARAGE — 400 SQ. FT.

TOTAL LIVING AREA:
1,373 SQ. FT.

BL

Brick Magnificence

Price Code: G

■ This plan features:

— Four bedrooms

— Three full baths

■ Large windows and brick detailing using segmented arches give fantastic curb appeal

■ Convenient Ranch layout allows for step-saving one floor ease

■ A fireplace in the Living Room adds a warm ambience

■ The Family Room has a second fireplace and built-in shelving

■ No materials list is available for this plan

MAIN FLOOR — 2,858 SQ. FT.
GARAGE — 768 SQ. FT.

TOTAL LIVING AREA:
2,858 SQ. FT.

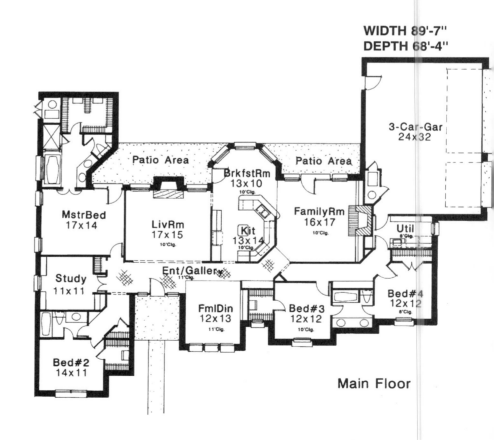

WIDTH 89'-7"
DEPTH 68'-4"

Main Floor

BL/ML

Smooth Traffic Flow

Price Code: G

- This plan features:
  — Four bedrooms
  — Two full and one half baths
- Two closets in the Garage and a Bonus Room provide abundant storage.
- The Bonus Room adds 388 square feet.
- Traffic flows easily between the Great Room and the spacious screened Porch.
- Tray ceilings decorate the front Bedroom/Study and Dining Room.
- This home is designed with a crawl space foundation.

MAIN FLOOR — 2,262 SQ. FT.
GARAGE — 542 SQ. FT.

TOTAL LIVING AREA:
2,262 SQ. FT.

©1998 Donald A. Gardner, Inc.

BL

Mix of Stucco and Brick

Price Code: C

- This plan features:
  — Three bedrooms
  — Two full baths
- In this home, 10-foot high ceilings top most of the living and sleeping areas.
- Ceilings slope at the edges of the Dining Room, the Living Room, and the Master Suite.
- The Garage includes two storage areas, one with access from the inside and the other from the backyard.
- This home is designed with crawl space and slab foundation options.

MAIN FLOOR — 1,890 SQ. FT.
GARAGE — 565 SQ. FT.

TOTAL LIVING AREA:
1,890 SQ. FT.

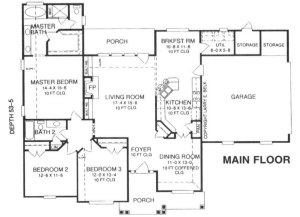

MAIN FLOOR

BL

A Collection of Gables

Price Code: L

■ This plan features:
— Four bedrooms
— Three full and one half baths
■ The offset Great Room provides interesting views of the house and site
■ Most of one wing is devoted to the Master Suite
■ Classic country European lines make the exterior a crowd pleaser
■ This home is designed with a slab foundation

MAIN FLOOR — 2,684 SQ. FT.
GARAGE — 638 SQ. FT.

TOTAL LIVING AREA:
2,684 SQ. FT.

MAIN FLOOR

BL/ML

Cabin in the Woods

Price Code: A

■ This plan features:
— Two bedrooms
— One full baths
■ The large Deck has a wood storage bin
■ The Living Room is warmed by a woodstove
■ The Kitchen is open to the Living Room and is fully appointed
■ Two large Bedrooms each have ample closet space
■ A full Bath completes this rustic cabin retreat

MAIN FLOOR — 728 SQ. FT.

TOTAL LIVING AREA:
728 SQ. FT.

MAIN FLOOR

To order your Blueprints, call 1-800-235-5700

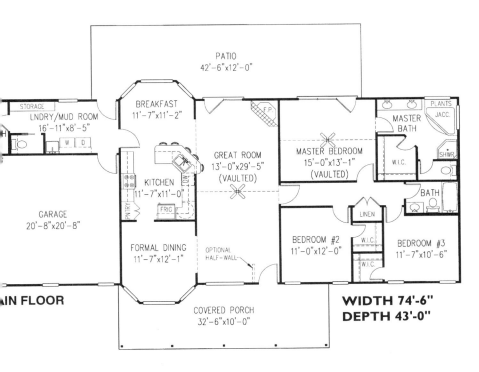

PATIO
42'-6"x12'-0"

STORAGE

LNDRY/MUD ROOM
16'-11"x8'-5"

W   D

BREAKFAST
11'-7"x11'-2"

F.P.

MASTER
BATH

PLANTS
JACC.

GREAT ROOM
13'-0"x29'-5"
(VAULTED)

MASTER BEDROOM
15'-0"x13'-1"
(VAULTED)

W.I.C.

SHWR

KITCHEN
11'-7"x11'-0"

PNTRY

DW

FRIG

GARAGE
20'-8"x20'-8"

BATH

LINEN

FORMAL DINING
11'-7"x12'-1"

OPTIONAL
HALF-WALL

BEDROOM #2
11'-0"x12'-0"

W.I.C.

BEDROOM #3
11'-7"x10'-6"

W.I.C.

IN FLOOR

COVERED PORCH
32'-6"x10'-0"

WIDTH 74'-6"
DEPTH 43'-0"

BL

Designed with the Family in Mind

Price Code: C

■ This plan features:

— Three bedrooms

— Two full and one half baths

■ The Garage leads through the Mud Room and Laundry

■ A bay window graces the Breakfast Nook and formal Dining Room

■ Behind the Master Bath's whirlpool tub is a shelf for plans

■ A corner fireplace warms the large Great Room

■ Efficiency is a hallmark of the well-designed Kitchen

■ Walk-in closets grace each Bedroom

MAIN FLOOR — 1,954 SQ. FT.
GARAGE — 411 SQ. FT.

TOTAL LIVING AREA:
1,954 SQ. FT

BL/ML

Ten Foot Entry

Price Code: B

- ■ This plan features:
- —Three bedrooms
- —Two full baths
- ■ Large volume Great Room highlighted by a fireplace flanked by windows
- ■ Decorative ceiling treatment giving elegance to the Dining Room
- ■ Fully equipped Kitchen with a planning desk and a Pantry
- ■ Roomy Master Bedroom suite has a volume ceiling and special amenities; a skylighted dressing bath area, plant shelf, a large walk-in closet, a double vanity and a whirlpool tub

MAIN FLOOR — 1,604 SQ. FT.
GARAGE — 466 SQ. FT.

TOTAL LIVING AREA:
1,604 SQ. FT.

MAIN FLOOR

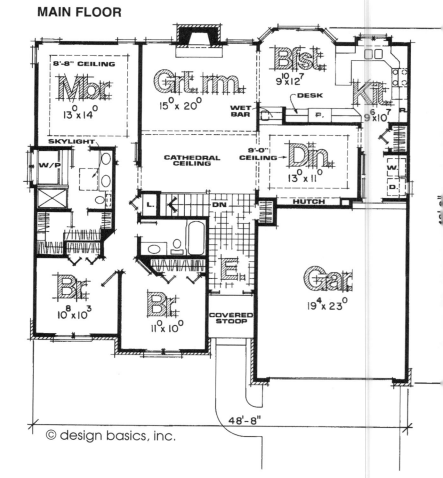

8'-8" CEILING
Mbr
13⁰ x 14⁰
SKYLIGHT
W/P

Grt. rm.
15⁰ x 20⁰
CATHEDRAL CEILING

Bfst.
9¹⁰x12⁷
DESK
WET BAR
P.
Kit
9⁶x10⁰

9'-0" CEILING
Dn.
13⁰ x 11⁰
HUTCH
W. D.

L.
DN

Br
10⁸ x 10³
Br
11⁰ x 10⁰
COVERED STOOP

Gar
19⁴ x 23⁰

48'-8"

© design basics, inc.

To order your Blueprints, call 1-800-235-5700

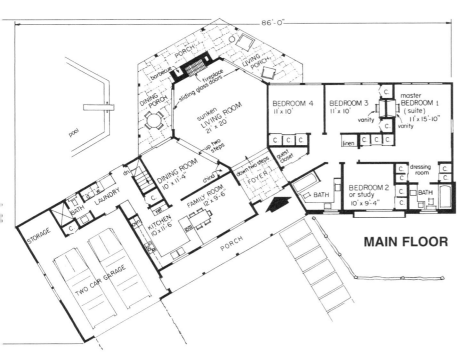

86'-0"

barbecue • DINING PORCH • LIVING PORCH

fireplace
sliding glass doors

pool

sunken
LIVING ROOM
21' x 20'

up two steps

DINING ROOM
10 x 11'-4"

china

down two steps

guest closet

FOYER

BEDROOM 4
11' x 10'

BEDROOM 3
11' x 10'

vanity

master
BEDROOM 1
(suite)
11' x 15'-10"
vanity

linen

dressing room

BATH

BEDROOM 2
or study
10' x 9'-4"

BATH

dn.

BATH LAUNDRY

FAMILY ROOM
12 x 9-6

KITCHEN
10 x 11-6

STORAGE

TWO CAR GARAGE

PORCH

MAIN FLOOR

BL/ML

Western Ranch House

Price Code: C

- This plan features:
— Four bedrooms
— Three full baths

- Authentic Ranch styling with long Loggia, posts and braces, hand-split shake roof and cross-buck doors

- A Texas-sized hexagonal, sunken Living Room with two solid walls, one with a fireplace

- A Porch surrounding the Living Room on three sides

- A Master Suite with a private Master Bath

- An efficient well-equipped Kitchen flowing into the Family Room

MAIN FLOOR — 1,830 SQ. FT.
BASEMENT — 1,830 SQ. FT.
GARAGE — 540 SQ. FT.

TOTAL LIVING AREA:
1,830 SQ. FT.

BL/ML/ZIP/RRR

Simple Lines Enhanced by Elegant Window Treatment

Price Code: A

- ■ This plan features:
  - — Three bedrooms
  - — Two full baths
- ■ A huge, arched window that floods the front room with natural light
- ■ A homey, well-lit Office or Den
- ■ An efficient Kitchen with easy access to the Dining Room
- ■ A Living Room with a sloped ceiling, a fireplace and a window wall
- ■ A Master Bedroom sporting a private Bath with a roomy walk-in closet and a whirlpool tub

MAIN AREA — 1,492 SQ. FT.
BASEMENT — 1,486 SQ. FT.
GARAGE — 462 SQ. FT.

TOTAL LIVING AREA:
1,492 SQ. FT.

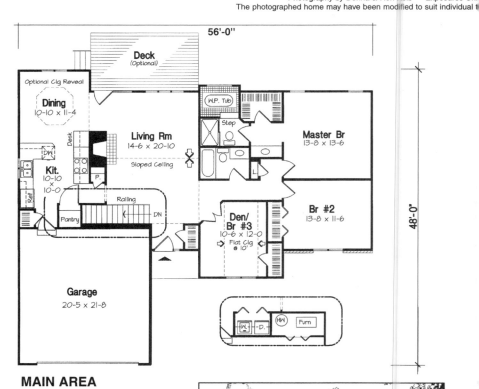

56'-0"

Deck (Optional)

Optional Clg Reveal

Dining
10-10 x 11-4

W.P. Tub

Living Rm
14-6 x 20-10

Step

Master Br
13-8 x 13-6

Sloped Ceiling

Desk

DW

Kit.
10-10 x 10-0

P.

Ref

Railing

DN

Den/
Br #3
10-6 x 12-0
Flat Clg
@ 10'

Br #2
13-8 x 11-6

Pantry

48'-0"

Garage
20-5 x 21-8

W.   D.   HW   Furn

MAIN AREA

BL/ML/ZIP

One Story Country Home

Price Code: A

■ This plan features:

— Three bedrooms

— Two full baths

■ A Living Room has a high ceiling and a heat-circulating fireplace

■ An efficient Kitchen accesses the Dining Room and rear Terrace

■ A Dinette Area for informal eating in the Kitchen can comfortably seat six people

■ A Master Suite is arranged with a large dressing area

MAIN AREA — 1,367 SQ. FT.
BASEMENT — 1,267 SQ. FT.
GARAGE — 431 SQ. FT.

TOTAL LIVING AREA:
1,367 SQ. FT.

Floor Plan

50'-0"   21'-4"

TERR.

whirlpool tub 5'-6"

heat-circul. f.p.

dw   sl. gl. dr.

DINETTE

M.B.R.

L. R.

KIT.
14'-8" x 12'-4"

TWO CAR GAR.
21'-0" x 19'-6"

glass blocks

16'-6 x 15'-2"
AVE.

13'-0" x 20'-6"
high ceiling

skylight above

ref.

w.   d.

dn.

DRESSING

D. R.
11'-4" x 10'-0"

STOR.

W.I.C.

c.

c.

B. R.
11'-0" x 12'-0"
high ceiling

B. R.
10'-6 x 10'-0"

P.

columns   FLOOR PLAN

railing

BL/ML/ZIP

Central Courtyard Features Pool

Price Code: D

■ This plan features:

— Three bedrooms

— One full bath and one three-quarter bath

■ A central Courtyard complete with a Pool

■ A secluded Master Bedroom accented by a skylight, a spacious walk-in closet, and a private Bath

■ A convenient Kitchen easily serving the Patio for comfortable outdoor entertaining

■ A detached two-car Garage

MAIN AREA — 2,194 SQ. FT.
GARAGE — 576 SQ. FT.

*TOTAL LIVING AREA:
2,194 SQ. FT.*

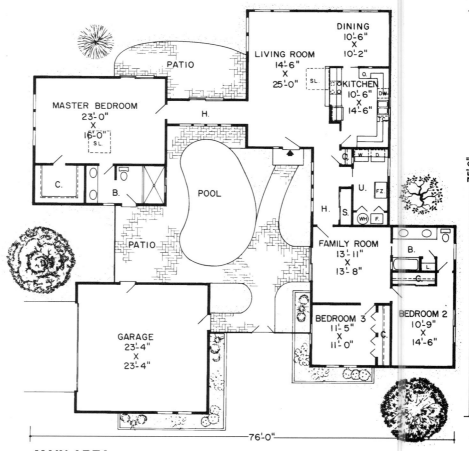

MAIN AREA

BL/ML/ZIP/RRR

Ranch Provides Great Kitchen Area

Price Code: A

■ This plan features:

— Three bedrooms

— Two full baths

■ A Dining Room with sliding glass doors to the backyard

■ Access to the Garage through the Laundry Room

■ A Master Bedroom with a private full Bath

■ A two-car Garage

MAIN AREA — 1,400 SQ. FT.
BASEMENT — 1,400 SQ. FT.
GARAGE — 528 SQ. FT.

TOTAL LIVING AREA:
1,400 SQ. FT.

Floor Plan

50'-0"

Garage
22 x 24

W D
L
Kit
Dining
9 x 13

DN
pantry

Living Rm
19 x 14

Br 2
11-6 x 13

Br 3
10-6 x 13

MBr 1
11-6 x 14

MAIN AREA

Alternate Plan
w/ Crawlspace

W D
L
Kit
10 x 13
Dining
9 x 13

F

BL/ML/ZIP

Easy One Floor Living

Price Code: B

■ This plan features:

— Three bedrooms

— Two full baths

■ A spacious Family Room topped by a vaulted ceiling and high-lighted by a large fireplace and a French door to the rear yard

■ A Pantry and a peninsula counter adding more efficiency to the Kitchen

■ A vaulted ceiling over the cozy Sitting Room in the Master Suite

■ An optional basement, crawl space or slab foundation — please specify when ordering

MAIN FLOOR — 1,671 SQ. FT.
BASEMENT — 1,685 SQ. FT.
GARAGE — 400 SQ. FT.

TOTAL LIVING AREA:
1,671 SQ. FT.

WIDTH 50'-0"
DEPTH 51'-0"

MAIN FLOOR

© Frank Betz Associates

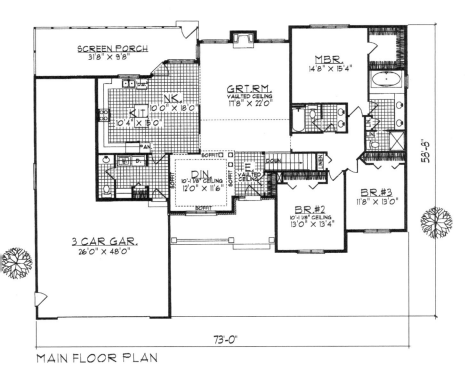

SCREEN PORCH
31'8" X 9'8"

NK.
10'0" X 18'0"

KIT.
10'4" X 15'0"

GRT. RM.
VAULTED CEILING
11'8" X 22'0"

M.B.R.
14'8" X 15'4"

PAN.

SOFFIT

DIN.
10'-1 1/8" CEILING
12'0" X 11'6"

SOFFIT

E.
VAULTED
CEILING

DOWN

SOFFIT

LIN.

LINEN

B.R. #3
11'8" X 13'0"

B.R. #2
10'-1 1/8" CEILING
13'0" X 13'4"

3 CAR GAR.
26'0" X 48'0"

73'-0"

58'-8"

MAIN FLOOR PLAN

BL/ML/ZIP

Luxury on One Level

Price Code: D

■ This plan features:

— Three bedrooms

— Two full and one half baths

■ Covered front Porch leads into entry and Great Room with vaulted ceiling

■ Arched soffits and columns impact the formal Dining Room

■ Country-size Kitchen with a Pantry, work island, eating Nook with Screen Porch beyond, and nearby Laundry/Garage entry

■ Master Bedroom offers a walk-in closet and a luxurious Bath

MAIN FLOOR — 2,196 SQ. FT.
BASEMENT — 2,196 SQ. FT.

TOTAL LIVING AREA:
2,196 SQ. FT.

BL/ML

Country Charmer

Price Code: A

■ This plan features:

—Three bedrooms

—Two full baths

■ Quaint front Porch is perfect for sitting and relaxing

■ Great Room opening into Dining Area and Kitchen

■ Master Suite with a private Bath, walk-in closet and built-in shelves

■ Two large secondary bedrooms in the front of the home share a hall Bath

■ Two car Garage located in the rear of the home

MAIN FLOOR — 1,438 SQ. FT.
GARAGE — 486 SQ. FT.

TOTAL LIVING AREA:
1,438 SQ. FT.

MAIN FLOOR

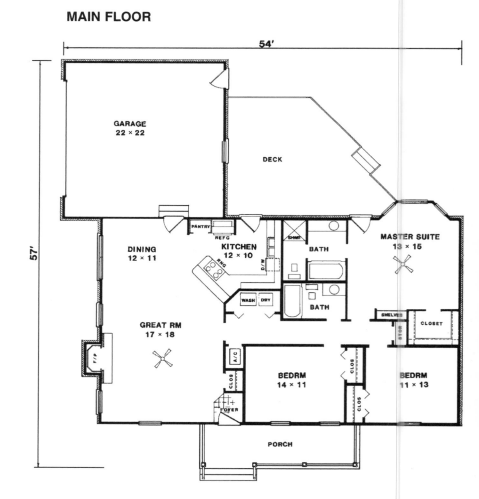

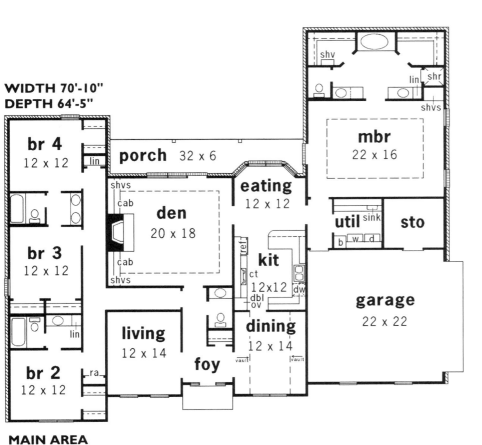

WIDTH 70'-10"
DEPTH 64'-5"

MAIN AREA

BL/ML

European Style

Price Code: F

■ This plan features:

— Four bedrooms

— Three full and one half baths

■ Central Foyer between spacious Living and Dining rooms

■ Hub Kitchen with extended counter and nearby Utility/Garage entry

■ Spacious Den with a hearth fireplace between built-ins

■ Master Bedroom wing with decorative ceiling, plush Bath with two walk-in closets

■ Three additional Bedrooms with ample closets and full Baths

■ Choice of basement or crawl space foundation — please specify when ordering

MAIN AREA — 2,727 SQ.
GARAGE — 569 SQ. FT.

TOTAL LIVING AREA:
2,727 SQ. FT.

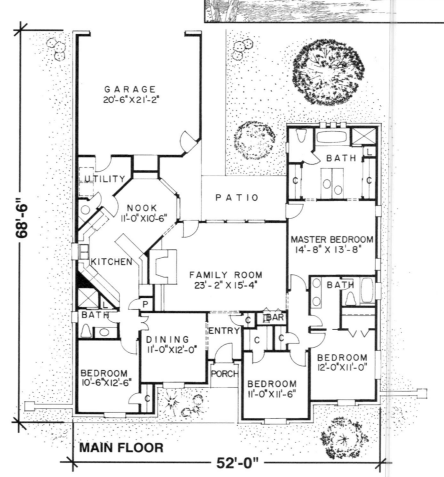

BL/ML/ZIP

Brick Home with Four Bedrooms

Price Code: D

■ This plan features:

— Four bedrooms

— Two full bath and one three-quarter bath

■ Four roomy bedrooms, including the Master Bedroom

■ A centrally located Family Room including a fireplace, wetbar and access to the Patio

■ A large Dining Room at the front of the home for entertaining

■ An interesting Kitchen and Nook with an adjoining Utility Room

MAIN FLOOR — 2,070 SQ. FT.
GARAGE — 474 SQ. FT.

TOTAL LIVING AREA:
2,070 SQ. FT.

GARAGE
20'-6" X 21'-2"

UTILITY

NOOK
11'-0" X 10'-6"

PATIO

BATH

KITCHEN

MASTER BEDROOM
14'-8" X 13'-8"

FAMILY ROOM
23'-2" X 15'-4"

BATH

P

BATH

BAR

ENTRY

DINING
11'-0" X 12'-0"

BEDROOM
10'-6" X 12'-6"

PORCH

BEDROOM
11'-0" X 11'-6"

BEDROOM
12'-0" X 11'-0"

68'-6"

MAIN FLOOR

52'-0"

To order your Blueprints, call 1-800-235-5700

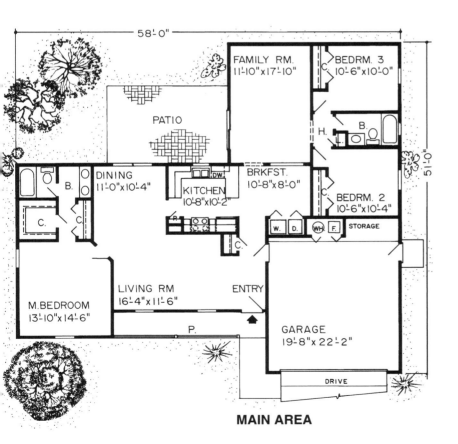

MAIN AREA

BL/ML/ZIP

Carefree Convenience

Price Code: B

■ This plan features:

— Three bedrooms

— Two full baths

■ A galley Kitchen centrally located between the Dining, Breakfast and Living Room areas

■ A Master Suite with two closets and a double vanity Bath

■ Two additional Bedrooms sharing a full Bath

MAIN AREA — 1,600 SQ. FT.
GARAGE — 465 SQ. FT.

TOTAL LIVING AREA:
1,600 SQ. FT.

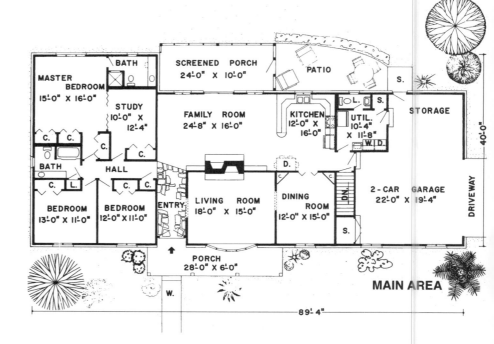

BL/ML/ZIP/RRR

Home Recalls the South

Price Code: E

■ This plan features:

— Three bedrooms

— One full, one half and one three-quarter baths

■ A Master Bedroom Suite with a private Study

■ Fireplaces enhancing the formal Living Room and spacious Family Room

■ A lovely, screened Porch/Patio skirting the Family Room and the Kitchen

■ A Utility Room with access into the Storage and Garage areas

MAIN AREA — 2,466 SQ. FT.
BASEMENT — 1,447 SQ. FT.
GARAGE — 664 SQ. FT.

TOTAL LIVING AREA:
2,466 SQ. FT.

Floor Plan — MAIN AREA

- BATH
- MASTER BEDROOM 15'-0" X 16'-0"
- STUDY 10'-0" X 12'-4"
- SCREENED PORCH 24'-0" X 10'-0"
- PATIO
- S.
- C. C. C.
- FAMILY ROOM 24'-8" X 16'-0"
- KITCHEN 12'-0" X 16'-0"
- L. L. S.
- UTIL. 10'-4" X 11'-8"
- W.D.
- STORAGE
- BATH
- C. L.
- HALL
- C. C.
- D.
- 40'-0"
- BEDROOM 13'-0" X 11'-0"
- BEDROOM 12'-0" X 11'-0"
- ENTRY
- LIVING ROOM 18'-0" X 15'-0"
- DINING ROOM 12'-0" X 15'-0"
- DN.
- 2 - CAR GARAGE 22'-0" X 19'-4"
- DRIVEWAY
- S.
- PORCH 28'-0" X 6'-0"
- W.
- 89'-4"
- **MAIN AREA**

BL

Gabled Roofline

Price Code: G

■ This plan features:
— Four bedrooms
— Two full and one three-quarter baths
■ The U-shaped Kitchen enjoys a center island and a service bar that opens to the Breakfast Nook.
■ 2,755 square feet on the main level; 440 square feet of bonus space
■ The bonus space above the three-car Garage offers an ideal location for a Grandparents' Suite.
■ This home is designed with a slab foundation.

MAIN FLOOR — 2,755 SQ. FT.

BONUS — 440 SQ. FT.

GARAGE — 724 SQ. FT.

TOTAL LIVING AREA:
2,755 SQ. FT.

WIDTH 73'-0"
DEPTH 82'-8"

MAIN FLOOR

BL/ML

Country Charm

Price Code: A

■ This plan features:
— Three bedrooms
— Two full and one half baths
■ 10-foot high ceilings in the Living Room, Family Room and Dinette Area
■ A heat-circulating fireplace
■ A Master Bath with separate stall shower and whirlpool tub
■ A two-car Garage with access through the Mudroom

UPPER LEVEL — 1,203 SQ. FT.

UNFINISHED BASEMENT — 676 SQ. FT.

GARAGE — 509 SQ. FT.

TOTAL LIVING AREA:
1,203 SQ. FT.

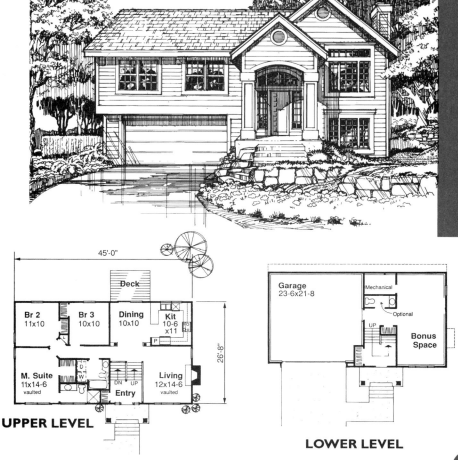

UPPER LEVEL

LOWER LEVEL

© 1999 Donald A. Gardner, Inc.

B. NATHAN

BL/ML

Compact and Elegant Design

Price Code: C

■ This plan features:
— Two bedrooms with an optional third bedroom
— Two full baths
■ A vaulted ceiling adds elegance and scale to the Great Room
■ Light and views flood the sunny Breakfast Nook
■ Over the Garage, a Bonus Room offers 280 sq. ft. of potential
■ Use the optional third Bedroom as a Study or Media Room

MAIN FLOOR — 1,828 SQ. FT.
BONUS — 352 SQ. FT.
GARAGE — 503 SQ. FT.

TOTAL LIVING AREA: 1,828 SQ. FT

BL

Unfinished Upper Level

Price Code: E

■ This plan features:
— Three bedrooms
— Two full and one half baths
■ A walk-in Pantry and long island with cooktop highlight the Kitchen.
■ Arched windows adorn each side of the fireplace in the Family Room.
■ The optional upper level adds 588 square feet.
■ This home is designed with basement and crawl-space foundation options.

MAIN FLOOR — 2,491 SQ. FT.
BONUS — 522 SQ. FT.
GARAGE — 588 SQ. FT.

TOTAL LIVING AREA: 2,491 SQ. FT

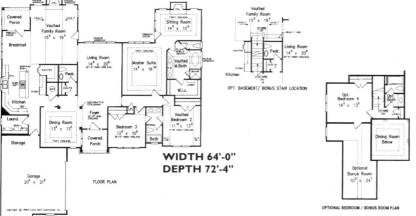

WIDTH 64'-0"
DEPTH 72'-4"

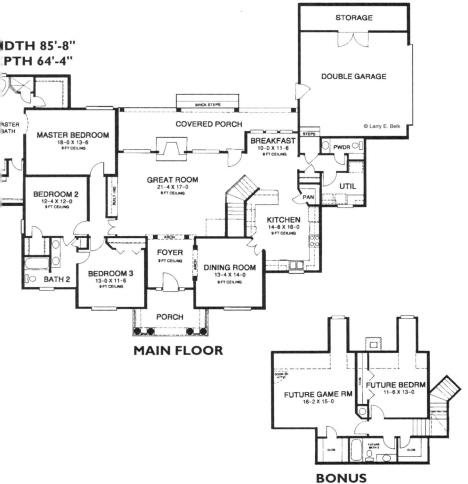

MAIN FLOOR

WIDTH 85'-8"
DEPTH 64'-4"

STORAGE

DOUBLE GARAGE

© Larry E. Belk

BRICK STEPS

COVERED PORCH

MASTER BATH

MASTER BEDROOM
18-0 X 13-6
9 FT CEILING

BREAKFAST
10-0 X 11-6
9 FT CEILING

PWDR

STEPS

BEDROOM 2
12-4 X 12-0
9 FT CEILING

GREAT ROOM
21-4 X 17-0
9 FT CEILING

UTIL

PAN

BUILT-INS

KITCHEN
14-6 X 16-0
9 FT CEILING

ARCH

BATH 2

FOYER
9 FT CEILING

BEDROOM 3
13-0 X 11-6
9 FT CEILING

ARCH

DINING ROOM
13-4 X 14-0
9 FT CEILING

PORCH

BONUS

DOOR TO ATTIC

FUTURE GAME RM
16-2 X 15-0

CLO.

FUTURE BEDRM
11-6 X 13-0

FUTURE BATH 3

CLO.

CLO.

BL/ML

Stately Elegance

Price Code: E

■ This plan features:

— Three bedrooms

— Two full and one half baths

■ Elegant columns frame Entry into Foyer and expansive Great Room beyond

■ Efficient Kitchen ideal for busy cook with walk-in Pantry, Breakfast Area and access to formal Dining Room, Laundry and Garage

■ A private Master Bedroom suite boasts a Bath with two walk-in closets and whirlpool tub

■ An optional slab or crawl space foundation — please specify when ordering

MAIN FLOOR — 2,409 SQ. FT.
GARAGE — 644 SQ. FT.

TOTAL LIVING AREA:
2,409 SQ. FT.

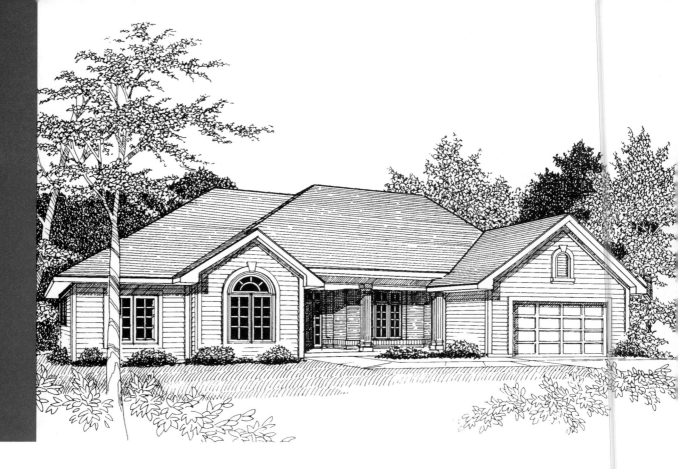

BL

Distinctive Ranch

Price Code: C

■ This plan features:

— Three bedrooms

— Two full baths

■ This hipped roofed Ranch has an exterior that mixes brick and siding

■ The Great room has a cathedral ceiling and a rear wall fireplace

■ The Dining Room features a high ceiling and a bright front window

■ The two-car Garage could easily be expanded to three with a door placed in the rear Storage Area

■ No materials list is available for this plan

MAIN FLOOR — 1,802 SQ. FT.
BASEMENT — 1,802 SQ. FT.

TOTAL LIVING AREA:
1,802 SQ. FT.

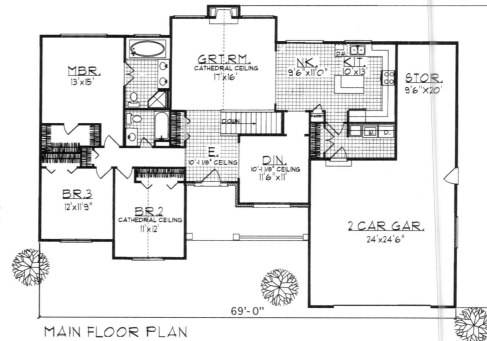

MBR.
13'x15'

GRT.RM.
CATHEDRAL CEILING
17'x16'

NK.
9'6"x11'0"

KIT.
10'x13'

STOR.
9'6"X20'

E.
10'-1 1/8" CEILING

DIN.
10'-1 1/8" CEILING
11'6"x11'

BR.3
12'x11'9"

BR.2
CATHEDRAL CEILING
11'x12'

2 CAR GAR.
24'x24'6"

69'-0"

MAIN FLOOR PLAN

To order your Blueprints, call 1-800-235-5700

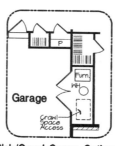

Slab/Crawl Space Option

BL/ML/ZIP/RRR

Easy Living

Price Code: A

- This plan features:
  - Three bedrooms
  - Two full baths
- A dramatic sloped ceiling and a massive fireplace in the Living Room
- A Dining Room crowned by a sloping ceiling and a plant shelf also having sliding doors to the Deck
- A U-shaped Kitchen with abundant cabinets, a window over the sink and a walk-in Pantry
- A Master Suite with a private full Bath, decorative ceiling and walk-in closet

MAIN FLOOR — 1,456 SQ. FT.
BASEMENT — 1,448 SQ. FT.
GARAGE — 452 SQ. FT.

TOTAL LIVING AREA:
1,456 SQ. FT.

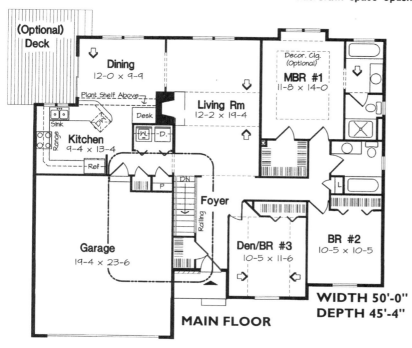

WIDTH 50'-0"
DEPTH 45'-4"

MAIN FLOOR

BL/ML

Formal Balance

Price Code: A

■ This plan features:

— Three bedrooms

— Two full baths

■ A cathedral ceiling in the Living Room with a heat-circulating fireplace as the focal point

■ A bow window in the Dining Room that adds elegance as well as natural light

■ A well-equipped Kitchen that serves both the Dinette and the formal Dining Room efficiently

■ A Master Bedroom with three closets and a private Master Bath with sliding glass doors to the Master Deck with a hot tub

MAIN FLOOR — 1,476 SQ. FT.
BASEMENT — 1,361 SQ. FT.
GARAGE — 548 SQ. FT.

TOTAL LIVING AREA:
1,476 SQ. FT.

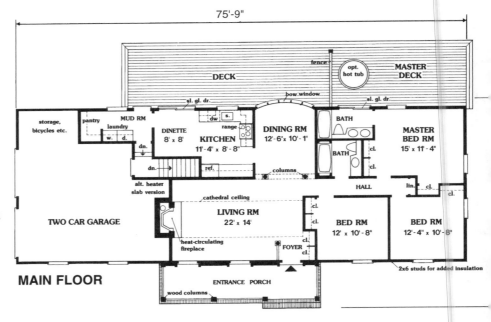

MAIN AREA

WIDTH — 58'-0"
DEPTH — 60'-0"

BL/ML/RRR

Four Bedroom Charmer

Price Code: D

■ This plan features:

— Four bedrooms

— Two full baths

■ A vaulted ceiling in the naturally lighted entry

■ A Living Room with a masonry fireplace, large windowed bay and vaulted ceiling

■ A coffered ceiling and built-in china cabinet in the Dining Room

■ A large Family Room with a wood stove alcove

■ An island cooktop and built-in Pantry in the Kitchen

■ A luxurious Master Bedroom with whirlpool garden tub

■ A Study with a window seat and built-in bookshelves

MAIN AREA— 2,185 SQ. FT.

TOTAL LIVING AREA:

BL/ML

Symmetrical and Stately

Price Code: E

■ This plan features:

— Four bedrooms

— Two full and one half baths

■ Double columned Porch leads into the open Foyer

■ Decorative ceiling crowns the Den with a hearth fireplace and built-in shelves

■ Large, efficient Kitchen with a peninsula serving counter, a Breakfast area, adjoining the Utility and the Garage

■ Master Bedroom suite has a decorative ceiling and dual vanity

■ An optional crawl space or slab foundation — please specify when ordering

MAIN FLOOR — 2,387 SQ. FT.
GARAGE — 505 SQ. FT.

TOTAL LIVING AREA:
2,387 SQ. FT.

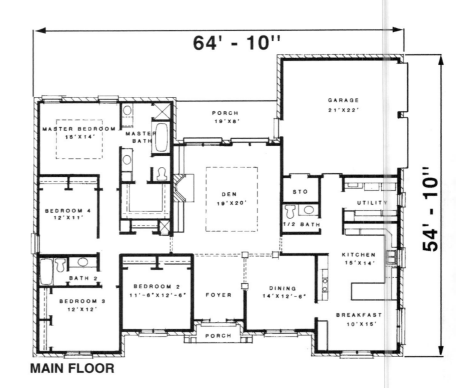

MAIN FLOOR

To order your Blueprints, call 1-800-235-5700

BL/ML/ZIP/RRR

Traditional Beauty

Price Code: D

■ This plan features:

— Three bedrooms

— Two full baths

■ Traditional beauty with large arched windows, round columns, covered porch, brick veneer and an open floor plan

■ Clerestory dormers above covered Porch

■ Convenient Kitchen with Breakfast Area and work island with sink

■ Tray ceiling over the Master Bedroom, Dining Room and Bedroom/Study

■ Dual vanity, separate shower and whirlpool tub in the Master Bath

MAIN FLOOR — 1,576 SQ. FT.
GARAGE — 465 SQ. FT.

TOTAL LIVING AREA:
1,576 SQ. FT

Floor Plan

- spa
- DECK
- MASTER BED RM. 13-4 x 13-8
- master bath
- skylights
- fireplace
- BRKFST. 11-4 x 7-8
- w / d
- walk-in closet
- storage
- BED RM. 11-4 x 11-0
- GREAT RM. 15-4 x 16-10 (cathedral ceiling)
- cl
- bath
- KITCHEN 11-4 x 10-0
- GARAGE 20-0 x 19-8
- cl
- FOYER 8-2 x 5-10
- cl
- BED RM./ STUDY 11-4 x 10-4
- PORCH
- DINING RM. 11-4 x 11-4

© 1993 DAGA
All rights reserved

47-3

60-6

FLOOR PLAN

BL/ML/ZIP

A Modern Slant On A Country Theme

Price Code: B

■ This plan features:

—Three bedrooms

—Two full baths

■ Country-styled front porch highlighting exterior enhanced by dormer windows

■ Modern open floor plan for a more spacious feeling

■ Great Room accented by a quaint corner fireplace and a ceiling fan

■ Dining Area adjacent to the Great Room for easy entertaining

■ Kitchen has a convenient snack bar for meals on the go

■ Two additional Bedrooms sharing full Bath in the hall

FIRST FLOOR — 1,648 SQ. FT.
GARAGE — 479 SQ. FT.

TOTAL LIVING AREA:
1,648 SQ. FT.

MAIN FLOOR

To order your Blueprints, call 1-800-235-5700

BL

Visual Impact

Price Code: E

- This plan features:
— Four bedrooms
— Two full and one half baths
- Two dormers centered over double arches announce the entrance of this stylish brick and siding one-story.
- Classic columns provide visual impact at the front door and a see-through fireplace adds a cozy feel to both the Dining Room and Great Room.
- Bedrooms two and three, both with walk-in closets, are located nearby.
- Bedroom four is situated for use as either a Bedroom or a Study.

MAIN FLOOR — 2,389 SQ. FT.
GARAGE — 543 SQ. FT.

TOTAL LIVING AREA:
2,389 SQ. FT.

WIDTH 75'-2"
DEPTH 61'-4"

MAIN FLOOR

BL/ML/ZIP/RRR

Windows Add Warmth To All Living Areas

Price Code: B

- This plan features:
— Three bedrooms
— Two full baths
- A Master Suite with huge his and her, walk-in closets and private bath
- A second and third Bedroom with ample closet space
- A Kitchen equipped with an island counter, and flowing easily into the Dining and Family Rooms
- A Laundry Room conveniently located near all three bedrooms
- An optional garage

MAIN FLOOR— 1,672 SQ. FT.
OPTIONAL GARAGE — 566 SQ. FT.

TOTAL LIVING AREA:
1,672 SQ. FT.

MAIN FLOOR

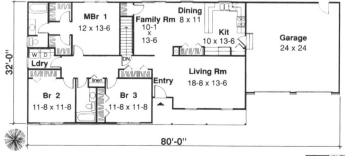

OPTIONAL ROOM

BL/ML

Small, Yet Lavishly Appointed

Price Code: C

■ This plan features:

— Three bedrooms

— Two full and one half baths

■ The Dining Room, Living Room, Foyer and Master Bath are all topped by high ceilings

■ Master Bedroom includes a decorative tray ceiling

■ Living Room has a large fireplace and a French door

■ An optional basement or crawl space foundation — please specify when ordering

MAIN FLOOR — 1,845 SQ. FT.
BONUS — 409 SQ. FT.
BASEMENT — 1,845 SQ. FT.
GARAGE — 529 SQ. FT.

TOTAL LIVING AREA: 1,845 SQ. FT.

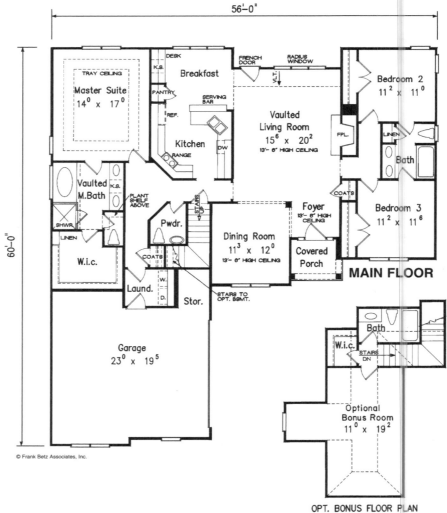

© Frank Betz Associates, Inc.

OPT. BONUS FLOOR PLAN

To order your Blueprints, call 1-800-235-5700

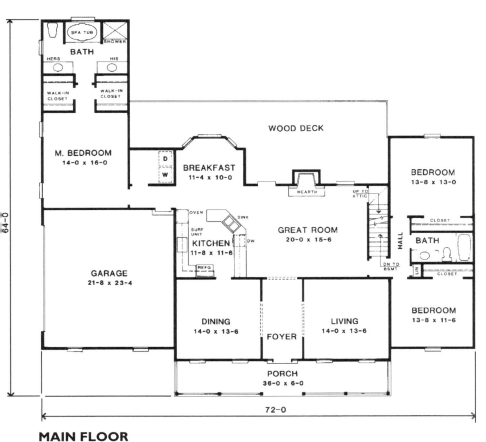

MAIN FLOOR

BL/ML

Traditional Ranch Plan

Price Code: D

■ This plan features:

—Three bedrooms

—Two full baths

■ Large Foyer set between the formal Living and Dining Rooms

■ Spacious Great Room adjacent to the open Kitchen /Breakfast Area

■ Secluded Master Bedroom highlighted by the Master Bath with a garden tub, separate shower, and his and her vanities

■ Bay window allowing bountiful natural light into the Breakfast Area

■ An optional basement or crawl space foundation — please specify when ordering

MAIN FLOOR — 2,218 SQ. FT.
BASEMENT — 1,658 SQ. FT.
GARAGE — 528 SQ. FT.

TOTAL LIVING AREA:
2,218 SQ. FT.

BL

Divided Three-Car Garage

Price Code: F

- This plan features:
— Three bedrooms
— Two full and one half baths
- A Shop Area connects the divided Garage, which provides room for three vehicles.
- The large Great Room is the hub of the home, sequestering the bedroom wing and providing access to the Kitchen and Breakfast Room.
- This home is designed with a slab foundation.

MAIN FLOOR — 2,551 SQ. FT.
GARAGE — 642 SQ. FT.

TOTAL LIVING AREA:
2,551 SQ. FT.

FLOOR PLAN

WIDTH 52'-0"
DEPTH 59'-4"

BL/ML

Accented by
Vaulted Ceilings & Columns

Price Code: D

- This plan features
—Three bedrooms
—Two full and one half baths
- Corner quoins, arched windows and keystones accent the exterior
- Columns defining the entrances to the Dining Room, Family Room and Breakfast Room
- Vaulted ceilings adding volume to the Foyer, Dining Room, Living Room, Family Room, Breakfast Room and the Master Bath
- An efficient and well-appointed Kitchen highlighted by serving bar to the family room
- A large focal point fireplace enhancing the Family Room
- Private Master Suite topped by a tray ceiling and enhanced by a lavish Bath
- Two additional Bedrooms sharing the full Bath in the hall

MAIN FLOOR — 2,094 SQ. FT.
BASEMENT — 2,108 SQ. FT.
GARAGE — 453 SQ. FT.

TOTAL LIVING AREA:
2,094 SQ. FT.

© Frank Betz Associates, Inc.

MAIN FLOOR

To order your Blueprints, call 1-800-235-5700

BL/ML/ZIP

Private Master Suite

Price Code: D

■ This plan features:

— Three bedrooms

— Two full and one half bath

■ Secluded Master Bedroom suite tucked into the rear left corner of the home with a five-piece bath and two walk-in closets

■ Two additional Bedrooms at the opposite side of the home sharing the full Bath in the hall

■ Expansive Living Room high-lighted by a corner fireplace and access to the rear Porch

■ Kitchen is sandwiched between the bright, bayed Nook and the formal Dining Room providing ease in serving

MAIN FLOOR — 2,069 SQ. FT.
GARAGE — 481 SQ. FT.

TOTAL LIVING AREA:
2,069 SQ. FT.

WIDTH 70'-0"
DEPTH 58'-0"

MAIN FLOOR

SHOWER
CLOSET
BATH
MASTER SUITE 13×19
FAN
CLOSET
R/A
1/2 BATH
GARAGE 20×23
WASH
DRY
UTIL
SINK
NOOK 9×9
F/P
BAR
D/W
RNG
REF
KIT'N 12×14
OVEN
PORCH
LIVING RM 17×25
FAN
11'-0" CEILING
DINING 12×12
CLO
CLO
FOYER
STUDY 8×9
BEDRM 11×12
CLOS
HALL
BATH
A/C
CLOS
BEDRM 12×12
PORCH

© 1997 Donald A. Gardner Architects, Inc.

BL/ML/ZIP/RRR

Country-Style Home With Corner Porch

Price Code: E

■ This plan features:

— Three bedrooms

— Two full baths

■ Dining Room has four floor to ceiling windows that overlook the front Porch

■ Great Room topped by a cathedral ceiling, enhanced by a fireplace and sliding doors to the back Porch

■ Master Bedroom has a walk in closet and private Bath

■ A skylight Bonus Room over the two-car Garage

MAIN FLOOR — 1,815 SQ. FT.
GARAGE — 522 SQ, FT.
BONUS — 336 SQ. FT.

TOTAL LIVING AREA:
1,815 SQ. FT.

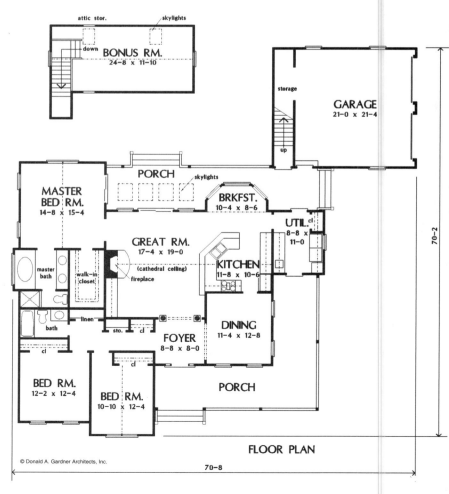

BL/ML/RRR

Secluded Master Suite

Price Code: G

- This plan features:
  — Three bedrooms plus an optional bedroom
  — Two full and one half baths
- A large fireplace and cathedral ceiling create an impressive Great Room
- Both the Great Room and Master Bedroom open onto the rear screened Porch
- Over the Garage, 354 sq. ft. of Bonus Space awaits its potential
- An angled Kitchen counter would be great for buffets

MAIN FLOOR — 2,282 SQ. FT.
BONUS — 354 SQ. FT.
GARAGE — 572 SQ. FT.
PORCH — 435 SQ. FT.

TOTAL LIVING AREA:
2,282 SQ. FT

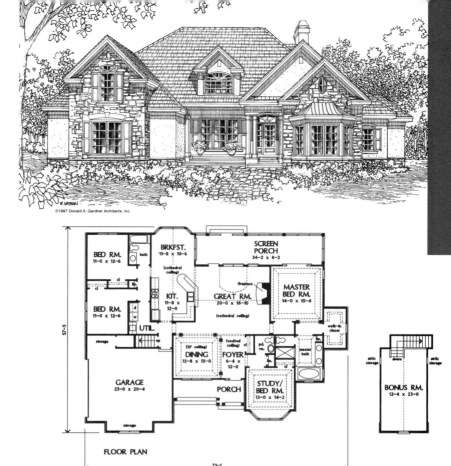

BL/ML/ZIP

Classic Ranch Has Contemporary Flavor

Price Code: A

- This plan features:
  — Three bedrooms
  — Two full baths
- A galley-styled Kitchen easily serving the Dining Room
- A Living Room with bump out window and fireplace
- Ample closet space
- A Master Bedroom with a private Bath and an individual shower

MAIN FLOOR — 1,268 SQ. FT.
BASEMENT — 1,248 SQ. FT.

TOTAL LIVING AREA:
1,268 SQ. FT.

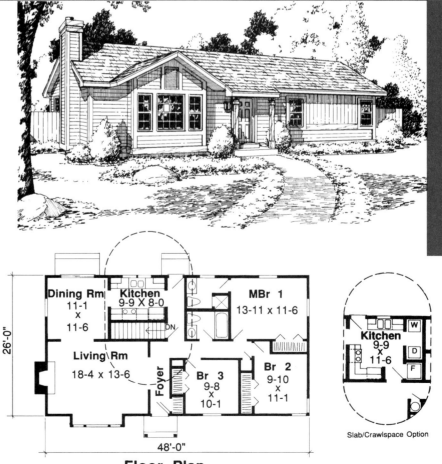

BL

Easy Living

Price Code: A

■ This plan features:

— Three bedrooms

— Two full baths

■ A covered front Porch shelters the entry to this home

■ Family Room is enlarged by vaulted ceiling above a cozy fire-place

■ The L-shaped Kitchen includes a work island and Dining Area

■ The Master Bedroom has two building options for its Bath

■ Both of the secondary Bedrooms have walk-in closets

MAIN FLOOR — 1,474 SQ. FT.
GARAGE — 454 SQ. FT.

TOTAL LIVING AREA:
1,474 SQ. FT.

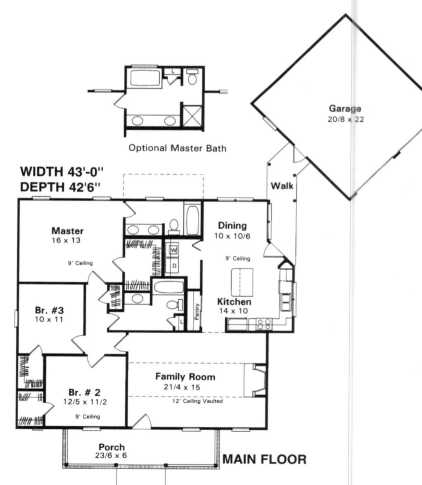

Optional Master Bath

WIDTH 43'-0"
DEPTH 42'6"

Garage
20/8 x 22

Walk

Master
16 x 13

9' Ceiling

Dining
10 x 10/6

9' Ceiling

Br. #3
10 x 11

W
D

Pantry

Kitchen
14 x 10

Br. # 2
12/5 x 11/2

9' Ceiling

Family Room
21/4 x 15

12' Ceiling Vaulted

Porch
23/6 x 6

MAIN FLOOR

To order your Blueprints, call 1-800-235-5700

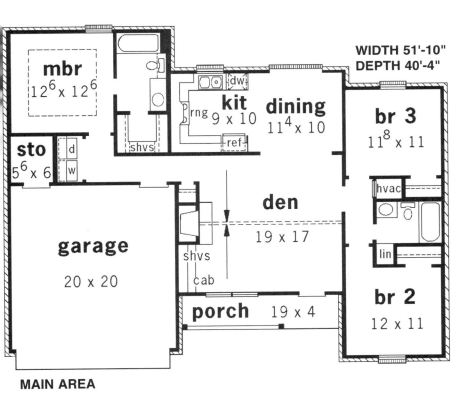

WIDTH 51'-10"
DEPTH 40'-4"

mbr
12^6 x 12^6

sto
5^6 x 6

garage
20 x 20

kit
rng 9 x 10

shvs

ref

dining
11^4 x 10

den
19 x 17

shvs

cab

porch   19 x 4

br 3
11^8 x 11

hvac

lin

br 2
12 x 11

MAIN AREA

BL/ML

Private Master Suite

Price Code: A

■ This plan features:

— Three bedrooms

— Two full baths

■ A spacious Great Room enhanced by a vaulted ceiling and fireplace

■ A well-equipped Kitchen with windowed double sink

■ A secluded Master Suite with decorative ceiling, private Master Bath, and walk-in closet

■ Two additional Bedrooms sharing hall Bath

■ An optional crawl space or slab foundation — please specify when ordering

MAIN FLOOR — 1,293 SQ. FT.
GARAGE — 433 SQ. FT.

TOTAL LIVING AREA:
1,293 SQ. FT.

BL/ML

Turret Study Creates Impact

Price Code: I

■ This plan features:

—Three bedrooms

—Two full, one half and one three-quarter baths

■ Entry doors opening into the formal Living Room focusing to the Lanai through sliding glass doors and a mitered glass corner

■ Double sided fireplace in the Living Room shared by the Master Suite

■ Spacious Master Suite including a fireplace, morning kitchen bar, and Lanai access

MAIN FLOOR — 3,477 SQ. FT.
GARAGE — 771 SQ. FT.

TOTAL LIVING AREA:
3,477 SQ. FT.

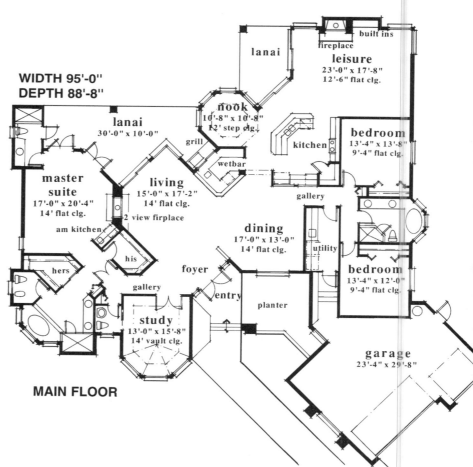

WIDTH 95'-0"
DEPTH 88'-8"

MAIN FLOOR

To order your Blueprints, call 1-800-235-5700

© Frank Betz Associates, Inc.

50'-0"

Master Suite
17⁵ x 14⁴
TRAY CEILING

FPL.

FRENCH DOOR   RADIUS WDW.

VAULT

ARCHED OPENING

Dining Room
11⁸ x 11⁰

Vaulted
Great Room
19³ x 18⁷
16'-0" HIGH CEILING

VAULT   VAULT

SHWR.

Vaulted
M.Bath

PLANT SHELF ABOVE

W.i.c.
LINEN

K.S.

DECORATIVE COLUMNS

SERVING BAR

ARCHED OPENINGS

Kitchen

RANGE

DW.

ISLAND

REF.

Breakfast

PAN.

TRAY CLG.

Bedroom 2
12⁰ x 11⁰

W.i.c.

COATS

Foyer
16'-0" HIGH CLG.

Pwdr. Laund.
W.
D.

Storage

55'-4"

VLT.   VLT.

LINEN

Bedroom 3
11¹⁰ x 10⁹

Garage
21⁵ x 20³

Bath

RADIUS WDW.

Main floor

GARAGE LOCATION W/ BASEMENT

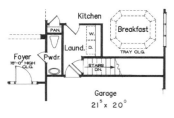

Kitchen

PAN.

Breakfast

Laund.
W.
D.

TRAY CLG.

Foyer
16'-0" HIGH CLG.

Pwdr.

STAIRS DN.

Garage
21⁵ x 20⁰

OPT. BASEMENT STAIRS LOCATION

BL/ML

With All the Amenities

Price Code: C

■ This plan features:

— Three bedrooms

— Two full and one half baths

■ Sixteen foot high ceiling over the Foyer

■ French door to the rear yard and decorative columns at its arched entrance

■ Vaulted ceiling in Dining Room

■ Expansive Kitchen features a center work island and a built-in Pantry and Breakfast Area

■ An optional basement, slab or crawl space foundation — please specify when ordering

MAIN FLOOR — 1,884 SQ. FT.
BASEMENT — 1,908 SQ. FT.
GARAGE — 495 SQ. FT.

TOTAL LIVING AREA:
1,884 SQ. FT.

BL/ML/RRR

Tremendous Curb Appeal

Price Code: C

■ This plan features:

— Three bedrooms

— Two full baths

■ Wrap-around Porch sheltering entry

■ Great Room, Dining Room and Kitchen open to each other for a feeling of spaciousness

■ Pantry, skylight and peninsula counter add to the comfort and efficiency of the Kitchen

■ Cathedral ceiling crowns the Master Suite, which also has walk-in and linen closets and a luxurious private Bath

MAIN FLOOR — 1,246 SQ. FT.
GARAGE — 420 SQ. FT.

TOTAL LIVING AREA: 1,246 SQ. FT.

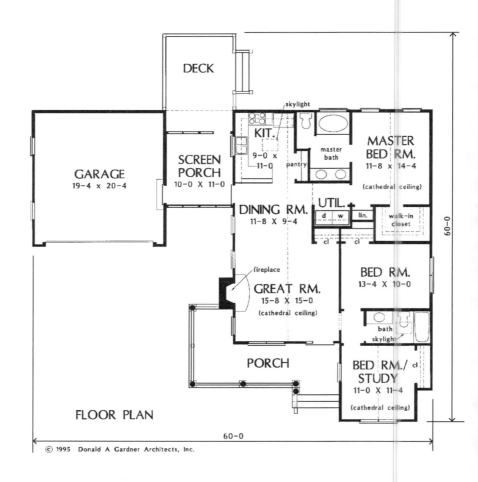

FLOOR PLAN

© 1995 Donald A Gardner Architects, Inc.

BL/ML/ZIP

Gazebo Porch Creates Old-Fashioned Feel

Price Code: A

■ This plan features:

— Three bedrooms

— Two full baths

■ An old-fashioned welcome is created by the covered Porch

■ The Breakfast Area overlooks the Porch and is separated from the Kitchen by an extended counter

■ The Dining Room and the Great Room are highlighted by a two sided fireplace

■ The roomy Master suite is enhanced by a whirlpool Bath with double vanity and a walk-in closet

■ No materials list is available for this plan

MAIN FLOOR — 1,452 SQ. FT.
GARAGE — 584 SQ. FT.

TOTAL LIVING AREA:
1,452 SQ. FT.

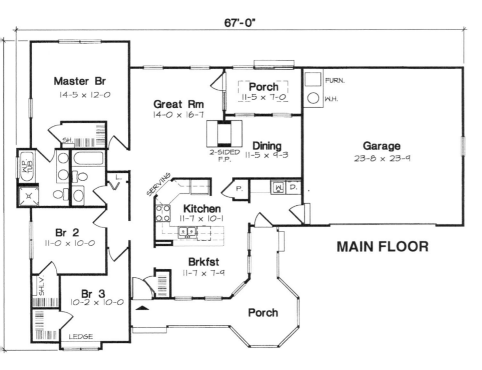

67'-0"

Master Br
14-5 x 12-0

Great Rm
14-0 x 16-7

Porch
11-5 x 7-0

FURN.

W.H.

2-SIDED F.P.

Dining
11-5 x 9-3

Garage
23-8 x 23-9

SERVING

P.

W   D.

Kitchen
11-7 x 10-1

MAIN FLOOR

Br 2
11-0 x 10-0

SHLV.

Br 3
10-2 x 10-0

LEDGE

Brkfst
11-7 x 7-9

Porch

SH.

WP. TUB

L.

BL

Spectacular Front Window

Price Code: C

■ This plan features:

— Three bedrooms

— Two full baths

■ The Family Room has a vaulted ceiling and is accented by a fireplace

■ The Master Suite features a tray ceiling over the Bedroom and a vaulted ceiling over the Bath

■ An optional basement, crawl space or slab foundation — please specify when ordering

■ No materials list is available for this plan

MAIN FLOOR — 1,875 SQ. FT.
BASEMENT — 1,891 SQ. FT.
GARAGE — 475 SQ. FT.

TOTAL LIVING AREA:
1,875 SQ. FT.

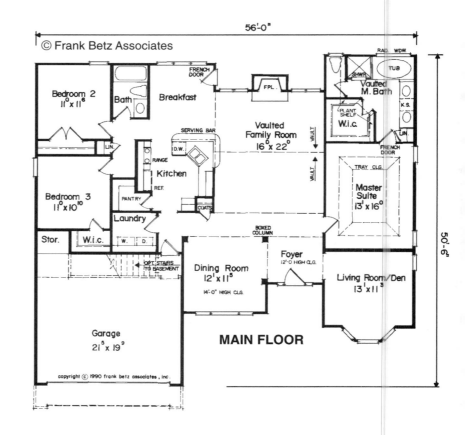

© Frank Betz Associates

56'-0"

50'-6"

Bedroom 2
11⁰ x 11⁶

Bath

Breakfast

FRENCH DOOR

FPL

RAD. WDW

Vaulted M. Bath

SHWR

TUB

PLANT SHELF

W.i.c.

K.S.

SERVING BAR

D.W.

RANGE

Kitchen

REF.

Vaulted Family Room
16⁰ x 22⁰

VAULT

VAULT

FRENCH DOOR

Bedroom 3
11⁰ x 10¹⁰

PANTRY

Laundry

COATS

TRAY CLG.

Master Suite
13¹ x 16⁰

Stor.

W.i.c.

W.

D.

OPT. STAIRS TO BASEMENT

BOXED COLUMN

Foyer
12'-0" HIGH CLG.

Dining Room
12¹ x 11⁵

14'-0" HIGH CLG.

Living Room/Den
13¹ x 11³

Garage
21⁵ x 19⁹

MAIN FLOOR

copyright © 1990 frank betz associates, inc.

BL

Wrapping Porch Highlights Ranch

Price Code: B

■ This plan features:
— Three bedrooms
— Two full baths
■ The front elevation is adorned in a wrapping front Porch
■ The expansive Family Room flows into the Dining Area, which in turn is open to the Kitchen
■ The Master Suite includes a recessed ceiling and a private five-piece Bath
■ Two additional Bedrooms share a full Bath

MAIN FLOOR — 1,550 SQ. FT.
GARAGE — 548 SQ. FT.

TOTAL LIVING AREA:
1,550 SQ. FT.

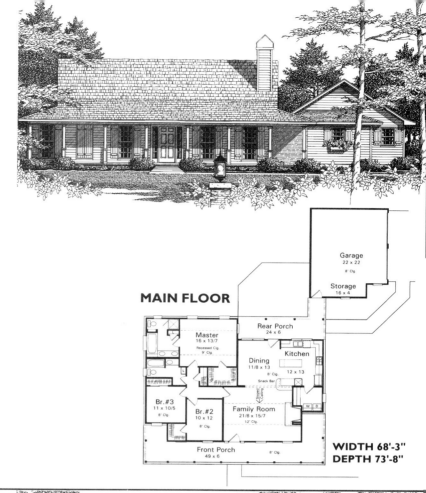

MAIN FLOOR

WIDTH 68'-3"
DEPTH 73'-8"

BL/ML

Decorative Ceilings Add Accents

Price Code: C

■ This plan features:
— Three bedrooms
— Two full baths
■ The cozy front Porch leads into the formal Foyer
■ A secluded Study is to the right of the Foyer
■ Colonial columns and a half wall separate the Dining area from the Foyer
■ The Great Room is accented by a fireplace and a tray ceiling
■ The Kitchen is laid out in an efficient U-shape and features an extended counter/eating bar
■ The Master Suite is tucked into the left rear corner of the home
■ A tray ceiling highlights the bedroom area of the Master Suite
■ Two additional Bedrooms, located on the opposite side of the home, share a full Bath in the hall

MAIN FLOOR — 1,771 SQ. FT.
GARAGE — 480 SQ. FT.

TOTAL LIVING AREA:
1,771 SQ. FT.

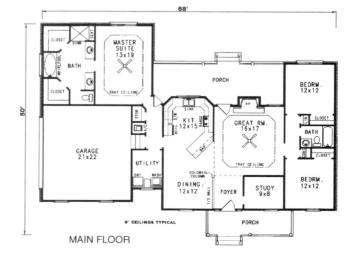

MAIN FLOOR

BL/ML

Lots of Views and Breezes

Price Code: D

■ This plan features:
— Three bedrooms
— Two full baths
■ Kitchen directly off Foyer with work island/cooktop and serving counter/snackbar
■ Sloped ceiling tops fireplace and sliding glass doors to Terrace in Living/Dining Rooms
■ Master Bedroom enhanced by outdoor access and a pampering Bath with a whirlpool tub
■ Two additional Bedrooms share a double vanity Bath

MAIN FLOOR — 2,189 SQ. FT.
GARAGE — 480 SQ. FT.

TOTAL LIVING AREA: 2,189 SQ. FT.

MAIN FLOOR

BL

Covered Patio

Price Code: D

■ This plan features:
— Four bedrooms
— Three full baths
■ The Great Room and Breakfast Room share a free-flowing space that offers access to the covered Patio.
■ The Master Suite features a sloped ceiling, a walk-in closet, and a Bath with a double vanity and whirlpool tub.
■ This home is designed with a slab foundation.

MAIN FLOOR — 2,169 SQ. FT.
GARAGE — 542 SQ. FT.

TOTAL LIVING AREA: 2,169 SQ. FT.

FLOOR PLAN

To order your Blueprints, call 1-800-235-5700

BL/ML

Cozy Three Bedroom

Price Code: B

■ This plan features:

— Three bedrooms

— Two full baths

■ The triple arched front Porch adds to the curb appeal of the home

■ The expansive Great Room is accented by a cozy gas fireplace

■ The Master Bedroom is high-lighted by a walk-in closet and a whirlpool Bath

■ Two secondary bedrooms share use of the full hall Bath

■ The rear Porch extends dining to the outdoors

MAIN FLOOR — 1,515 SQ. FT.
GARAGE — 528 SQ. FT.

TOTAL LIVING AREA:
1,515 SQ. FT.

MAIN FLOOR

51'

60'

GARAGE
22x24

MASTER SUITE
15x13

WHIRLPOOL

UTILITY

BATH

DRY   WASH

RANGE

KITCHEN
14x10

SINK D/W

REFG.

PORCH

BAR

SHOWER

BATH

LIN.

EATING

CLOSET

A/C

LIN.

CLOSET

BEDRM.
13x12

CLOSET

BEDRM./STUDY
13x12

GREAT ROOM
22x22

GAS
F/P

OPTIONAL DOOR

FOYER

9' CEILINGS

PORCH

BL/ML/ZIP

Master Suite Sitting Room

Price Code: D

■ This plan features:
— Four bedrooms
— Three full baths
■ The Living Room can be open to the Foyer or can be altered for use as a bedroom by including a door off the hallway.
■ The Master Suite includes a Sitting Area, a full Bath, and a walk-in closet.
■ The bonus room adds 400 square feet.
■ This home is designed with basement and crawl-space foundation options.

MAIN AREA — 2,193 SQ. FT.
GARAGE — 522 SQ. FT.

TOTAL LIVING AREA:
2,193 SQ. FT.

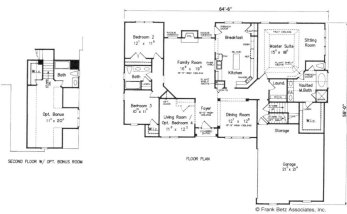

SECOND FLOOR W/ OPT. BONUS ROOM

FLOOR PLAN

© Frank Betz Associates, Inc.

BL/ML

Columned Elegance

Price Code: E

■ This plan features:
— Three bedrooms
— Two full and one half baths
■ This traditional home is enhanced by elegant columns on the large front Porch
■ The Study and the Dining Room both overlook the front Porch
■ The Great Room has a fireplace, built-in book shelves and access to the rear Deck
■ The modern Kitchen has an angled serving bar with a double sink
■ The Breakfast Nook has a bright wall of windows that overlooks the rear yard
■ The secluded Master Suite has dual walk-in closets, and a Bath with a spa tub
■ Two additional Bedrooms are located on the opposite side of the home, and they share a full Bath
■ This plan is available with a basement or a crawl space foundation, please specify when ordering this plan

MAIN FLOOR — 2,485 SQ. FT.
BASEMENT — 2,485 SQ. FT.
GARAGE — 484 SQ. FT.

TOTAL LIVING AREA:
2,485 SQ. FT.

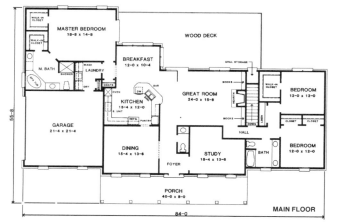

MAIN FLOOR

To order your Blueprints, call 1-800-235-5700

BL/ML

Classic Lines

Price Code: E

■ This plan features:
— Two bedrooms plus an optional third bedroom
— Three full baths
■ A clever U-shaped Kitchen counter lets mom survey the Great Room and Dining Room
■ The Master Suite includes its own private Porch
■ Plan includes options for a second Master Suite, each with private Porch
■ The third Bedroom could be a Study or even a Game Room

MAIN FLOOR — 1,792 SQ. FT.
BONUS — 338 SQ. FT.
GARAGE — 504 SQ. FT.

TOTAL LIVING AREA:
1,792 SQ. FT

© 1998 Donald A. Gardner, Inc.

© 1996 Donald A. Gardner, Inc.

BL/ML/ZIP

Fireplace Adds a Cozy Touch

Price Code: B

■ This plan features:
— Three bedrooms
— One full and one three-quarter baths
■ A Garage level that includes a basement recreation and workshop area, perfect for the household hobbyist
■ A large bow window and a wide opening to the formal Dining Room, adding to the feeling of spaciousness
■ Access to a raised Deck from the spacious Kitchen

MAIN FLOOR — 1,676 SQ. FT.
BASEMENT RECREATION AREA — 592 SQ. FT.
WORKSHOP — 144 SQ. FT.
GARAGE — 697 SQ. FT.

TOTAL LIVING AREA:
1,676 SQ. FT.

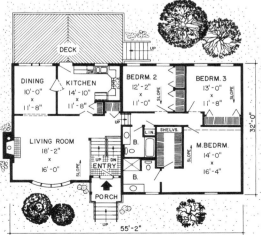

MAIN FLOOR

BL/ML/ZIP

Split Bedroom Ranch

Price Code: C

■ This plan features:

— Three bedrooms

— Two full baths

■ The Foyer opens into the Great Room with a vaulted ceiling and a hearth fireplace

■ The U-shaped Kitchen is located between the Dining room and the Breakfast Nook

■ The secluded Master Bedroom is spacious and includes a full Bath

■ The covered front Porch and rear Deck provide additional space for entertaining

■ An optional basement, slab or a crawl space foundation — please specify when ordering

MAIN FLOOR — 1,804 SQ. FT.
BASEMENT — 1,804 SQ. FT.
GARAGE — 506 SQ. FT.

TOTAL LIVING AREA:
1,804 SQ. FT.

MAIN FLOOR

To order your Blueprints, call 1-800-235-5700

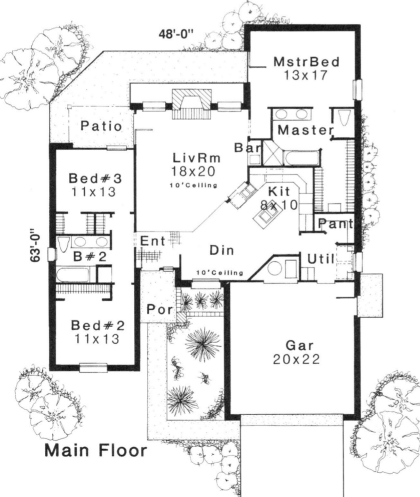

48'-0"

MstrBed
13x17

Patio

Master

Bar

LivRm
18x20
10'Ceiling

Bed#3
11x13

Kit
8x10

63'-0"

B#2

Ent

Din

Pant

Util

10'Ceiling

Bed#2
11x13

Por

Gar
20x22

Main Floor

BL/ZIP

Easy Everyday Living

Price Code: B

■ This plan features:

— Three bedrooms

— Two full baths

■ Front entrance accented by segmented arches, sidelight and transom windows

■ Open Living Room with fireplace and a wetbar

■ Dining Area open to both the Living Room and Kitchen

■ Efficient Kitchen with a cooktop island and a walk-in Pantry

■ Large walk-in closet, double vanity bath and access to Patio featured in the Master Bedroom

■ No materials list is available for this plan

MAIN FLOOR — 1,664 SQ. FT.
BASEMENT — 1,600 SQ. FT.
GARAGE — 440 SQ. FT

TOTAL LIVING AREA:
1,664 SQ. FT.

BL

Vaulted Ceilings Define Public Spaces

Price Code: A

- This plan features:
  — Three bedrooms
  — Two full baths
- A Pantry adds storage to the U-shaped Kitchen
- The drive-under Garage leads up to the Great Room
- Display shelves are widely used throughout the house
- A tray ceiling adds height to the Master Bedroom
- Visitors are protected from the weather by a small covered Porch
- The Master Bath offers a large tub and a separate shower

MAIN FLOOR — 1,166 SQ. FT.
BASEMENT — 1,166 SQ. FT.

TOTAL LIVING AREA:
1,166 SQ. FT

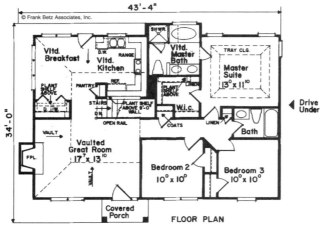

© Frank Betz Associates, Inc.

FLOOR PLAN

PLAN NO. 98424

BL/ML

Sprawling Ranch

Price Code: D

- This plan features:
  — Three bedrooms
  — Two full and one half baths
- Foyer with a 12-foot high ceiling and flows into the Dining and Living Rooms
- Family Room in rear of home with a fireplace and radius windows on either side
- The Kitchen is L-shaped and has a center island with a cooktop
- The Breakfast bay area includes a walk-in Pantry
- The Master Suite is beyond belief with a tray ceiling, a Sitting Area, a walk in closet and a luxurious Bath
- Two other Bedrooms are large in size and share access to a full Bath
- An optional basement or crawl space foundation — please specify when ordering

MAIN FLOOR — 2,236 SQ. FT.
BASEMENT — 2,236 SQ. FT.
GARAGE — 517 SQ. FT.

TOTAL LIVING AREA:
2,236 SQ. FT.

MAIN FLOOR

To order your Blueprints, call 1-800-235-5700

BL

One-Level Living at its Finest

Price Code: L

■ This plan features:
— Four bedrooms
— Three full, one half and one three-quarter baths
■ Luxurious Master Suite includes huge closet, Bath and Exercise Area
■ All secondary Bedrooms feature private Baths and walk-in closets
■ Off the rounded Breakfast Room is a covered Patio for outdoor meals
■ The three-car Garage features plenty of extra storage
■ A formal Dining Room comes with a tall pullman ceiling

MAIN FLOOR — 4,615 SQ. FT.
GARAGE — 748 SQ. FT.

TOTAL LIVING AREA:
4,615 SQ. FT

MAIN FLOOR

BL/ZIP

Traditional Ranch

Price Code: B

■ This plan features:
— Three bedrooms
— Two full baths
■ A large front palladium window that gives this home great curb appeal, and allows a view of the front yard from the Living Room
■ A vaulted ceiling in the Living Room, adding to the architectural interest and the spacious feel of the room
■ Sliding glass doors in the Dining Room that lead to a wood Deck
■ A built-in Pantry, double sink and breakfast bar in the efficient Kitchen
■ A Master Suite that includes a walk-in closet and a private Bath with a double vanity
■ Two additional Bedrooms that share a full hall Bath

MAIN AREA —1,568 SQ. FT.
BASEMENT — 1,568 SQ. FT.
GARAGE — 509 SQ. FT.

TOTAL LIVING AREA:
1,568 SQ. FT.

MAIN FLOOR

BL/ML

Split Bedroom Plan

Price Code: D

- This plan features:
  — Three bedrooms
  — Two full baths
- Dining Room is crowned by a tray ceiling
- Living Room/Den privatized by double doors at its entrance
- The Kitchen includes a walk-in Pantry and a corner double sink
- The Master Suite is topped by a tray ceiling and contains a compartmental Bath
- An optional basement, slab or crawl space foundation — please specify when ordering

MAIN FLOOR — 2,051 SQ. FT.
BASEMENT — 2,051 SQ. FT.
GARAGE — 441 SQ. FT.

TOTAL LIVING AREA:
2,051 SQ. FT.

WIDTH 56'-0"
DEPTH 60'-6"

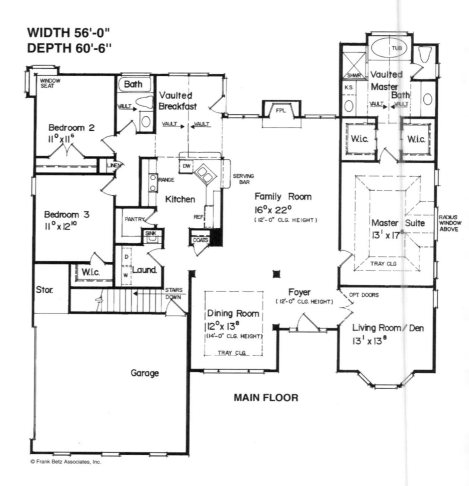

MAIN FLOOR

© Frank Betz Associates, Inc.

94

BL/ML/ZIP

Expansive, Not Expensive

Price Code: C

■ This plan features:

— Three bedrooms

— Two full baths

■ A Master Suite with his and her closets and a private Master Bath

■ Two additional Bedrooms that share a full Bath with a dressing area

■ A pleasant Dining Room that overlooks a rear garden

■ A well-equipped Kitchen with a large pantry and a serving counter

■ An optional basement, slab or crawl space foundation — please specify when ordering

MAIN FLOOR — 1,773 SQ. FT.

TOTAL LIVING AREA:
1,773 SQ. FT.

MAIN FLOOR

PATIO
16-0x10-0

GARAGE
21-0x21-0

SCR. PORCH
12-0x20-4

DINING
12-0x13-4

KITCHEN
10x13

UTILITY

W D

PANTRY

BEDROOM
11-0x13-4

CLOSET

M. BATH

SEAT

CLOSET

CLOSET

M. BEDROOM
12-0x18-0

43'-8"

LIVING ROOM
15-6x17-8

DOWN

CLOSET

COATS

FOYER

BEDROOM
12-0x11-4

LINEN

DRESSING

LINEN

BATH

PORCH
26-0x6-0

88'-8"

BL/ML

Luxury in One-story Plan

Price Code: B

■ This plan features:

__ Three bedrooms

— Two full baths

■ Covered Stoop leads into dynamic Activity Room with fireplace, recessed ceiling and adjacent Dining Room and Sun Deck

■ Open Kitchen/Breakfast Room offers loads of counter space and light with nearby Pantry, Laundry and Garage

■ An optional basement, slab or crawl space — please specify when ordering

MAIN FLOOR — 1,595 SQ. FT.
BASEMENT — 1,595 SQ. FT.
GARAGE — 491 SQ. FT.

TOTAL LIVING AREA:
1,595 SQ. FT.

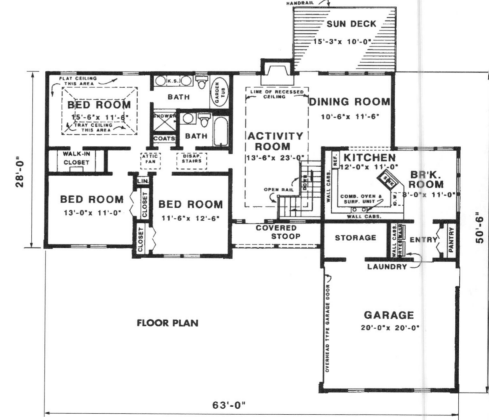

BL/ML

Keystone and Arched Windows

Price Code: B

■ This plan features:
— Three bedrooms
— Two full baths

■ An arched window in the Dining Room offers eye-catching appeal

■ A fireplace and French door to the rear yard are in the Great Room

■ An efficient Kitchen includes a serving bar, Pantry and pass-through to the Great Room

■ A plush Master Suite includes a private Bath and a walk-in closet

■ An optional basement, slab or crawl space foundation — please specify when ordering

MAIN FLOOR — 1,670 SQ. FT.

TOTAL LIVING AREA:
1,670 SQ. FT.

MAIN FLOOR

© Frank Betz Associates, Inc.

BL

Open and Airy

Price Code: C

■ This plan features:
— Three bedrooms
— Two full baths

■ Less formal and more spacious, the Great Room is a contemporary masterpiece.

■ A corner window, walk-in closet and soaking tub make the Master Suite complete.

■ While the family's young, the Study can double as a Nursery.

■ Empty nesters or couples just getting started will feel at home in this house.

■ A gourmet Kitchen looks straight through the Breakfast Area's bay window to views beyond.

MAIN FLOOR — 1,869 SQ. FT.
GARAGE — 470 SQ. FT.

TOTAL LIVING AREA:
1,869 SQ. FT.

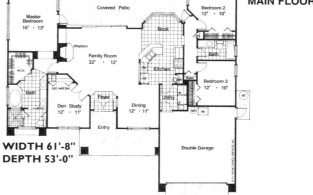

MAIN FLOOR

WIDTH 61'-8"
DEPTH 53'-0"

To order your Blueprints, call 1-800-235-5700

©1995 Donald A. Gardner Architects, Inc.

BL/ML/ZIP/RRR

Cathedral Ceiling

Price Code: C

■ This plan features:

— Three bedrooms

— Two full baths

■ Cathedral ceiling expanding the Great room, Dining Room and Kitchen

■ A versatile Bedroom or Study topped by a cathedral ceiling accented by double circle-top windows

■ Master Suite complete with a cathedral ceiling, including a bath with a garden tub, linen closet and a walk-in closet

MAIN FLOOR — 1,417 SQ. FT.
GARAGE — 441 SQ. FT.

TOTAL LIVING AREA:
1,417 SQ. FT.

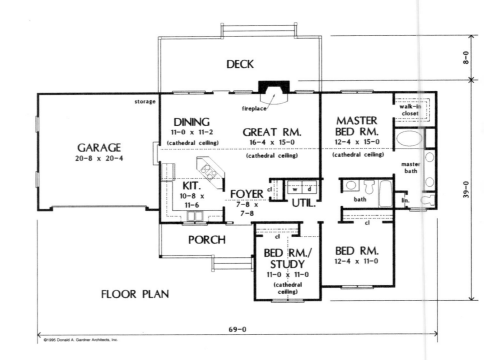

©1995 Donald A. Gardner Architects, Inc.

To order your Blueprints, call 1-800-235-5700

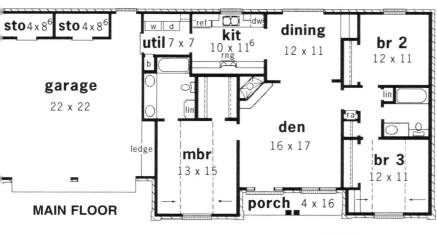

MAIN FLOOR

sto 4 x 8⁶ sto 4 x 8⁶

util 7 x 7

kit 10 x 11⁶

dining 12 x 11

br 2 12 x 11

garage 22 x 22

mbr 13 x 15

den 16 x 17

br 3 12 x 11

ledge

porch 4 x 16

WIDTH 67'-4"
DEPTH 32'-10"

BL/ML

Elegant Brick Exterior

Price Code: A

■ This plan features:

—Three bedrooms

—Two full baths

■ Detailing and accenting columns highlighting the covered front Porch

■ Den is enhanced by a corner fireplace and adjoins Dining Room

■ Efficient Kitchen well-appointed and has easy access to the Utility/Laundry Room

■ Master Bedroom topped by a vaulted ceiling and has a private Bath and walk-in closet

■ An optional slab or crawl space foundation — please specify when ordering

MAIN FLOOR — 1,390 SQ. FT.
GARAGE — 590 SQ. FT.

TOTAL LIVING AREA:
1,390 SQ. FT.

BL/ML

Home For the Discriminating Buyer

Price Code: B

■ This plan features:

— Three bedrooms

— Two full baths

■ A sloped ceiling and a corner fireplace enhancing the Great Room

■ A Kitchen with a garden window above the double sink

■ A peninsula counter joins the Kitchen and the Breakfast Room

■ A Master Suite with a large walk-in closet, a private Bath with an oval corner tub, and a separate shower and double vanity

MAIN AREA — 1,746 SQ. FT.
BASEMENT — 1,560 SQ. FT.
GARAGE — 455 SQ. FT.

TOTAL LIVING AREA:
1,746 SQ. FT.

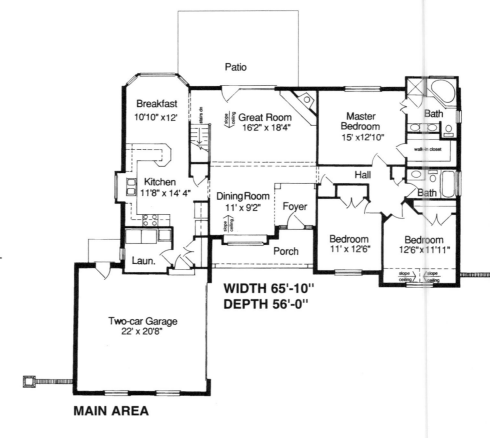

WIDTH 65'-10"
DEPTH 56'-0"

MAIN AREA

To order your Blueprints, call 1-800-235-5700

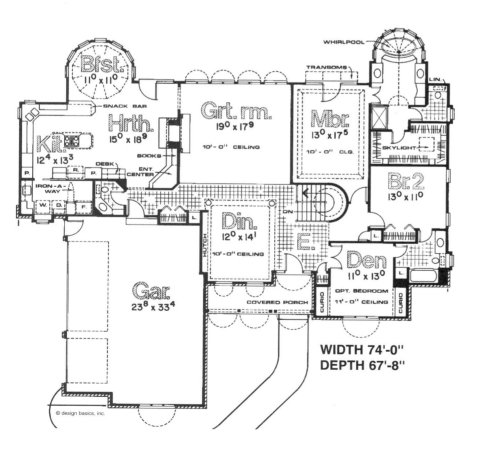

WIDTH 74'-0"
DEPTH 67'-8"

BL/ML/RRR

Bricks and Arches Detail this Ranch

Price Code: F

■ This plan features:

— Two bedrooms

— Two full and one half baths

■ A Master Bedroom with a vaulted ceiling and luxurious Bath complimented by a skylit walk-in closet

■ A second bedroom shares a full Bath with the Den/optional Bedroom

■ A Great Room sharing a see-through fireplace with the Hearth Room, which also has a built-in entertainment center

■ A gazebo-shaped nook opening into the Kitchen with a center island, snack bar and desk

MAIN FLOOR — 2,512 SQ. FT.
GARAGE — 783 SQ. FT.

TOTAL LIVING AREA:
2,512 SQ. FT.

B. NATHAN

© 1990 Donald A. Gardner Architects, Inc.

BL/ML/ZIP/RRR

Compact Three Bedroom

Price Code: C

■ This plan features:

— Three bedrooms

— Two full baths

■ Dormers above the covered Porch light the foyer leading to the dramatic Great Room crowned in a cathedral ceiling and enhanced by a fireplace

■ Great Room opens to the island Kitchen with Breakfast Area and access to a spacious rear Deck

■ Tray ceilings adding interest to the Bedroom/Study, Dining Room and the Master Bedroom

MAIN FLOOR — 1,452 SQ. FT.
GARAGE AND STORAGE — 427 SQ. FT.

TOTAL LIVING AREA
1,452 SQ. FT.

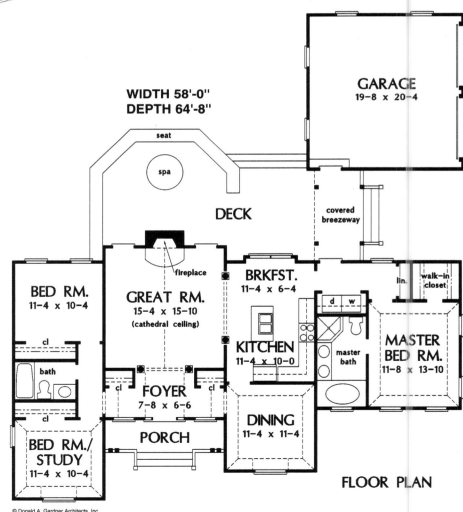

WIDTH 58'-0"
DEPTH 64'-8"

FLOOR PLAN

© Donald A. Gardner Architects, Inc.

BL/ML

Classic Country Good Looks

Price Code: D

■ This plan features:
— Two bedrooms and an optional third bedroom
— Two full baths
■ The two-car Garage features extra, separate storage
■ A Two-rocker Porch greets all visitors
■ The extra space can be Study, Bedroom, Media Room or Game Room
■ A large walk-in closet graces the Master Suite

MAIN FLOOR — 1,650 SQ. FT.
BONUS — 394 SQ. FT.
GARAGE — 554 SQ. FT.

TOTAL LIVING AREA:
1,650 SQ. FT

© 1999 Donald A. Gardner, Inc.

BL/ML/ZIP

Exclusive Master Suite

Price Code: C

■ This plan features:
— Three bedrooms
— Two full and one half baths
■ Front Porch entry into Foyer and open Living and Dining Room
■ Huge fireplace and double window highlight Living Room
■ Convenient Kitchen with cooktop island/snack-bar, pantry, and bright Breakfast Area with back yard access
■ Corner Master Bedroom offers a decorative ceiling, walk-in closets and a double vanity Bath
■ Two additional Bedrooms with ample closets and private access to a full Bath

MAIN FLOOR — 1,831 SQ. FT.
GARAGE — 484 SQ. FT.

TOTAL LIVING AREA:
1,831 SQ. FT.

OPTION

MAIN FLOOR

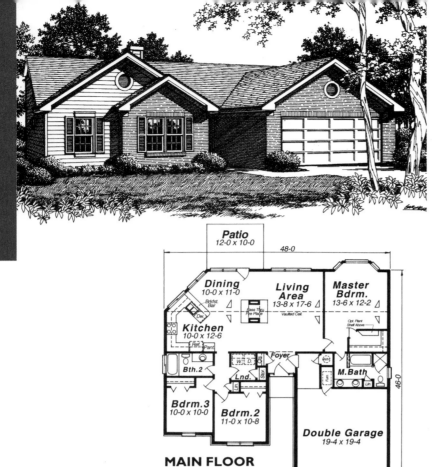

BL/ML/ZIP

Wonderful Open Spaces

Price Code: A

■ This plan features:
— Three bedrooms
— Two full baths
■ A Family Room, Kitchen and Breakfast Area that all connect
■ A central fireplace adds warmth and atmosphere to the Family Room, Kitchen and the Breakfast Area
■ The Master Suite includes a walk-in closet, a double vanity, separate shower and a tub
■ A wooden Deck that can be accessed from the Breakfast Area
■ An optional crawl space or slab foundation — please specify when ordering

MAIN FLOOR — 1,388 SQ. FT.
GARAGE — 400 SQ. FT.

TOTAL LIVING AREA:
1,388 SQ. FT.

Patio
12-0 x 10-0

Dining
10-0 x 11-0

Living Area
13-8 x 17-6

Master Bdrm.
13-6 x 12-2

Kitchen
10-0 x 12-6

Bth.2

Bdrm.3
10-0 x 10-0

Bdrm.2
11-0 x 10-8

M.Bath

Foyer

Double Garage
19-4 x 19-4

MAIN FLOOR

© 1988, Jannis Vann & Associates, Inc.

BL

Traditional Family Comfort

Price Code: C

■ This plan features:
— Three bedrooms
— Two full baths
■ A huge Family Room is at the heart of this family-first home
■ A large Kitchen and generously sized Breakfast area flank the Family Room
■ French doors welcome you home to the Den, which offers the potential to also be a Nursery or Guest Room
■ Traditional brick siding brings warmth and appeal to the street view
■ Ceilings throughout are spacious 10 and 11 feet high
■ This home is designed with a slab foundation

MAIN FLOOR — 1,898 SQ. FT.
GARAGE — 541 SQ. FT.

TOTAL LIVING AREA:
1,898 SQ. FT.

Master Bedroom
volume ceiling
13⁰ x 16⁰

Covered Patio

Bedroom 2
volume ceiling
11⁴ x 11⁰

Breakfast

Family Room
volume ceiling
17⁴ x 12⁸

Kitchen

Bedroom 3
volume ceiling
14⁴ x 11⁴

Bath

Den Study
volume ceiling
11⁰ x 12⁰

Foyer

Dining
volume ceiling
10⁰ x 12⁸

Entry

Double Garage

MAIN FLOOR

WIDTH 60'-0"
DEPTH 59'-4"

© Donald A. Gardner Architects, Inc.

B. NATHAN

BL/ML/RRR

Stately Home

Price Code: H

■ This plan features:

— Four bedrooms

— Two full and one half baths

■ Light floods through the arched window in the clerestory dormer above the foyer

■ Great Room topped by a cathedral ceiling boasting built-in cabinets and bookshelves

■ Master Suite includes a fireplace, access to the deck, his and her vanity, a shower and a whirlpool tub

MAIN FLOOR — 2,526 SQ. FT.
GARAGE — 611 SQ. FT.

TOTAL LIVING AREA:
2,526 SQ. FT.

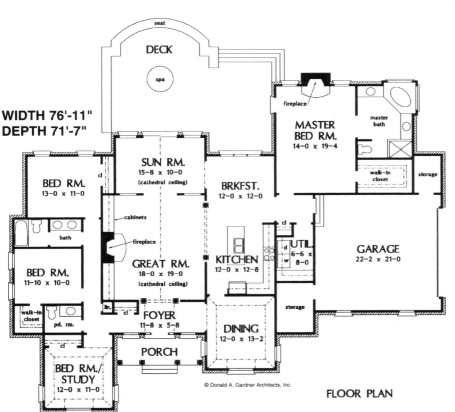

WIDTH 76'-11"
DEPTH 71'-7"

DECK

seat

spa

SUN RM.
15-8 x 10-0
(cathedral ceiling)

BED RM.
13-0 x 11-0

BRKFST.
12-0 x 12-0

fireplace

MASTER
BED RM.
14-0 x 19-4

master
bath

cabinets

fireplace

walk-in
closet

storage

bath

GREAT RM.
18-0 x 19-0
(cathedral ceiling)

KITCHEN
12-0 x 12-8

UTIL
6-6 x
8-0

GARAGE
22-2 x 21-0

BED RM.
11-10 x 10-0

walk-in
closet

pd. rm.

FOYER
11-8 x 5-8

DINING
12-0 x 13-2

storage

PORCH

BED RM./
STUDY
12-0 x 11-0

© Donald A. Gardner Architects, Inc.

FLOOR PLAN

BL/ML

Country Ranch

Price Code: A

■ This plan features:

— Three bedrooms

— Two full baths

■ A covered, wrap-around Porch, adding charm to this Country-styled home

■ A high vaulted ceiling in the Living Room

■ A smaller Kitchen with ample cupboard and counter space, that is augmented by a large pantry

■ An informal Family Room with access to the Deck

■ A private Master Suite with a spa tub and a walk-in closet

■ A Shop and Storage Area in the two-car Garage

MAIN AREA — 1,485 SQ. FT.
GARAGE — 701 SQ. FT.

TOTAL LIVING AREA:
1,485 SQ. FT.

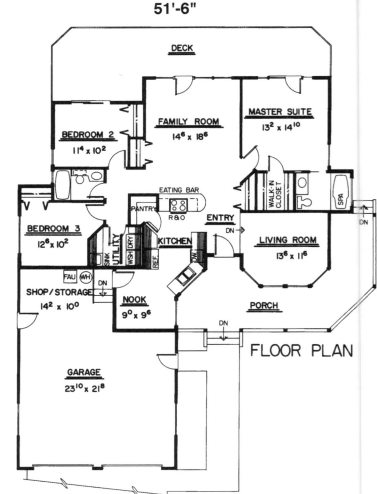

51'-6"

63'-0"

FLOOR PLAN

To order your Blueprints, call 1-800-235-5700

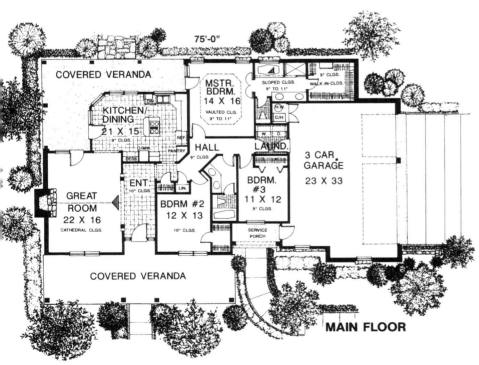

75'-0"

COVERED VERANDA

KITCHEN/
DINING
21 X 15
9" CLGS.

MSTR.
BDRM.
14 X 16
VAULTED CLG.
9" TO 11"

SLOPED CLGS.
9" TO 11"

WALK-IN-CLOS.

9" CLGS.

HALL
9" CLGS.

LAUND.

3 CAR.
GARAGE
23 X 33

GREAT
ROOM
22 X 16
CATHEDRAL CLGS.

ENT.
10" CLGS.

BDRM #2
12 X 13
10" CLGS.

BDRM.
#3
11 X 12
9" CLGS.

SERVICE
PORCH

COVERED VERANDA

MAIN FLOOR

BL/ML/ZIP

Southern Hospitality

Price Code: C

■ This plan features:

— Three bedrooms

— Two full baths

■ Welcoming covered Veranda

■ Easy-care, tiled Entry leads into
Great Room with a fieldstone
fireplace and an atrium door to
another covered Veranda

■ A bright Kitchen/Dining Room
includes a cooktop island/
snackbar, built-in pantry and
desk, and access to covered
Veranda

■ Vaulted ceiling crowns Master
Bedroom that offers a plush Bath
and a huge walk-in closet

MAIN FLOOR — 1,830 SQ. FT.
GARAGE — 759 SQ. FT.

TOTAL LIVING AREA:
1,830 SQ. FT.

© 1995 Donald A. Gardner Architects, Inc.

BL/ML/ZIP/RRR

Casually Elegant

Price Code: D

- ■ This plan features:
- — Three bedrooms
- — Two full baths
- ■ Arched windows, dormers and charming front and back Porches with columns creating Country flavoring
- ■ Central Great Room topped by a cathedral ceiling, a fireplace and a clerestory window
- ■ Breakfast Bay for casual dining is open to the Kitchen
- ■ Cathedral ceiling crowning the Master Bedroom
- ■ Master Bath with skylights, whirlpool tub, shower, and a double vanity

MAIN FLOOR — 1,561 SQ. FT.
GARAGE & STORAGE — 446 SQ. FT.

TOTAL LIVING AREA:
1,561 SQ. FT.

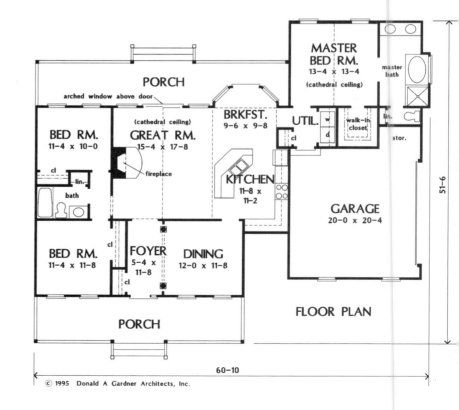

FLOOR PLAN

© 1995 Donald A Gardner Architects, Inc.

BL/ML/RRR

Country Charm and Convenience

Price Code: D

■ This plan features:
— Three bedrooms
— Two full baths
■ The open design pulls the Great Room, Kitchen and Breakfast Bay into one common area
■ Cathedral ceilings in the Great Room , Master Bedroom and a secondary Bedroom
■ The rear Deck expands the living and entertaining space
■ The Dining Room provides a quiet place for relaxed family dinners
■ Two additional Bedrooms share a full Bath

MAIN FLOOR — 1,512 SQ. FT.
GARAGE & STORAGE — 455 SQ. FT.

TOTAL LIVING AREA:
1,512 SQ. FT.

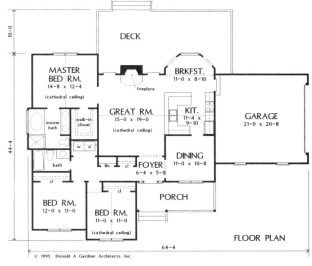

©1995 Donald A. Gardner Architects, Inc.

DECK

MASTER BED RM.
14-8 x 12-4
(cathedral ceiling)

master bath

walk-in closet

bath

BRKFST.
11-0 x 8-10

fireplace

GREAT RM.
15-0 x 19-0
(cathedral ceiling)

KIT.
11-4 x 9-10

GARAGE
21-0 x 20-8

w   d

DINING
11-0 x 10-8

lin. cl   FOYER
6-4 x 5-8

cl

BED RM.
12-0 x 11-0

cl

BED RM.
11-0 x 11-0
(cathedral ceiling)

PORCH

10-0

44-4

64-4

FLOOR PLAN

© 1995 Donald A Gardner Architects, Inc.

BL

Clean Country Appeal

Price Code: C

■ This plan features:
— Three bedrooms
— Two full baths
■ A vaulted-ceiling Great Room offers an impressively large family space.
■ Skylights flood the Great Room and Breakfast Room with natural light.
■ A large soaking tub in the Master Bath offers quiet comfort at the end of a long day.
■ The Kids' Wing includes a separate Bath and quick access to the covered Patio out back.
■ This home is designed with a slab foundation.

MAIN FLOOR — 1,901 SQ. FT.
GARAGE — 484 SQ. FT.

TOTAL LIVING AREA:
1,902 SQ. FT.

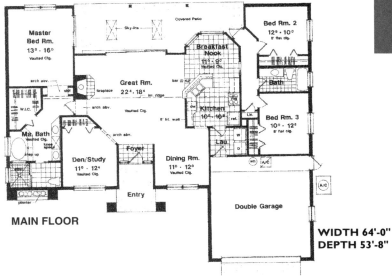

Covered Patio

Master Bed Rm.
13⁰ · 16⁰
Vaulted Clg.

Sky-lts

Bed Rm. 2
12⁵ · 10⁰
8' flat clg.

Breakfast Nook
11⁵ · 9⁰
Vaulted Clg.

Great Rm.
22⁴ · 18⁴
int. ridge
Vaulted Clg.

bar @ 42

W.I.C.

Bath

Ma. Bath
Vaulted Clg.
knee space

Kitchen
10⁴ · 10⁰

Bed Rm. 3
10⁰ · 12⁵
8' flat clg.

Lau.

Den/Study
11⁰ · 12⁴
Vaulted Clg.

Foyer

Dining Rm.
11⁰ · 12⁰
Vaulted Clg.

A/C

A/C

planter

Entry

Double Garage

MAIN FLOOR

WIDTH 64'-0"
DEPTH 53'-8"

PLAN NO. 96463

©1995 Donald A. Gardner Architects, Inc.   B. NATHAN

BL/ML/RRR

Your Family Will Grow In Style

Price Code: D

■ This plan features:

— Three bedrooms

— Two full baths

■ Open Great Room and Kitchen enlarged by a cathedral ceiling

■ Wooden rear Deck expand entertaining to the outdoors

■ Cathedral ceiling adding volume and drama to the Master Suite

■ Flexible Bedroom/Study includes a cathedral ceiling and a double window with an arched top

■ Second floor Bonus Space may be finished with two more Bedrooms

FIRST FLOOR — 1,633 SQ. FT.
GARAGE & STORAGE — 512 SQ. FT.
BONUS — 595 SQ. FT.

TOTAL LIVING AREA:
1,633 SQ. FT.

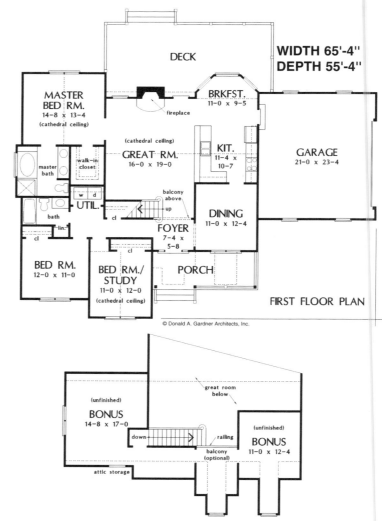

WIDTH 65'-4"
DEPTH 55'-4"

FIRST FLOOR PLAN

© Donald A. Gardner Architects, Inc.

110

To order your Blueprints, call 1-800-235-5700

Donald A. Gardner Architects, Inc.

B. NATHAN

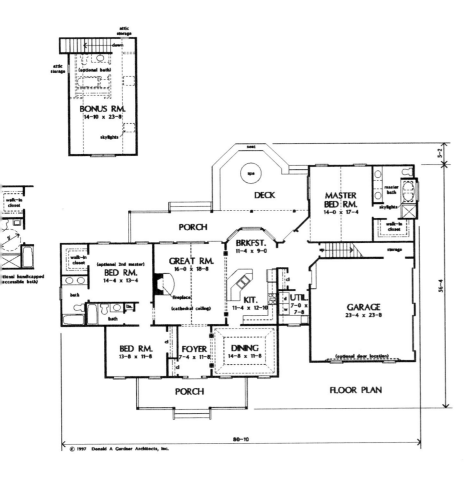

attic storage

attic storage

(optional bath)

down

BONUS RM.
14-10 x 23-8

skylights

walk-in closet

tional handicapped accessible bath)

seat

spa

DECK

PORCH

BRKFST.
11-4 x 9-0

MASTER BED RM.
14-0 x 17-4

master bath

skylights

walk-in closet

storage

walk-in closet

(optional 2nd master)
BED RM.
14-4 x 13-4

GREAT RM.
16-0 x 18-8

bath

bath

fireplace
(cathedral ceiling)

KIT.
11-4 x 12-10

cl

UTIL
7-0 x 7-8

up

dn

GARAGE
23-4 x 23-8

BED RM.
13-8 x 11-8

FOYER
7-4 x 11-8

DINING
14-8 x 11-8

d

ln.

cl

(optional door location)

PORCH

FLOOR PLAN

5-2

56-4

80-10

© 1997 Donald A Gardner Architects, Inc.

BL/ML/RRR

Grace and Style

Price Code: F

■ This plan features:

—Three bedrooms

—Three full baths

■ Foyer, accented by columns, gives entry into the formal Dining Room

■ Kitchen with angled serving island is open to the Breakfast Bay

■ Great Room is topped by a cathedral ceiling and enhanced by a fireplace

■ Secluded Master Suite has a walk-in closet and a skylit Bath

■ Bonus Room could be a terrific fourth Bedroom and Bath

MAIN FLOOR — 2,057 SQ. FT.
GARAGE & STORAGE — 622 SQ. FT.
BONUS ROOM — 444 SQ. FT.

TOTAL LIVING AREA:
2,057 SQ. FT.

BL/ML

Secluded Master Suite

Price Code: B

■ This plan features:

— Three bedrooms

— Two full baths

■ A convenient one-level design with an open floor plan between the Kitchen, Breakfast Area and Great Room

■ A vaulted ceiling and a large cozy fireplace in the Great Room

■ A well-equipped Kitchen using a peninsula counter as an eating bar

■ A Master Suite with a luxurious Master Bath

■ An optional crawl space or slab foundation — please specify when ordering

MAIN AREA — 1,680 SQ. FT.
GARAGE — 538 SQ. FT.

TOTAL LIVING AREA:
1,680 SQ. FT.

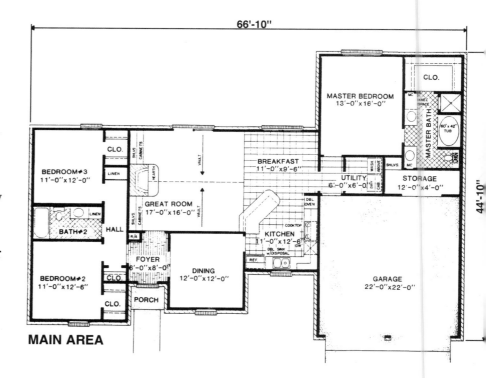

MAIN AREA

To order your Blueprints, call 1-800-235-5700

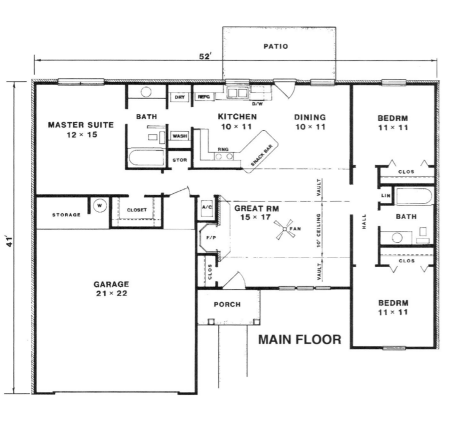

52'

PATIO

MASTER SUITE
12 × 15

BATH

DRY   REFG
D/W

KITCHEN
10 × 11

DINING
10 × 11

BEDRM
11 × 11

WASH

RNG

STOR

SNACK BAR

CLOS

LIN

BATH

41'

STORAGE   W

CLOSET

A/C

GREAT RM
15 × 17

FAN

VAULT

10' CEILING

VAULT

HALL

CLOS

F/P

CLOS

GARAGE
21 × 22

PORCH

VAULT

BEDRM
11 × 11

MAIN FLOOR

BL

Split-Bedroom Floor Plan

Price Code: A

■ This plan features:

— Three bedrooms

— Two full baths

■ A split-bedroom floor plan gives the Master Bedroom ultimate privacy

■ The Patio is accessed from the Dining Room and expands dining to the outdoors

■ No materials list is available for this plan

■ An optional crawl space or slab foundation — please specify when ordering

MAIN FLOOR — 1,234 SQ. FT.
GARAGE — 423 SQ. FT.

TOTAL LIVING AREA:
1,243 SQ. FT.

BL/RRR

A Traditional Ranch

Price Code: C

■ This plan features:
— Three bedrooms
— Two full and one half baths
■ The two-car Garage offers the option of a third bay or extra storage space.
■ 1,859 square feet of living space.
■ Columns and a lowered soffit define the separation of Kitchen from Living Room.
■ This home is designed with a basement foundation.

MAIN FLOOR — 1,859 SQ. FT.
GARAGE — 750 SQ. FT.

TOTAL LIVING AREA:
1,859 SQ. FT.

MAIN FLOOR

BL/ML/RRR

Appealing Brick Elevation

Price Code: D

■ This plan features:
— Three bedrooms
— Two full and one three-quarter bath
■ Formal Living and Dining Room flanking the Entry
■ Impressive Great Room topped by an eleven-foot ceiling
■ Awing windows framing the raised hearth fireplace
■ Attractive Kitchen/Dinette Area includes an island, desk, wrapping counters, a walk-in Pantry and access to the covered Patio
■ Pampering Master Suite with a skylight dressing area, a walk-in closet, double vanity, a whirlpool tub and a decorative plant shelf

MAIN FLOOR — 2,172 SQ. FT.
GARAGE — 680 SQ. FT.

TOTAL LIVING AREA:
2,172 SQ. FT.

MAIN FLOOR

© design basics inc.

To order your Blueprints, call 1-800-235-5700

© 1996 Donald A. Gardner Architects, Inc.

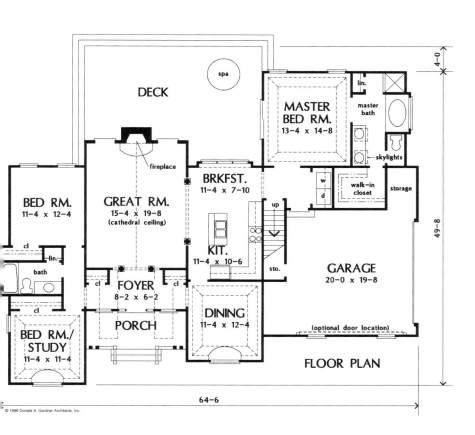

© 1996 Donald A. Gardner Architects, Inc.

BL/ML/ZIP/RRR

Cathedral Ceiling Enlarges Great Room

Price Code: D

- This plan features:
— Three bedrooms
— Two full baths

- Two dormers add volume to the Foyer

- Great Room, topped by a cathedral ceiling, is open to the Kitchen and Breakfast area

- Private Master Suite crowned in a tray ceiling and highlighted by a skylit Bath

- Front Bedroom topped by a tray ceiling

MAIN FLOOR — 1,699 SQ. FT.
GARAGE — 498 SQ. FT.
BONUS — 336 SQ. FT.

TOTAL LIVING AREA:
1,699 SQ. FT.

BL

Easy Maintenance

Price Code: A

■ This plan features:

— Two bedroom

— Two three-quarter baths

■ Abundant glass and a wrap-around Deck to enjoy the outdoors

■ A tiled entrance into a large Great Room with a fieldstone fireplace and Dining Area under a sloped ceiling

■ A compact tiled Kitchen open to Great Room and adjacent to the Utility Area

MAIN AREA — 786 SQ. FT.
DECK — 580 SQ. FT.

TOTAL LIVING AREA:
786 SQ. FT.

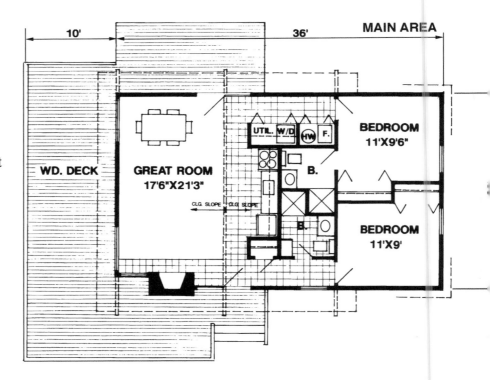

To order your Blueprints, call 1-800-235-5700

BL/ML

An Affordable, Stylish Floor Plan

Price Code: A

■ This plan features:

— Three bedrooms

— One full and one three quarter baths

■ A covered Porch entry

■ An old-fashioned hearth fireplace in the vaulted ceiling Living Room

■ A handy Kitchen with U-shaped counter that is accessible from the Dining Room

■ A Master Bedroom with a large walk-in closet and private Bath

■ An optional crawl space or slab foundation — please specify when ordering

MAIN AREA — 1,410 SQ. FT.
GARAGE — 484 SQ. FT.

TOTAL LIVING AREA:
1,410 SQ. FT.

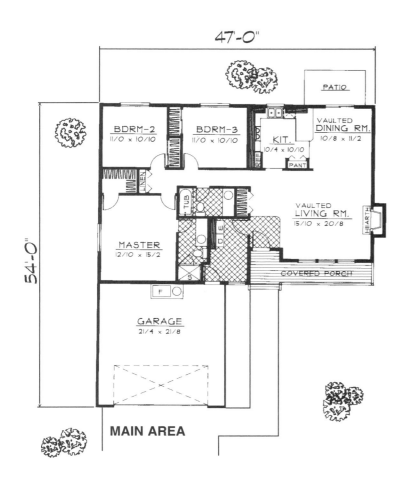

47'-0"

54'-0"

PATIO

BDRM-2
11/0 × 10/10

BDRM-3
11/0 × 10/10

KIT.
10/4 × 10/10

VAULTED
DINING RM.
10/8 × 11/2

REF

PANT

LINEN

TUB

VAULTED
LIVING RM.
15/10 × 20/8

HEARTH

MASTER
12/10 × 15/2

COVERED PORCH

F

GARAGE
21/4 × 21/8

MAIN AREA

© 1998 Donald A Gardner, Inc.

B. NATHAN

BL/ML

Carpenter Gothic Details

Price Code: D

- This plan features:
  — Three bedrooms
  — Two full baths
- The Master Suite is subtly removed from the other Bedrooms
- A Laundry in the Kid's Wing puts it where it's needed
- The small front Porch is adorned with graceful arches
- Three skylights flood the Great Room with natural light

MAIN FLOOR — 1,511 SQ. FT.
BONUS — 549 SQ. FT.
GARAGE — 655 SQ. FT.

TOTAL LIVING AREA:
1,511 SQ. FT.

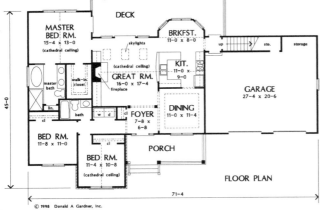

DECK

MASTER BED RM.
15-4 x 13-0
(cathedral ceiling)

BRKFST.
11-0 x 8-0
skylights

up   sto.   storage

KIT.
11-0 x 9-0

GREAT RM.
16-0 x 17-4
(cathedral ceiling)
fireplace

GARAGE
27-4 x 20-6

walk-in closet

master bath

lin.

bath   w d   cl

DINING
11-0 x 11-4

FOYER
7-8 x 6-8

BED RM.
11-8 x 11-0

BED RM.
11-4 x 10-8
(cathedral ceiling)

PORCH

FLOOR PLAN

71-4

45-0

(optional opening)

BONUS RM.
23-6 x 20-6

attic storage

attic storage

down

© 1998 Donald A Gardner, Inc.

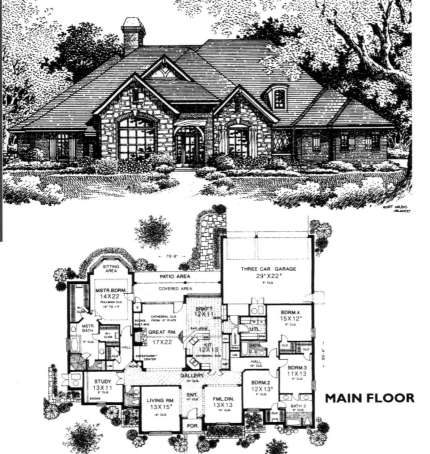

KURT VALES
ORLANDO

BL

English Country Elegance

Price Code: I

- This plan features:
  — Four bedrooms
  — Three full and one half baths
- When you're relaxing in this spectacular Master-Suite wing, you know you've arrived.
- The fourth Bedroom, with private Bath, is great for overnight guests.
- Imagine entertaining in your cathedral-ceiling Great Room with stone fireplace and impressive built-ins.
- Take your breakfast in the window-walled Breakfast Area or more formally in the Dining Room.
- The classic three-car Garage gives you all the extra space you need.
- This home was designed with a slab foundation.

MAIN FLOOR — 3,262 SQ. FT
GARAGE — 662 SQ. FT
PORCH — 285 SQ. FT
DECK — 172 SQ. FT

TOTAL LIVING AREA:
3,262 SQ. FT.

SITTING AREA

PATIO AREA
COVERED AREA

THREE CAR GARAGE
29'X22'

MSTR.BDRM.
14X22
PULLMAN CLG.

MSTR. BATH

CATHEDRAL CLG. FROM 10' PLATE

GREAT RM.
17X22

BRKFT.
12X11

BDRM.4
15X12

UTL.

KIT.
12X18

ENTERTAINMENT CENTER

STUDY
13X11

GALLERY

HALL

BDRM.3
11X13

BDRM.2
12X13'

LIVING RM.
13X15'

ENT.

FML.DIN.
13X13

BATH 2

POR.

79'-8"

65'-4"

MAIN FLOOR

To order your Blueprints, call 1-800-235-5700

BL/ML/ZIP

Porches Expands Living Space

Price Code: D

■ This plan features:

— Three bedrooms

— Two full and one half baths

■ Porches on the front and the rear of this home expand the living space to the outdoors

■ The spacious Great Room is enhanced by a twelve foot ceiling and a fireplace

■ The well-appointed Kitchen has an extended counter/eating bar

■ The Master Suite is enhanced by his and her walk-in closets

■ There is a Bonus Room for the future expansion

MAIN FLOOR — 2,089 SQ. FT.
BONUS ROOM — 497 SQ. FT.
GARAGE — 541 SQ. FT.

TOTAL LIVING AREA:
2,089 SQ. FT.

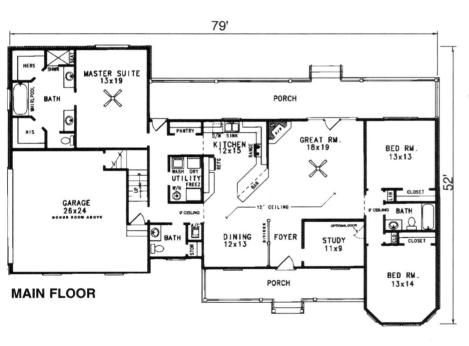

MAIN FLOOR

PLAN NO. 97857

BL

Timeless Country Elegance

Price Code: E

- This plan features:
  — Three bedrooms
  — Two full baths and one half bath
- A deep Porchiere leads to separate one-car Garages
- The walled Courtyard greets visitors
- A secluded shelf-lined Study offers peaceful reading enjoyment
- Stretching from one side the other, a long Gallery connects all
- The two children's Bedrooms are connected by a double-vanity Bath
- For shady relaxation, a covered area joins the Patio and Living Room

MAIN FLOOR — 2,332 SQ. FT.
GARAGE — 620 SQ. FT.

TOTAL LIVING AREA:
2,332 SQ. FT

PLAN NO. 82011

BL

Garage Storage

Price Code: B

- This plan features:
  — Three bedrooms
  — Two full baths
- At the heart of the home, the Kitchen opens to a DiningRoom/Hearth Room with a fireplace.
- A sloped ceiling and a fireplace enhance the Great Room, located next to the Foyer.
- Glass block decorates the Master Bath.
- This home is designed with basement, crawl space and slab foundation options.

MAIN FLOOR — 1,654 SQ. FT.
GARAGE — 400 SQ. FT.

TOTAL LIVING AREA:
1,654 SQ. FT.

MAIN FLOOR

./ML/ZIP

Multiple Gables and a Cozy Front Porch

Price Code: B

This plan features:

- Three bedrooms

- Two full baths

Multiple gables and a cozy front porch

The Foyer leads to a Great Room capped by a sloped ceiling and a fireplace

The Dining Area includes double hung windows

A Kitchen providing an abundance of counter space with a breakfast bar

A Master Bedroom Suite including a walk-in closet and private Bath

MAIN FLOOR — 1,508 SQ. FT.
BASEMENT — 1,439 SQ. FT.
GARAGE — 440 SQ. FT.

TOTAL LIVING AREA:
1,508 SQ. FT.

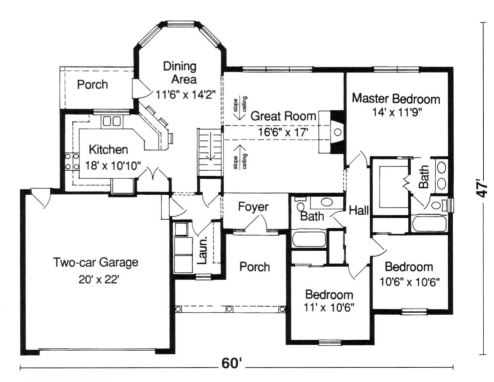

MAIN FLOOR

BL
Classic Spanish Elegance

Price Code: I

- This plan features:
- — Five bedrooms
- — Four full and one three-quarter baths
- Octagonal Family Room offers views in every direction.
- This home is designed with a slab foundation.

MAIN AREA — 3,434 SQ. FT.
GARAGE — 814 SQ. FT.
BONUS — 512 SQ. FT.

**TOTAL LIVING AREA:
3,434 SQ. FT.**

**WIDTH 82'-4"
DEPTH 83'-8"**

MAIN FLOOR

BL
Tall Ceilings

Price Code: B

- This plan features:
- — Three bedrooms
- — Two full baths
- The vaulted ceiling and open layout of the Living Room add drama to the home.
- The Garage storage alcove provides room for sports or lawn equipment.
- One of the secondary Bedrooms has a more than 10-foot-high ceiling.
- This home is designed with a basement foundation.

MAIN FLOOR — 1,537 SQ. FT.

**TOTAL LIVING AREA:
1,537 SQ. FT.**

MAIN FLOOR

To order your Blueprints, call 1-800-235-5700

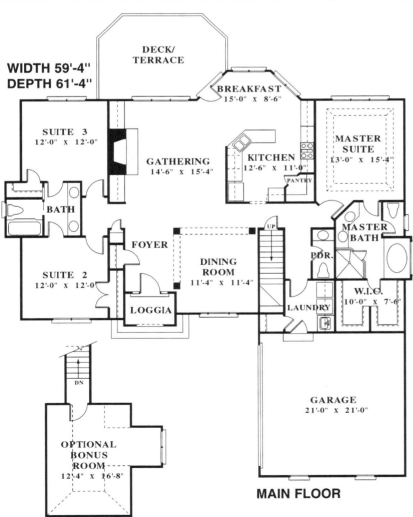

WIDTH 59'-4"
DEPTH 61'-4"

DECK/TERRACE

BREAKFAST
15'-0" x 8'-6"

SUITE 3
12'-0" x 12'-0"

GATHERING
14'-6" x 15'-4"

KITCHEN
12'-6" x 11'-0"

MASTER SUITE
13'-0" x 15'-4"

PANTRY

BATH

FOYER

MASTER BATH

SUITE 2
12'-0" x 12'-0"

DINING ROOM
11'-4" x 11'-4"

UP

PDR.

W.I.C.
10'-0" x 7'-6"

LOGGIA

LAUNDRY

DN

GARAGE
21'-0" x 21'-0"

OPTIONAL BONUS ROOM
12'-4" x 16'-8"

MAIN FLOOR

BL

Step-Saving Floor Plan

Price Code: C

■ This plan features:

— Three bedrooms

— Two full and one half baths

■ Recessed entrance leads into Foyer, Dining Room defined by columns, and Gathering Room beyond

■ Expansive Gathering Room with an inviting fireplace, opens to Deck/Terrace and Breakfast/Kitchen Area for comfortable gatherings

MAIN FLOOR — 1,950 SQ. FT.
BASEMENT — 1,287 SQ. FT.
GARAGE — 466 SQ. FT.
BONUS — 255 SQ. FT.

TOTAL LIVING AREA:
1,950 SQ. FT.

BL/ML

Expansive Living Room

Price Code: A

■ This plan features:

— Three bedrooms

— Two full baths

■ Vaulted ceiling crowns spacious Living Room highlighted by a fireplace

■ Walk-in closet and a private five-piece Bath topped by a vaulted ceiling in the Master Bedroom

■ An optional basement, crawl space or slab foundation — please specify when ordering

MAIN FLOOR — 1,346 SQ. FT.
GARAGE — 395 SQ. FT.
BASEMENT — 1358 SQ. FT.

TOTAL LIVING AREA:
1,346 SQ. FT.

MAIN FLOOR

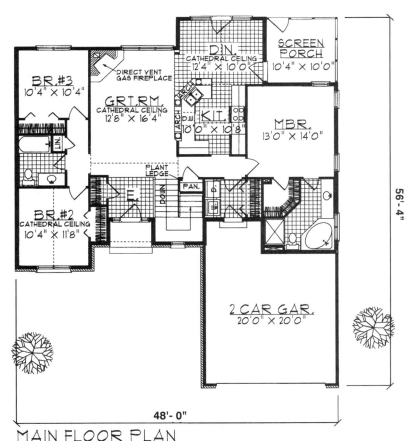

MAIN FLOOR PLAN

48'-0"

56'-4"

BL

Brick Details Add Class

Price Code: A

■ This plan features:

— Three bedrooms

— Two full baths

■ Keystone entrance leads into easy-care, tile Entry

■ Expansive Great Room has a cathedral ceiling

■ Hub Kitchen is accented by arches and columns

■ Adjoining Dining Area with large windows and outdoor access

■ Master Bedroom suite has a plush Bath

■ No materials list is available for this plan

MAIN FLOOR — 1,472 SQ. FT.
BASEMENT — 1,472 SQ. FT.
GARAGE — 424 SQ. FT.

TOTAL LIVING AREA:
1,472 SQ. FT.

© 1996 Donald A. Gardner Architects, Inc.

B. NATHAN

PLAN NO. 99810

BL/ML/ZIP/RRR

Dramatic Dormers

Price Code: D

■ This plan features:

— Three bedrooms

— Two full baths

■ A Foyer open to the dramatic dormer, defined by columns

■ A Dining Room augmented by a tray ceiling

■ A Great Room expands into the Kitchen and Breakfast Room

■ A privately located Master Suite is topped by a tray ceiling

■ Two additional Bedrooms, located at the opposite side share a full Bath and linen closet

MAIN FLOOR — 1,685 SQ. FT.
GARAGE & STORAGE — 536 SQ. FT.
BONUS — 331 SQ. FT.

TOTAL LIVING AREA:
1,685 SQ. FT.

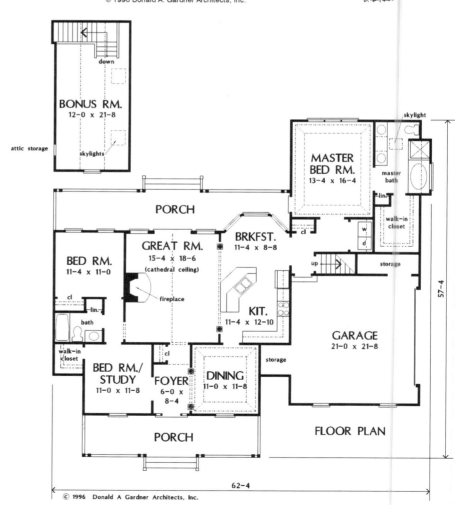

BONUS RM.
12-0 x 21-8

attic storage

skylights

down

skylight

MASTER BED RM.
13-4 x 16-4

master bath

lin.

walk-in closet

PORCH

cl

w
d

storage

GREAT RM.
15-4 x 18-6
(cathedral ceiling)

BRKFST.
11-4 x 8-8

up

BED RM.
11-4 x 11-0

fireplace

KIT.
11-4 x 12-10

GARAGE
21-0 x 21-8

cl
lin.

bath

walk-in closet

cl

storage

BED RM./
STUDY
11-0 x 11-8

FOYER
6-0 x 8-4

DINING
11-0 x 11-8

PORCH

FLOOR PLAN

57-4

62-4

© 1996 Donald A Gardner Architects, Inc.

126

To order your Blueprints, call 1-800-235-5700

BL

A Versatile Back Porch

Price Code: A

- This plan features:
— Three bedrooms
— Two full baths
- Clever open bar connects the Kitchen and Great Room
- One wall of the Breakfast Room contains a built-in computer desk
- A large bay window creates a light-filled Dining Room
- The Bedroom near the front entrance could be used as a Study or Playroom
- A glass-block window lights the Master Bath's whirlpool tub
- The Master Suite features his-and-hers walk-in closets

MAIN FLOOR — 1,485 SQ. FT.
GARAGE — 415 SQ. FT.

TOTAL LIVING AREA:
1,485 SQ. FT.

MAIN FLOOR

BL/ML/ZIP/RRR

Master Retreat Welcomes You Home

Price Code: A

- This plan features:
— Three bedrooms
— Two full baths
- Foyer opens into an huge Living Room with a fireplace below a sloped ceiling and Deck access
- Efficient Kitchen with a Pantry, serving counter, Dining Area, Laundry closet and Garage entry
- Corner Master Bedroom offers a walk-in closet and pampering Bath with a raised tub
- Two more Bedrooms, one with a Den option, share a full Bath

MAIN FLOOR — 1,486 SQ. FT.
GARAGE — 462 SQ. FT.

TOTAL LIVING AREA:
1,486 SQ. FT.

MAIN FLOOR

Slab/Crawlspace Option

© 1997 Donald A. Gardner Architects, Inc.

BL/ML/ZIP/RRR

Illusion of Spaciousness

Price Code: C

- ■ This plan features:
- — Three bedrooms
- — Two full baths
- ■ Open living spaces and vaulted ceilings create an illusion of spaciousness
- ■ Kitchen features a skylight and a serving counter/breakfast bar
- ■ The well-equipped Master Suite is located in the rear for privacy
- ■ Two additional Bedrooms in front share a full Bath

MAIN FLOOR — 1,246 SQ. FT.
GARAGE — 420 SQ. FT.

TOTAL LIVING AREA: 1,246 SQ. FT.

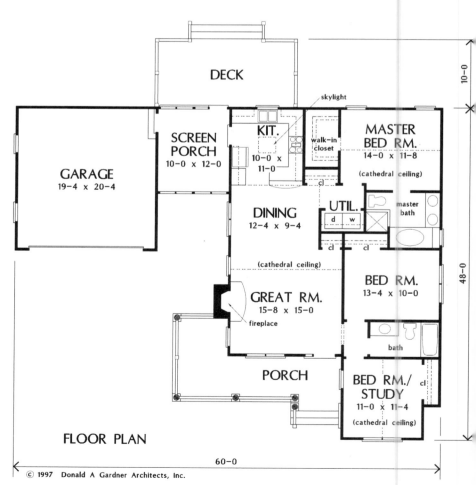

DECK

skylight

GARAGE
19-4 x 20-4

SCREEN PORCH
10-0 x 12-0

KIT.
10-0 x 11-0

walk-in closet

MASTER BED RM.
14-0 x 11-8
(cathedral ceiling)

master bath

DINING
12-4 x 9-4

UTIL.
d   w

(cathedral ceiling)

GREAT RM.
15-8 x 15-0

fireplace

BED RM.
13-4 x 10-0

bath

PORCH

BED RM./ STUDY
11-0 x 11-4
(cathedral ceiling)

10-0

48-0

60-0

FLOOR PLAN

© 1997 Donald A Gardner Architects, Inc.

To order your Blueprints, call 1-800-235-5700

BL

Outstanding Elevation

Price Code: F

■ This plan features:
— Three bedrooms
— One full, two three-quarter and one half baths
■ Grand double door entrance into Foyer and formal Dining Room and Grand Room defined by columns
■ Efficient Kitchen with Pantry and cooktop island easily serves Breakfast Area, Deck and Keeping Den
■ No materials list is available for this plan

MAIN FLOOR — 2,677 SQ. FT.
GARAGE — 543 SQ. FT.
BONUS — 319 SQ. FT.

TOTAL LIVING AREA: 2,677 SQ. FT.

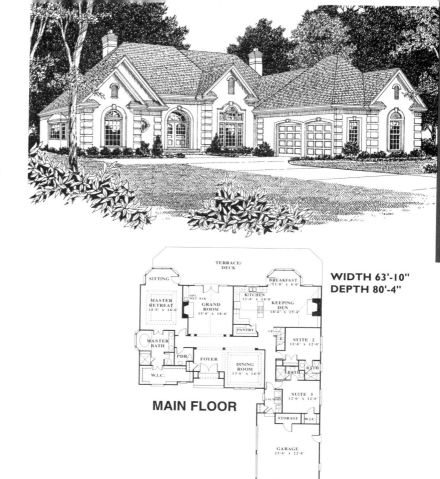

PLAN NO. 96913

WIDTH 63'-10"
DEPTH 80'-4"

MAIN FLOOR

BL

Grow Into This Home

Price Code: D

■ This plan features:
— Two bedrooms
— Two full and one half baths
■ Extend the Kitchen/Dining Area with an optional bay window for backyard views.
■ A complete Master Suite includes an option for soaking tub and linen closet.
■ Twelve-foot ceilings add drama to the spacious Family Room.
■ Create inviting appeal with the luxurious entry.
■ This home was designed with a slab foundation, crawl space or basement options.

MAIN FLOOR — 2,142 SQ. FT.
GARAGE — 574 SQ. FT.

TOTAL LIVING AREA: 2,142 SQ. FT.

PLAN NO. 65611

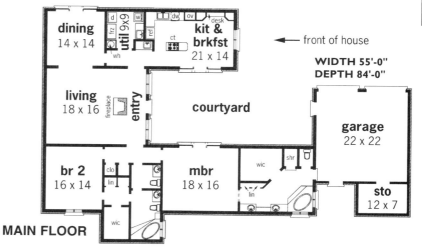

← front of house

WIDTH 55'-0"
DEPTH 84'-0"

MAIN FLOOR

BL/ML/ZIP

Moderate Ranch

Price Code: C

■ This plan features:

— Three bedrooms

— Two full baths

■ A large Great Room with a vaulted ceiling and a stone fireplace with bookshelves on either side

■ A spacious Kitchen, with ample cabinet space, conveniently located next to the large Dining Room

■ A Master Suite having a large Bath with a garden tub, double vanity and a walk-in closet

■ An optional basement, slab or crawl space foundation — please specify when ordering

MAIN FLOOR — 1,811 SQ. FT.
BASEMENT — 1,811 SQ. FT.
GARAGE — 484 SQ. FT.

TOTAL LIVING AREA:
1,811 SQ. FT.

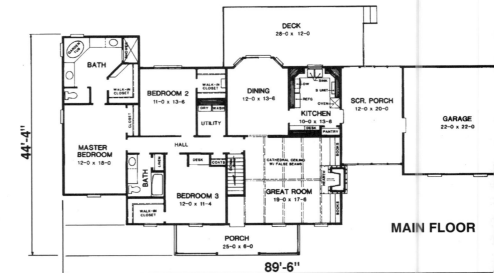

To order your Blueprints, call 1-800-235-5700

©1986 Donald A. Gardner Architects, Inc.

nny Dormer
ightens Foyer

Price Code: C

his plan features:

Three bedrooms

Two full baths

Open Great Room, Dining Room
and Kitchen topped by a
cathedral ceiling emphasizing
spaciousness

Master Bedroom crowned in
cathedral ceiling and pampered
by a private Bath with garden
tub, dual vanity and a walk-in
closet

Skylit Bonus Room above the
garage offering flexibility and
opportunity for growth

IN FLOOR — 1,386 SQ. FT.
RAGE — 517 SQ. FT.
NUS ROOM — 314 SQ. FT.

TOTAL LIVING AREA:
1,386 SQ. FT.

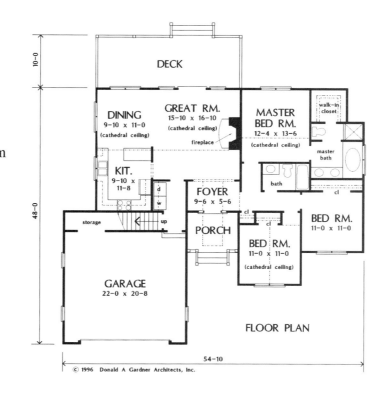

DECK

10-0

48-0

DINING
9-10 x 11-0
(cathedral ceiling)

GREAT RM.
15-10 x 16-10
(cathedral ceiling)

fireplace

MASTER
BED RM.
12-4 x 13-6
(cathedral ceiling)

walk-in
closet

master
bath

KIT.
9-10 x
11-8

FOYER
9-6 x 5-6

bath

cl

d
w

storage

up

PORCH

cl

cl

BED RM.
11-0 x 11-0

BED RM.
11-0 x 11-0
(cathedral ceiling)

GARAGE
22-0 x 20-8

FLOOR PLAN

54-10

© 1996   Donald A Gardner Architects, Inc.

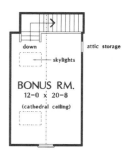

down

attic storage

skylights

BONUS RM.
12-0 x 20-8
(cathedral ceiling)

To order your Blueprints, call 1-800-235-5700

BL

A Must See Design

Price Code: D

- This plan features:
- — Three bedrooms
- — Two full baths
- Attractive, arched entrance leads into Great Room with a wall of windows and an expansive cathedral ceiling above a cozy fireplace
- Convenient Kitchen easily accesses Nook and Dining areas, Laundry and Garage
- Corner Master Bedroom is enhanced by two large, walk-in closets, a cathedral ceiling and a double vanity Bath
- No materials list is available for this plan

MAIN FLOOR — 2,229 SQ. FT.
BASEMENT — 2,229 SQ. FT.
GARAGE — 551 SQ. FT.

TOTAL LIVING AREA:
2,229 SQ. FT.

MAIN FLOOR

BL/ML

Simply Irresistible

Price Code: B

- This plan features:
- — Three bedrooms
- — Two full baths
- An 11-foot ceiling in the entry welcomes visitors with scope and scale.
- A serving bar between Kitchen and Family Room is great for entertaining.
- The luxurious Master Suite includes deluxe Bath and Sitting Area among its amenities.
- Secondary Bedrooms measure a roomy 13x11 feet.
- This home was designed with a slab foundation.

MAIN FLOOR — 1,681 SQ. FT.
GARAGE — 427 SQ. FT.

TOTAL LIVING AREA:
1,681 SQ. FT.

WIDTH 55'-8"
DEPTH 53'-2"

MAIN FLOOR

To order your Blueprints, call 1-800-235-5700

BL/ML/ZIP/RRR

Varied Roof Heights Create Interesting Lines

Price Code: B

■ This plan features:

— Three bedrooms

— Two full and one half baths

■ A spacious Family Room with a heat-circulating fireplace

■ A large Kitchen with a cooktop island, opening into the Dinette Bay

■ A Master Suite with his-n-her closets and a private Master Bath

■ Two additional Bedrooms which share a full hall Bath

■ Formal Dining and Living Rooms, flow into each other for easy entertaining

MAIN AREA — 1,613 SQ. FT.
BASEMENT — 1,060 SQ. FT.
GARAGE — 461 SQ. FT.

TOTAL LIVING AREA:
1,613 SQ. FT.

Floor Plan

PATIO 83'-8''

LAV

mud rm laund.

DINETTE 7'-8'' x 12'-4''

KIT 8'-6'' x 13'

island cook top

dw | s

sl. gl. dr.

FAMILY RM 15'-8'' x 13'-0''

fireplace

wd bin

BATH

MASTER BED RM 14'-6'' x 13'-0''

cl

BATH

cl

HALL

27'-4''

TWO CAR GARAGE 22'-0'' x 20'-0''

up

dn

cl | pantry

ref

DINING RM 11'-0'' x 12'-0''

LIVING RM 17'-6'' x 13'-4''

cl

FOYER

BED RM 10'-0'' x 10'-0''

lin

d

BED RM 10'-0'' x 13'-4''

cl

MAIN AREA

COVERED PORCH

BL/ML

Keystone Arches and Decorative Windows

Price Code: B

■ This plan features:

— Three bedrooms

— Two full baths

■ Brick and stucco enhance the dramatic front elevation and volume entrance

■ Inviting Entry leads into expansive Great Room with hearth fireplace framed by transom windows

■ Corner Master Suite enjoys a tr ceiling, roomy walk-in closet a a plush Bath with a double van and whirlpool window tub

■ Two additional Bedrooms, with large closets, share a full Bath

MAIN FLOOR — 1,666 SQ. FT.
BASEMENT — 1,666 SQ. FT.
GARAGE — 496 SQ. FT.

TOTAL LIVING AREA:
1,666 SQ. FT.

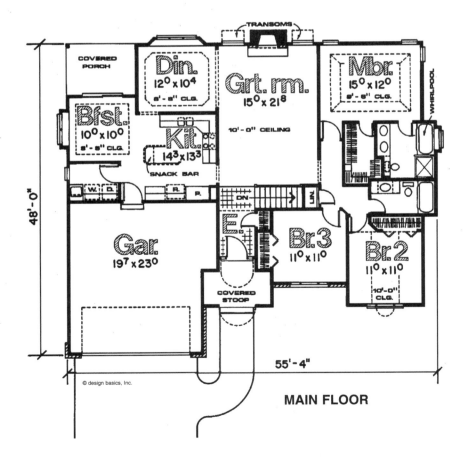

MAIN FLOOR

© design basics, Inc.

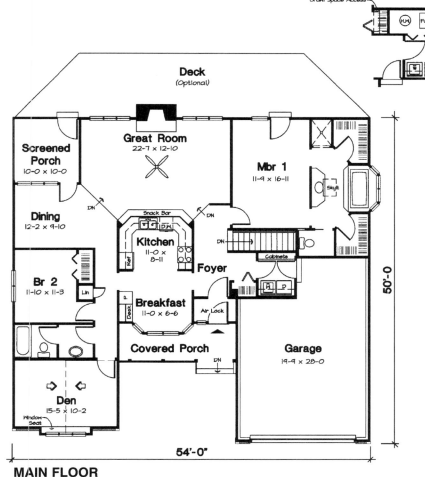

Crawl Space Access

BL/ML/ZIP

Energy Efficient Air-Lock Entry

Price Code: C

- ■ This plan features:
- — Two bedrooms
- — Two full baths
- ■ The attractive covered Porch highlights the curb appeal of this charming home
- ■ A window seat and a vaulted ceiling enhance the private Den
- ■ The sunken Great Room is accented by a fireplace
- ■ A screened Porch, accessed from the Dining Room, extends the living space to the outdoors
- ■ The Master Bath features a garden tub, separate shower, his-n-her walk-in closets and a skylight

MAIN FLOOR — 1,771 SQ. FT.
BASEMENT — 1,194 SQ. FT.
GARAGE — 517 SQ. FT.

TOTAL LIVING AREA:
1,771 SQ. FT.

MAIN FLOOR

BL/ML

Traditional Ranch

Price Code: E

■ This plan features:

— Three bedrooms

— Two full baths

■ A tray ceiling over Master Suite which is equipped with his and her walk-in closets and a private Master Bath with a cathedral ceiling

■ A formal Living Room with a cathedral ceiling

■ A decorative tray ceiling in the elegant formal Dining Room

■ A spacious Family Room with a vaulted ceiling and a fireplace

■ A modern, well-appointed Kitchen with snack bar and bayed Breakfast Area

MAIN AREA — 2,275 SQ. FT.
BASEMENT — 2,207 SQ. FT.
GARAGE — 512 SQ. FT.

TOTAL LIVING AREA:
2,275 SQ. FT.

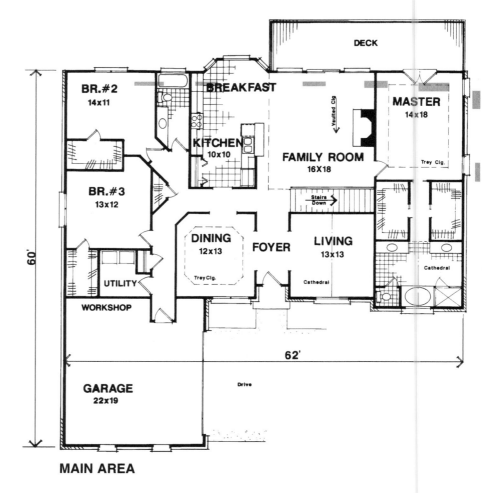

BL

Country Flair

Price Code: A

■ This plan features:
— Three bedrooms
— Two full baths
■ An inviting front Porch leads into a tiled
  Entry and Great Room with focal point fireplace
■ Open layout of Great Room, Dining Area,
  Wood Deck and Kitchen easily accommodates
  a busy family
■ Master Bedroom set in a quiet corner, offers
  a huge walk-in closet and double vanity Bath
■ Two additional Bedrooms, one an optional
  Den, share a full hall Bath
■ No materials list is available for this plan

MAIN FLOOR — 1,461 SQ. FT.
BASEMENT — 1,461 SQ. FT.
GARAGE — 458 SQ. FT.

TOTAL LIVING AREA: 1,461 SQ. FT.

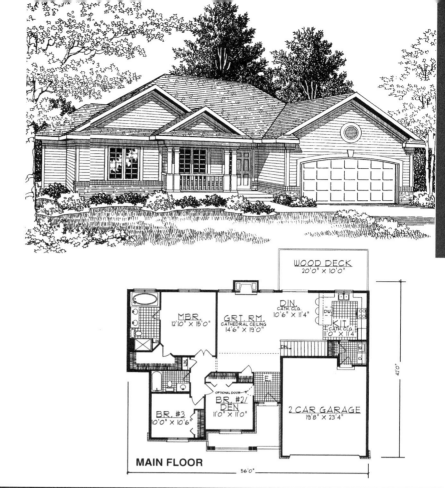

BL

Grow Into This Home

Price Code: A

■ This plan features:
— Three bedrooms
— Two full baths
■ Extend the Kitchen/Dining Area with an optional
  bay window for backyard views.
■ A complete Master Suite includes an option for
  soaking tub and linen closet.
■ Twelve-foot ceilings add drama to the spacious
  Family Room.
■ Create inviting appeal with the luxurious entry.
■ This home was designed with a slab foundation,
  crawlspace or basement options.

MAIN FLOOR — 1,296 SQ. FT.
GARAGE — 380 SQ. FT.
UNFINISHED BASEMENT — 1,336 SQ. FT.

TOTAL LIVING AREA: 1,296 SQ. FT.

WIDTH 46'-0"
DEPTH 42'-0"

PLAN NO. 98008

©1997 Donald A. Gardner Architects, Inc.

BL/ML/RRR

Pretty as a Picture

Price Code: E

■ This plan features:

— Three bedrooms

— Two full baths

■ The wrapping front Porch is beautiful and functional

■ The Dining Room has a tray ceiling and windows that overlook the front Porch

■ The Kitchen has a convenient layout with a work triangle

■ The Master Bedroom is isolated and features a galley Bath that leads into the walk-in closet

■ There is a bonus room over the Garage

MAIN FLOOR — 1,911 SQ. FT.
BONUS — 406 SQ. FT.
GARAGE — 551 SQ. FT.

TOTAL LIVING AREA:
1,911 SQ. FT.

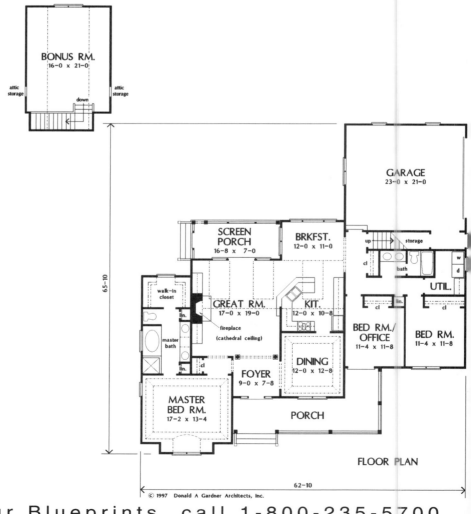

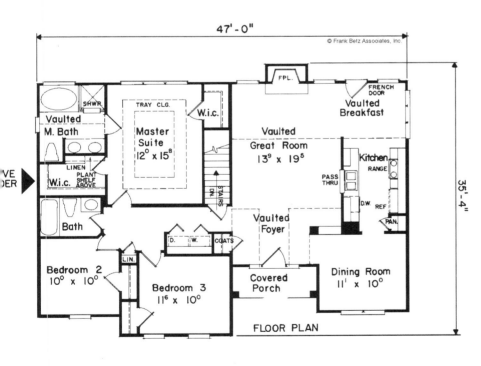

© Frank Betz Associates, Inc.

47'-0"

35'-4"

FLOOR PLAN

SHWR

Vaulted
M. Bath

TRAY CLG.

W.i.c.

FPL.

FRENCH
DOOR

Vaulted
Breakfast

LINEN

PLANT
SHELF
ABOVE

W.i.c.

Master
Suite
12⁰ x 15⁸

Vaulted
Great Room
13⁹ x 19⁵

Kitchen
RANGE

Bath

PASS
THRU

D.W. REF

PAN.

STAIRS
DN

Vaulted
Foyer

LIN.

D.   W.   COATS

Bedroom 2
10⁰ x 10⁰

Bedroom 3
11⁶ x 10⁰

Covered
Porch

Dining Room
11' x 10⁰

BL

Vaulted Ceilings Create Spacious Feelings

Price Code: A

■ This plan features:

— Three bedrooms

— Two full baths

■ Open layout with vaulted ceilings in Foyer, Great Room and Breakfast Area

■ Kitchen with pass-thru and Pantry, efficiently serves bright Breakfast Area, Great Room and formal Dining Room

MAIN FLOOR — 1,363 SQ. FT.
BASEMENT — 715 SQ. FT.
GARAGE — 677 SQ. FT.

TOTAL LIVING AREA:
1,363 SQ. FT.

BL/ML/ZIP

Compact and Beautiful

Price Code: C

■ This plan features:
— Three bedrooms
— Two full baths
■ Only 30-foot wide, this unique home fits on the narrowest of lots
■ Even with it's slender design, the home's master suite is fully loaded
■ The ample, one and a-half car garage offers plenty of auxiliary storage space
■ The efficient though complete galley kitchen anchors the home
■ This home is designed with a slab foundation

MAIN FLOOR — 1,118 SQ. FT.

TOTAL LIVING AREA:
1,118 SQ. FT.

WIDTH 30'-0"
DEPTH 60'-0"

MAIN FLOOR

BL

Open Areas
For Entertaining

Price Code: B

■ This plan features:
— Three bedrooms
— Two full baths
■ The Great-Room features a 9-foot-high raised ceiling, a hearth fireplace, and access to the backyard
■ The Kitchen includes a Pantry and is only steps away from both the Laundry and Dining Rooms
■ This home is designed with basement, slab, and crawlspace foundation options

MAIN FLOOR — 1,538 SQ. FT.
GARAGE — 441 SQ. FT.

TOTAL LIVING AREA:
1,538 SQ. FT.

MAIN FLOOR

To order your Blueprints, call 1-800-235-5700

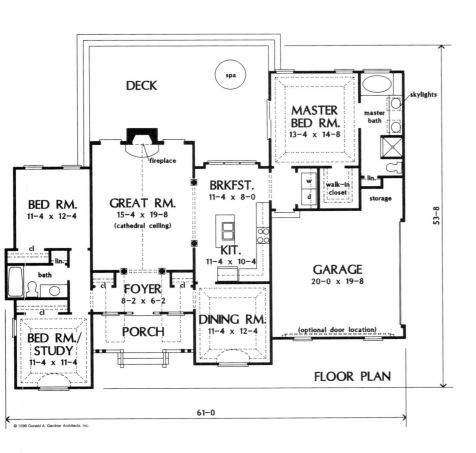

DECK

spa

MASTER
BED RM.
13-4 x 14-8

skylights

master
bath

fireplace

BRKFST.
11-4 x 8-0

w

d

walk-in
closet

lin.

storage

53-8

BED RM.
11-4 x 12-4

GREAT RM.
15-4 x 19-8
(cathedral ceiling)

cl

lin.

bath

KIT.
11-4 x 10-4

GARAGE
20-0 x 19-8

cl

FOYER
8-2 x 6-2

cl

BED RM./
STUDY
11-4 x 11-4

PORCH

DINING RM.
11-4 x 12-4

(optional door location)

FLOOR PLAN

61-0

© 1996 Donald A. Gardner Architects, Inc.

BL/ML/ZIP/RRR

Charm and Personality

Price Code: D

■ This plan features:

— Three bedrooms

— Two full baths

■ Interior columns dramatically open the Foyer and Kitchen to the spacious Great Room

■ The Great Room has a cathedral ceiling and a fireplace

■ Master Suite with a tray ceiling combines privacy with access to the rear Deck with Spa

■ Tray ceilings with round-top picture windows bring a special elegance to the Dining Room and the front Swing Room

MAIN FLOOR — 1,655 SQ. FT.
GARAGE — 434 SQ. FT.

TOTAL LIVING AREA:
1,655 SQ. FT.

BL

Those Fabulous Details

Price Code: E

- ■ This plan features:
- — Four bedrooms
- — Two full and one half baths
- ■ Hub of home is vaulted Family Room with French door
- ■ Vaulted Breakfast Area expands efficient Kitchen
- ■ Spacious Master Suite boasts a Sitting Area with fireplace
- ■ An optional basement or crawl space foundation — please specify when ordering
- ■ No materials list is available for this plan

MAIN FLOOR — 2,311 SQ. FT.
BONUS — 425 SQ. FT.
BASEMENT — 2,311 SQ. FT.
GARAGE — 500 SQ. FT.

TOTAL LIVING AREA:
2,311 SQ. FT.

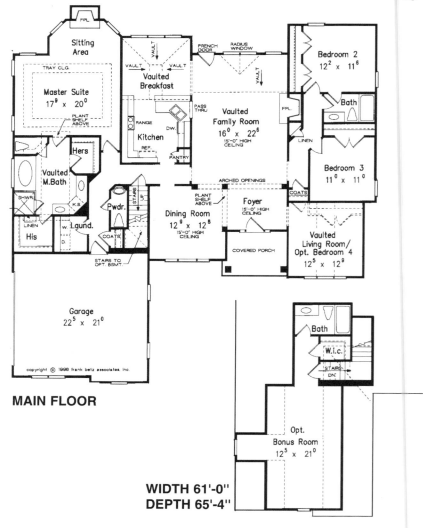

MAIN FLOOR

WIDTH 61'-0"
DEPTH 65'-4"

OPT. BONUS FLOOR PLAN

BL

High Ceilings and Arched Windows

Price Code: B

- This plan features:
  - Three bedrooms
  - Two full baths
- Kitchen with a serving bar to the Breakfast Room
- Tray ceiling in the Master Suite and a vaulted ceiling over the Sitting Room and the Master Bath
- No materials list is available for this plan
- An optional basement or crawl space foundation — please specify when ordering

MAIN FLOOR — 1,502 SQ. FT.
GARAGE — 448 SQ. FT.
BASEMENT — 1,555 SQ. FT.

TOTAL LIVING AREA:
1,502 SQ. FT.

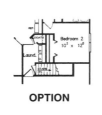

OPTION

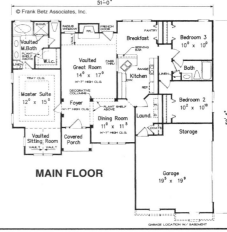

© Frank Betz Associates, Inc.

MAIN FLOOR

GARAGE LOCATION W/ BASEMENT

BL

Complete Efficiency

Price Code: A

- This plan features:
  - Three bedrooms
  - Two full baths
- Careful design makes this home "live" much bigger than it really is.
- A vaulted ceiling in the family room adds scale and drama.
- The laundry room is conveniently placed between kitchen and garage.
- A soaking tub, double vanity and vaulted ceiling add to the elegance of the master bath.
- The master suite includes a large walk-in closet for ample storage.
- This home was designed with a slab or crawl space foundation options.

MAIN FLOOR — 1,197 SQ. FT.
GARAGE — 380 SQ. FT.

TOTAL LIVING AREA:
1,197 SQ. FT.

WIDTH 52'-0"
DEPTH 42'-0"

MAIN FLOOR

PLAN NO. 97254

BL

Elegant Ceiling Treatments

Price Code: B

- ■ This plan features:
- — Three Bedrooms
- — Two full baths
- ■ Dining Room defined by columns
- ■ Kitchen highlighted by a peninsula counter/serving bar
- ■ Vaulted ceiling highlighting the Great Room which also includes a fireplace between radius windows
- ■ No materials list is available for this plan
- ■ An optional crawl space or slab foundation — please specify when ordering

First floor — 1,692 sq. ft.
Bonus room — 358 sq. ft.
Basement — 1,705 sq. ft.
Garage — 472 sq. ft.

TOTAL LIVING AREA:
1,692 SQ. FT.

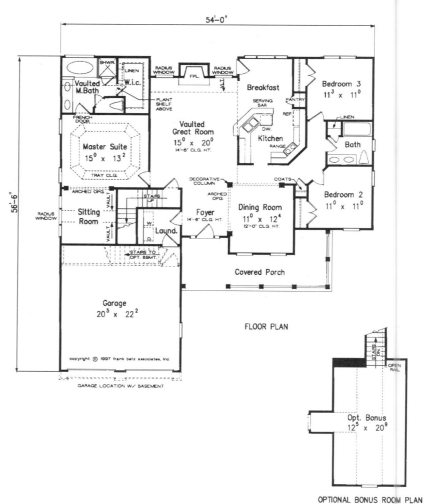

FLOOR PLAN

OPTIONAL BONUS ROOM PLAN

To order your Blueprints, call 1-800-235-5700

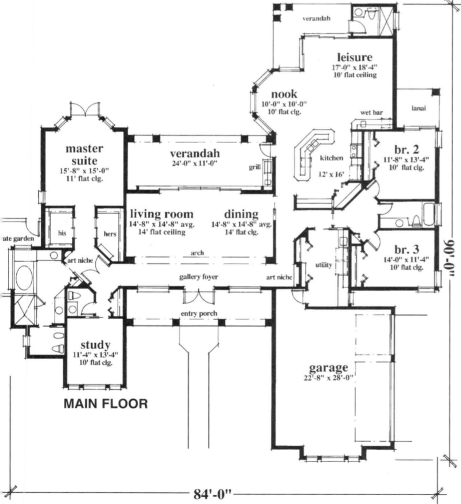

MAIN FLOOR

verandah

leisure
17'-0" x 18'-4"
10' flat ceiling

nook
10'-0" x 10'-0"
10' flat clg.

wet bar

lanai

kitchen
12' x 16'

br. 2
11'-8" x 13'-4"
10' flat clg.

master
suite
15'-8" x 15'-0"
11' flat clg.

verandah
24'-0" x 11'-0"

grill

his

hers

living room
14'-8" x 14'-8" avg.
14' flat ceiling

dining
14'-8" x 14'-8" avg.
14' flat clg.

br. 3
14'-0" x 11'-4"
10' flat clg.

art niche

arch

utility

ate garden

art niche

gallery foyer

entry porch

study
11'-4" x 13'-4"
10' flat clg.

garage
22'-8" x 28'-0"

90'-0"

84'-0"

BL/ML

A Custom Look

Price Code: G

■ This plan features:

— Three bedrooms

— Two full, one half, and one three quarter baths

■ Exterior highlighted by triple arched glass in entry Porch

■ Triple arches lead into Formal Living and Dining rooms, Verandah and beyond

■ Owners' wing has a Master Suite with glass alcove to rear yard, a lavish Bath and a Study

■ Two additional Bedrooms with corner windows and over-sized closets access a full Bath

■ No materials list is available for this plan

MAIN FLOOR — 2,978 SQ. FT.
GARAGE — 702 SQ. FT.

TOTAL LIVING AREA:
2,978 SQ. FT.

BL/ML

European Styling with a Georgian Flair

Price Code: C

■ This plan features:

— Four bedrooms

— Two full baths

■ Arched windows, quoins and shutters on the exterior, a columned covered front and a rear Porch

■ Kitchen flows into the informal Eating Area

■ Split Bedroom plan, Master Suite privately place to the rear

■ An optional crawl space or slab foundation — please specify when ordering

MAIN FLOOR — 1,873 SQ. FT.
GARAGE — 613 SQ. FT.
BONUS — 145 SQ. FT.

TOTAL LIVING AREA:
1,873 SQ. FT.

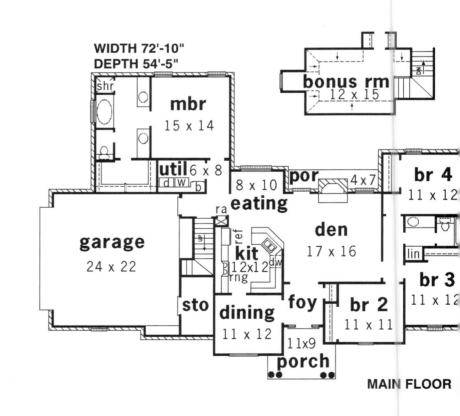

WIDTH 72'-10"
DEPTH 54'-5"

bonus rm
12 x 15

mbr
15 x 14

util 6 x 8

por
4 x 7

br 4
11 x 12

eating

garage
24 x 22

kit
12x12

den
17 x 16

sto

dining
11 x 12

foy

br 2
11 x 11

br 3
11 x 12

11x9

porch

MAIN FLOOR

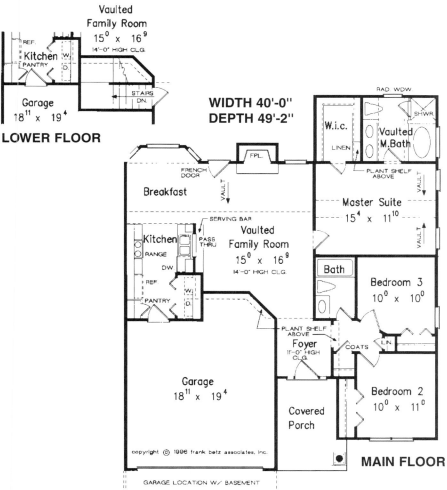

Vaulted Family Room
15⁰ x 16⁹
14'-0" HIGH CLG.

REF.
Kitchen
PANTRY
W.
D.

Garage
18¹¹ x 19⁴

STAIRS DN.

LOWER FLOOR

WIDTH 40'-0"
DEPTH 49'-2"

RAD. WDW

W.i.c.
LINEN
Vaulted M.Bath
SHWR.

PLANT SHELF ABOVE

FPL.

FRENCH DOOR

VAULT

Breakfast

Master Suite
15⁴ x 11¹⁰

SERVING BAR

Kitchen
RANGE
DW.
REF.
PANTRY

PASS THRU

Vaulted Family Room
15⁰ x 16⁹
14'-0" HIGH CLG.

Bath

Bedroom 3
10⁰ x 10⁰

W. D.

PLANT SHELF ABOVE

Foyer
11'-0" HIGH CLG.

COATS
LIN.

Garage
18¹¹ x 19⁴

Bedroom 2
10⁰ x 11⁰

Covered Porch

copyright © 1996 frank betz associates, inc.

GARAGE LOCATION W/ BASEMENT

MAIN FLOOR

BL

Charming Three-Bedroom

Price Code: A

■ This plan features:

— Three bedrooms

— Two full baths

■ Covered Porch leads into Foyer with plant shelves and Vaulted Family Room beyond

■ Efficient Kitchen with Pantry, Laundry and pass thru opens to bright Breakfast Area

■ An optional basement or crawl space foundation — please specify when ordering

■ No materials list is available for this plan

MAIN FLOOR — 1,222 SQ. FT.
LOWER FLOOR — 1,218 SQ. FT.
GARAGE — 410 SQ. FT.

TOTAL LIVING AREA: 1,222 SQ. FT.

BL

Definitely Detailed

Price Code: C

■ This plan features:

— Three bedrooms

— Two full baths

■ An artistically detailed brick exterior adds to the appeal of this home

■ The Great Room has a wall of windows and a warming fireplace

■ The Kitchen is arranged in a U-shape and features a center island plus a walk-in Pantry

■ An optional plan for the basement includes a Recreation Room, an Exercise Room, and a Bath

■ No materials list is available for this plan

MAIN FLOOR — 1,963 SQ. FT.
LOWER FLOOR — 1,963 SQ. FT.

TOTAL LIVING AREA:
1,963 SQ. FT.

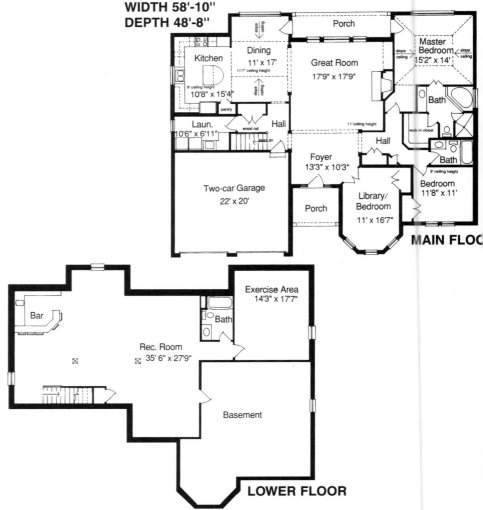

WIDTH 58'-10''
DEPTH 48'-8''

Porch

Dining
11' x 17'
11'7" ceiling height

Kitchen
10'8" x 15'4"
9' ceiling height

Great Room
17'9" x 17'9"

Master Bedroom
15'2" x 14'
slope ceiling

Bath

Laun.
10'6" x 6'11"

Hall

11' ceiling height

walk-in closet

Hall

Bath
9' ceiling height

Two-car Garage
22' x 20'

Foyer
13'3" x 10'3"

Porch

Library/ Bedroom
11' x 16'7"

Bedroom
11'8" x 11'

MAIN FLOOR

Bar

Exercise Area
14'3" x 17'7"

Bath

Rec. Room
35' 6" x 27'9"

Basement

LOWER FLOOR

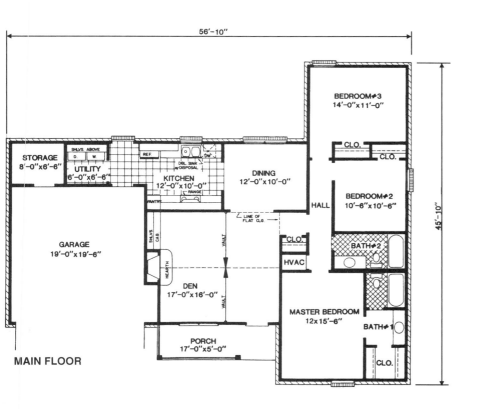

56'–10"

STORAGE
8'–0"x6'–6"

SHLVS. ABOVE
D. W.

UTILITY
6'–0"x6'–6"

REF.

KITCHEN
12'–0"x10'–0"

DBL. SINK
DISPOSAL

RANGE

PANTRY

DINING
12'–0"x10'–0"

BEDROOM#3
14'–0"x11'–0"

CLO.

CLO.

HALL

BEDROOM#2
10'–6"x10'–6"

GARAGE
19'–0"x19'–6"

SHLVS
CAB

HEARTH

DEN
17'–0"x16'–0"

LINE OF
FLAT CLG.

VAULT

VAULT

CLO.

HVAC

BATH#2

MASTER BEDROOM
12x15'–6"

PORCH
17'–0"x5'–0"

BATH#1

CLO.

45'–10"

MAIN FLOOR

BL/ML

Warm and Inviting

Price Code: A

■ This plan features:

— Three bedrooms

— Two full baths

■ A Den with a cozy fireplace and vaulted ceiling

■ A well-equipped Kitchen that contains a double sink and built-in Pantry

■ A spacious Master Bedroom with a private Master Bath and walk-in closet

■ Additional Bedrooms sharing full hall Bath

■ An optional crawl space or slab foundation — please specify when ordering

MAIN FLOOR — 1,363 SQ. FT.
GARAGE — 434 SQ. FT.

TOTAL LIVING AREA:
1,363 SQ. FT.

BL/ML

Striking Style

Price Code: A

- This plan features:
  — Three bedrooms
  — Two full baths

- Windows and exterior detailing create a striking elevation

- The Dining Room has a front window wall and arched openings

- The Great Room has a vaulted ceiling and a fireplace

- The Master Suite features a tray ceiling, a walk-in closet and a private Bath

- An optional basement or crawlspace foundation — please specify when ordering

FIRST FLOOR — 1,432 SQ. FT.
BASEMENT — 1,454 SQ. FT.
GARAGE — 440 SQ. FT.

TOTAL LIVING AREA: 1,432 SQ. FT.

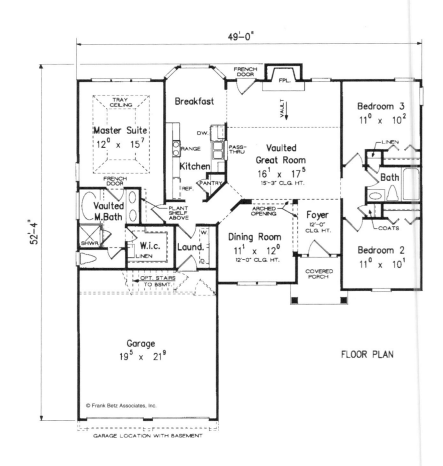

FLOOR PLAN

© Frank Betz Associates, Inc.

GARAGE LOCATION WITH BASEMENT

To order your Blueprints, call 1-800-235-5700

BL

Offset Gables Add Curb Appeal

Price Code: F

■ This plan features:
— Four bedrooms
— Three full baths
■ A big walk-in closet is conveniently placed off the Master Bath
■ A tall cathedral ceiling rises above the Family Room
■ Drop off the Laundry on the way to the Garage
■ Formal and informal Dining Rooms for any occasion
■ A wrap-around Patio embellishes the rear elevation

MAIN FLOOR — 2,579 SQ. FT.
GARAGE — 630 SQ. FT.

TOTAL LIVING AREA:
2,579 SQ. FT

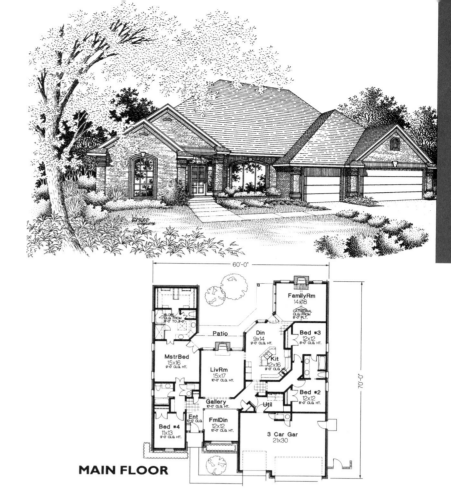

MAIN FLOOR

BL

A Big Country Space

Price Code: D

■ This plan features:
— Three bedrooms
— Two full baths
■ This plan is great for corner lots with its two-car Garage set toward the rear.
■ A large Family Room adjoining Kitchen are separated from the Dining Room by a lowered soffit.
■ Luxurious appoints in the Master Suite include large walk-in closet with attached, extra storage.
■ A two-Bedroom Kid's Suite features Bath and Study Room.
■ This home is designed with a slab foundation.

MAIN FLOOR — 2,077 SQ. FT.
GARAGE — 524 SQ. FT.

TOTAL LIVING AREA:
2,077 SQ. FT

WIDTH 70'-8"
DEPTH 69'-0"

MAIN FLOOR

PLAN NO. 98000

©1997 Donald A. Gardner Architects, Inc.

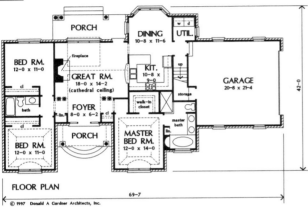

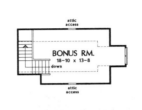

FLOOR PLAN

© 1997 Donald A. Gardner Architects, Inc.

BL/ML

Gentle Arches Adorn This Home

Price Code: C

■ This plan features:
— Three bedrooms
— Two full baths
■ Front and back Porches provide the right Country feel
■ Columns subtly separate the Great Room from the Foyer
■ A nearly 340 sq. ft. Bonus Space is available over the Garage
■ There's a pass-through from Kitchen to Great Room
■ A tray ceiling creates openness in the Master Bedroom

MAIN FLOOR — 1,488 SQ. FT.
BONUS — 338 SQ. FT.
GARAGE — 534 SQ. FT.

TOTAL LIVING AREA: 1,488 SQ. FT

PLAN NO. 24721

MAIN FLOOR

BL/ML/ZIP

Ranch with Country Appeal

Price Code: B

■ This plan features:
— Three bedrooms
— Two full baths
■ Tiled Foyer leading into the Living Room
■ Sloped ceiling topping the Living Room also accented by a fireplace
■ Built-in shelves on either side of the arched opening between the Living Room and the Dining Room
■ Efficient U-shaped Kitchen highlighted by breakfast bar
■ French door accessing rear Deck from Dining Area
■ Master Suite crowned with a decorative ceiling and contains a private whirlpool Bath
■ Roomy secondary Bedrooms share a full Bath in the hall

MAIN FLOOR — 1,539 SQ. FT.
BASEMENT — 1,530 SQ. FT.

TOTAL LIVING AREA: 1,539 SQ. FT.

BL

Luxurious Masterpiece

Price Code: K

■ This plan features:

— Four bedrooms

— Three full and one half baths

■ Expansive formal Living Room with a fourteen foot ceiling and a raised hearth fireplace

■ Family Room with a fireplace, wetbar and cathedral ceiling

■ Hub Kitchen with a cooktop island, peninsula counter/snackbar, and a bright Breakfast Area

■ French doors leads into Study

■ Private Master Bedroom enhanced by pullman ceiling and lavish his and her Baths

■ No materials list is available for this plan

MAIN FLOOR — 3,818 SQ. FT.
GARAGE — 816 SQ. FT.

TOTAL LIVING AREA:
3,818 SQ. FT.

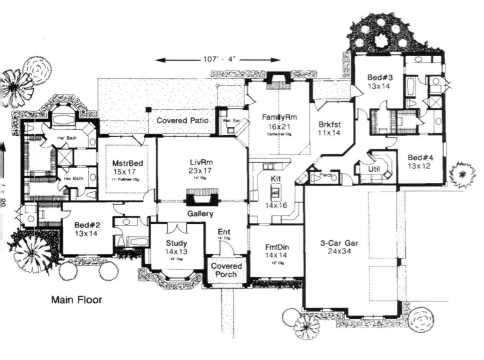

Main Floor

BL/ML/ZIP

Inviting Porch

Price Code: A

■ This plan features:

— Three bedrooms

— Two full baths

■ A large and spacious Living Room that adjoins the Dining Room for ease in entertaining

■ A private Bedroom wing offering a quiet atmosphere

■ A Master Bedroom with his and her closets and a private Bath

■ An efficient Kitchen with a walk-in Pantry

MAIN AREA — 1,243 SQ. FT.
BASEMENT — 1,103 SQ. FT.
GARAGE — 490 SQ. FT.

TOTAL LIVING AREA:
1,243 SQ. FT.

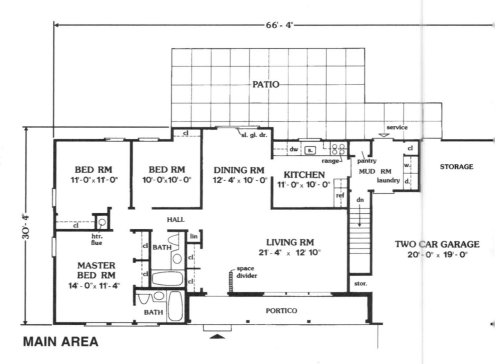

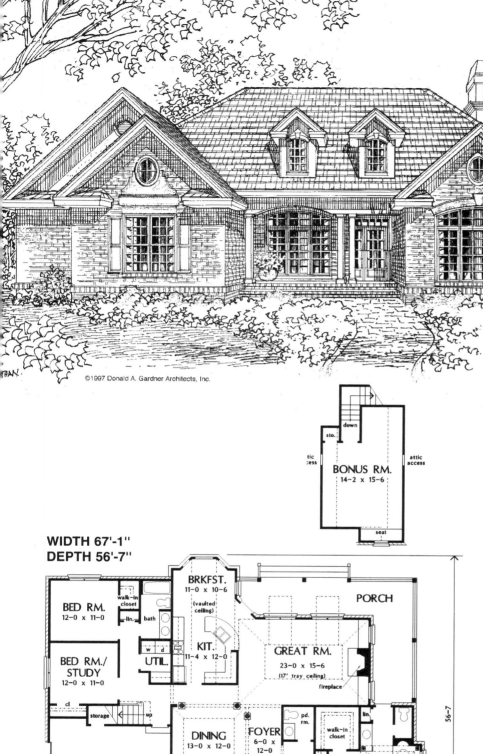

©1997 Donald A. Gardner Architects, Inc.

BONUS RM.
14-2 x 15-6

sto.

down

tic cess

attic access

seat

WIDTH 67'-1"
DEPTH 56'-7"

BED RM.
12-0 x 11-0

walk-in closet

lin.

bath

BRKFST.
11-0 x 10-6
(vaulted ceiling)

PORCH

BED RM./STUDY
12-0 x 11-0

w d

UTIL.

KIT.
11-4 x 12-0

GREAT RM.
23-0 x 15-6
(17' tray ceiling)

fireplace

cl

storage

up

DINING
13-0 x 12-0

FOYER
6-0 x 12-0

pd. rm.

cl

walk-in closet

lin.

master bath

56-7

GARAGE
21-4 x 24-8

PORCH

MASTER BED RM.
13-4 x 16-0
(vaulted ceiling)

storage

FLOOR PLAN

© 1997 Donald A Gardner Architects, Inc.

67-1

BL/ML/RRR

Elegant Brick Veneer

Price Code: D

■ This plan features:

— Three bedrooms

— Two full and one half baths

■ Arched and oval windows enhance the elegance of this home

■ Open, formal Dining Room defined by columns and topped with tray ceiling

■ Expansive Great Room offers a tray ceiling, and a cozy fireplace

■ Curved serving counter, vaulted ceiling and bright Breakfast Area highlight Kitchen

■ Separate Master Bedroom accented by a vaulted ceiling, roomy walk-in closet and lavish Bath

MAIN FLOOR — 2,198 SQ. FT.
BONUS ROOM — 325 SQ. FT.
GARAGE — 588 SQ. FT.

TOTAL LIVING AREA:
2,198 SQ. FT.

© Donald A. Gardner Architects, Inc.

BL/ML/ZIP/RRR

Great As A Mountain Retreat

Price Code: E

■ This plan features:

— Three bedrooms

— Two full baths

■ Board and batten siding, stone, and stucco combine to give this popular plan a casual feel

■ Casual family meals in sunny Breakfast bay; formal gatherings in the columned Dining Area

■ Master Suite is topped by a deep tray ceiling, has a large walk-in closet, an extravagant private Bath and direct access to back Porch

MAIN FLOOR — 1,912 SQ. FT.
GARAGE — 580 SQ. FT.
BONUS — 398 SQ. FT.

TOTAL LIVING AREA:
1,912 SQ. FT.

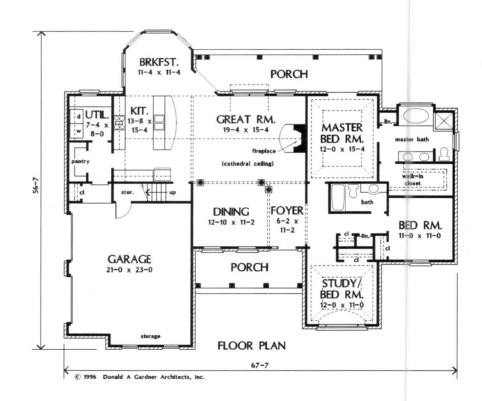

FLOOR PLAN

© 1996 Donald A Gardner Architects, Inc.

To order your Blueprints, call 1-800-235-5700

©1997 Donald A. Gardner Architects, Inc.

s plan is not to be built in Greenville County, SC.
d as reproducible only.

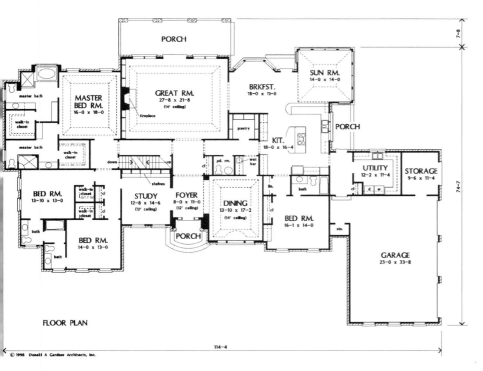

FLOOR PLAN

© 1998 Donald A Gardner Architects, Inc.

BL/ML/RRR

Always in Style

Price Code: L

■ This plan features:

— Four bedrooms

— Four full and two half baths

■ Brick, gables and a traditional hip roof always seem to be in style

■ Inside find dramatic spaces that include the Dining Room and the Great Room both with 14′ ceilings

■ The Study features a wall of built in bookshelves

■ The Kitchen has a center island with a cooktop

■ The Master Bedroom is opulent with dual Baths and closets

MAIN FLOOR — 4,523 SQ. FT.
GARAGE — 1,029 SQ. FT.

TOTAL LIVING AREA:
4,523 SQ. FT.

©1997 Donald A. Gardner Architects, Inc.

Floor Plan

DECK

11-0

master bath

lin.

(cathedral ceiling)

fireplace

DINING
12-0 x 12-0

walk-in closet

bath

lin.

BED RM.
11-0 x 11-0

GREAT RM.
15-0 x 17-10

MASTER BED RM.
13-0 x 15-0

walk-in closet

FOYER
6-2 x 6-0

KIT.
12-0 x 12-2

UTIL.
6-4 x 6-0

w
d

cl

BED RM.
11-0 x 11-0

cl

up

storage

48-6

PORCH

GARAGE
20-0 x 20-4

FLOOR PLAN

61-4

© 1997 Donald A Gardner Architects, Inc.

down

BONUS RM.
12-8 x 18-4

attic storage

attic storage

skylight

BL/ML/RRR

Compact Country

Price Code: D

■ This plan features:

— Three bedrooms

— Two full baths

■ Economical squared off design still stylish with gables and arches

■ Welcoming front Porch leads in Foyer, Great Room and Deck beyond

■ Comfortable gathering area created by open layout of Great Room, Dining Area and Kitchen

■ Master Suite provides privacy, elegant tray ceiling, walk-in closet and lavish Bath with two vanities

MAIN FLOOR — 1,517 SQ. FT.
BONUS ROOM — 287 SQ. FT.
GARAGE — 447 SQ. FT.

TOTAL LIVING AREA:
1,517 SQ. FT.

BL

High Ceilings and Open Spaces

Price Code: E

■ This plan features:
— Three bedrooms
— Three full baths
■ A tiled Foyer leads into the Dining Area that flows uninhibited into the Great Room
■ The Kitchen has a snack bar, a built-in Pantry, a Breakfast Area, and is adjacent to the Keeping Room with a fireplace
■ This plan is available with a basement, slab or crawl space foundation, please specify when ordering

MAIN FLOOR — 2,330 SQ. FT.
BASEMENT — 2,330 SQ. FT.
GARAGE — 416 SQ. FT.

TOTAL LIVING AREA:
2,330 SQ. FT.

WIDTH 50'-0"
DEPTH 70'-0"

MAIN FLOOR

BL

Built Around a Truly Great Room

Price Code: H

■ This plan features:
— Four bedrooms
— Three full baths
— Two full, one half and one three-quarter baths
■ Elegant Study contains private fireplace.
■ 3,162 square feet of living space.
■ Master Bedroom leads opens to Gallery and covered Patio.
■ This home is designed with a slab foundation.

MAIN FLOOR — 3,162 SQ. FT.
GARAGE — 662 SQ. FT.

TOTAL LIVING AREA:
3,162 SQ. FT.

WIDTH 85'-10"
DEPTH 66'-3"

MAIN FLOOR

© 1998 Donald A. Gardner, Inc.

BL/ML/RRR

Efficient Design

Price Code: C

- This plan features:
  — Three bedrooms
  — Two full baths
- Foyer introduces a wonderful Great Room with cathedral ceiling, inviting fireplace with built-in cabinets, and rear Porch access
- Comfortable family gatherings created by open layout of Great Room, Dining Area and Kitchen
- Compact Kitchen easy to work in with Pantry and angled breakfast bar
- Expansion and attic storage provided by bonus room over Garage

MAIN FLOOR — 1,476 SQ. FT.
BONUS ROOM — 340 SQ. FT.
GARAGE & STORAGE — 567 SQ. FT.

TOTAL LIVING AREA:
1,476 SQ. FT.

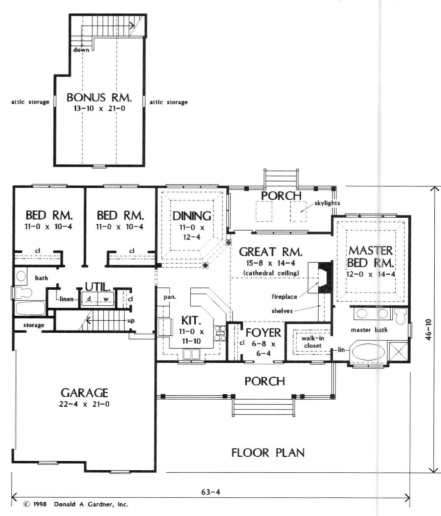

© 1998 Donald A Gardner, Inc.

To order your Blueprints, call 1-800-235-5700

BL

Brick Abounds

Price Code: B

■ This plan features:

— Three bedrooms

— Two full baths

■ The covered front Porch opens into the entry that has a 10-foot ceiling and a coat closet

■ The Dining Room features a 10-foot ceiling and access to the Patio

■ The Kitchen is angled and has a Pantry and a cooktop island

■ The Master Bedroom is located in the rear for privacy and boasts a triangular walk-in closet

■ No materials list is available for this plan

MAIN FLOOR — 1,528 SQ. FT.
GARAGE — 440 SQ. FT.

TOTAL LIVING AREA: 1,528 SQ. FT.

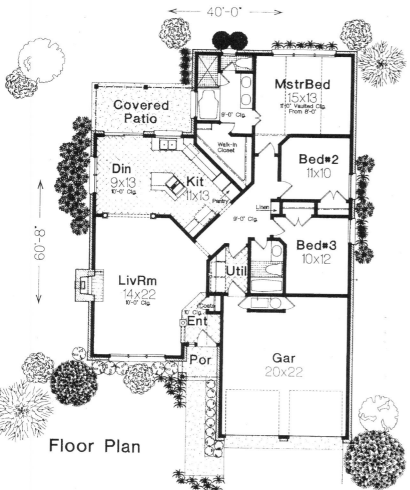

40'-0"

60'-8"

MstrBed
15x13
11'0" Vaulted Clg.
From 8'-0"

9'-0" Clg.

Covered Patio

Walk-In Closet

Bed#2
11x10

Din
9x13
10'-0" Clg.

Kit
11x13
Pantry

Linen

9'-0" Clg.

Bed#3
10x12

LivRm
14x22
10'-0" Clg.

Util

Ent
Coats

Por

Gar
20x22

Floor Plan

© 1998 Donald A. Gardner Architects, Inc.

BL/ML/ZIP/RRR

Compact Plan

Price Code: C

- **This plan features:**

— Three bedrooms

— Two full baths

- **A Great Room topped by a cathedral ceiling adjoins the Dining Room and Kitchen to create a spacious Living Area**

- **A bay window highlights the Dining Room and a palladian window allowing ample light into the Great Room**

- **A Master Suite is highlighted by ample closet space and a private skylit Bath enhanced by a dual vanity and a separate tub and shower**

MAIN FLOOR — 1,372 SQ. FT.
GARAGE & STORAGE — 537 SQ. FT.

TOTAL LIVING AREA:
1,372 SQ. FT.

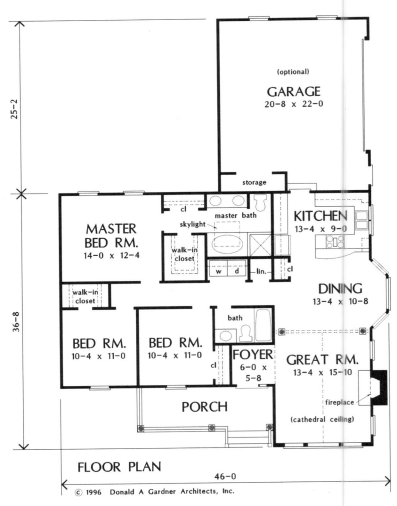

(optional)
GARAGE
20-8 x 22-0

25-2

storage

MASTER
BED RM.
14-0 x 12-4

cl

skylight

master bath

walk-in
closet

w d lin.

cl

KITCHEN
13-4 x 9-0

DINING
13-4 x 10-8

walk-in
closet

36-8

BED RM.
10-4 x 11-0

BED RM.
10-4 x 11-0

bath

FOYER
6-0 x
5-8

cl

GREAT RM.
13-4 x 15-10

fireplace

PORCH

(cathedral ceiling)

FLOOR PLAN

46-0

© 1996 Donald A Gardner Architects, Inc.

©1997 Donald A. Gardner Architects, Inc.

attic storage

skylights

down

BONUS RM.
21-0 x 12-6

attic storage

storage

GARAGE
21-0 x 21-4

up

MASTER
BED RM.
16-0 x 15-0

PORCH

BRKFST.
11-8 x 9-0

covered
breezeway

master
bath

walk-in
closet

fireplace

cl

pd.
rm.

linen

KIT.
14-8 x 12-8

UTIL.
8-8 x 6-4

GREAT RM.
17-4 x 20-4

lin.

(cathedral ceiling)

d w

BED RM.
11-0 x 12-6

lin.

cl

bath

lin.

d

FOYER
8-8 x
7-10

DINING
13-0 x 15-10

BED RM./
STUDY
12-0 x 12-4

PORCH

BED RM.
12-4 x 12-0

21-0

54-10

60-8

14-0

FLOOR PLAN

© 1997 Donald A Gardner Architects, Inc.

BL/ML/RRR

An Exciting Mixture

Price Code: G

■ This plan features:

— Four bedrooms

— Two full and one half baths

■ The exterior is an exciting mixture of brick, and siding

■ The Dining Room has five windows that view the Porch

■ A fireplace with built-ins adds character to the Great Room

■ The walk in closet in the Master Bedroom is a clothes hounds delight

■ There is a bonus room over the Garage awaiting your finishing touches

MAIN FLOOR — 2,273 SQ. FT.
BONUS — 342 SQ. FT.
GARAGE — 528 SQ. FT.

TOTAL LIVING AREA:
2,273 SQ. FT.

BL

One Floor Convenience

Price Code: F

■ This plan features:

— Four bedrooms

— Three full baths

■ A distinguished brick exterior adds curb appeal

■ Formal Entry/Gallery opens to the large Living Room with a hearth fireplace

■ Efficient Kitchen with angled counters and serving bar easily serves Breakfast Room, Patio and formal Dining Room

■ Corner Master Bedroom is enhanced by a vaulted ceiling and pampering Bath with a large walk-in closet

■ No materials list is available for this plan

MAIN FLOOR —2,675 SQ. FT.
GARAGE — 638 SQ. FT.

TOTAL LIVING AREA:
2,675 SQ. FT.

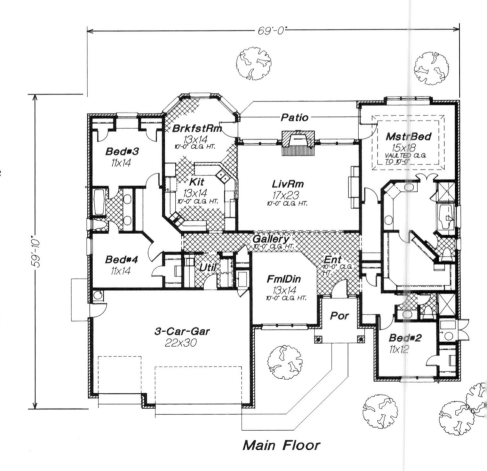

Main Floor

To order your Blueprints, call 1-800-235-5700

BL

Open Air Ranch

Price Code: C

■ This plan features:
— Four bedrooms
— Two full baths

■ The Dining Room features doors to the rear Patio

■ A convenient U-shaped Kitchen is highlighted by a double sink, a Pantry, and ample counter space

■ A Laundry/Utility Room is located off of the two-car Garage

■ Three Bedrooms share a full Bath

■ The Master Bedroom has two closets and a private Bath with dual vanities

■ There is no materials list available for this plan

MAIN FLOOR — 1,901 SQ. FT.
GARAGE — 420 SQ. FT.

TOTAL LIVING AREA:
1,901 SQ. FT.

MAIN FLOOR

BL

Especially Surprising

Price Code: A

■ This plan features:
— Three bedrooms
— Two full baths

■ Graceful columns support the covered entry

■ The tiled Foyer leads directly into the Great Room that has a rear wall fireplace and a cathedral ceiling

■ The Kitchen has an arched pass through to the Great Room and is open to the Dining Room with a cathedral ceiling

■ The screen Porch is accessed from the Dining Room

■ The Master Suite has a plant ledge, a fireplace, a tray ceiling, a walk-in closet and a fully appointed Bath

■ Two other Bedrooms have access to a full Bath in the hall

■ A two-car Garage

■ No materials list is available for this plan

MAIN FLOOR — 1,495 SQ. FT.
BASEMENT — 1,495 SQ. FT.

TOTAL LIVING AREA:
1,495 SQ. FT.

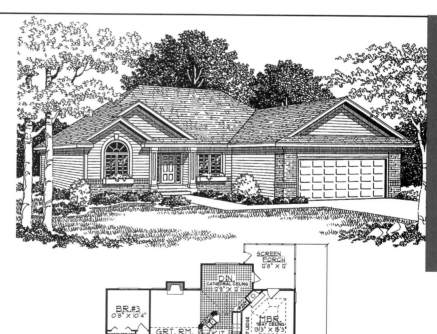

MAIN FLOOR PLAN

BL/ML/ZIP/RRR

Delightful, Compact Home

Price Code: A

■ This plan features:

— Three bedrooms

— Two full baths

■ A fireplaced Living Room further enhanced by a wonderful picture window

■ A counter island featuring double sinks separating the Kitchen and Dining areas

■ A Master Bedroom that includes a private Master Bath and double closets

■ Two additional Bedrooms with ample closet space that share a full Bath

MAIN AREA — 1,146 SQ. FT.

TOTAL LIVING AREA: 1,146 SQ. FT.

slab/crawlspace option

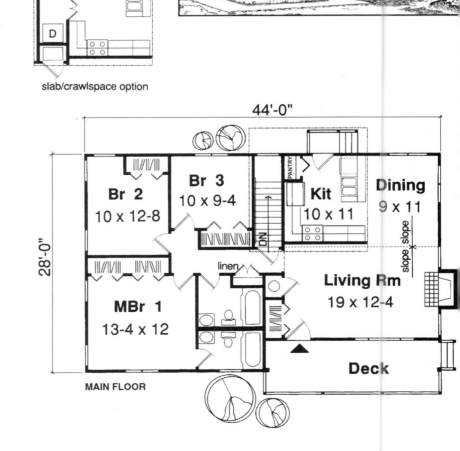

44'-0"

28'-0"

Br 2
10 x 12-8

Br 3
10 x 9-4

PANTRY

Kit
10 x 11

Dining
9 x 11

DN

slope slope

MBr 1
13-4 x 12

linen

Living Rm
19 x 12-4

Deck

MAIN FLOOR

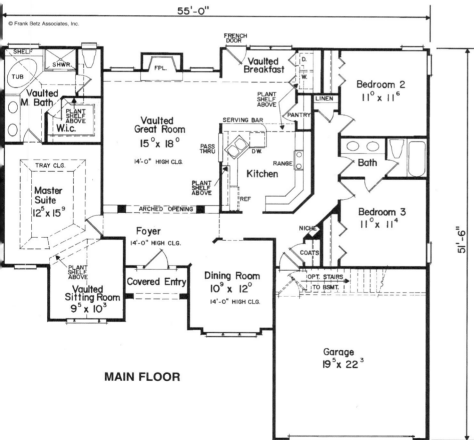

MAIN FLOOR

© Frank Betz Associates, Inc.

55'-0"

51'-6"

Vaulted M. Bath

Master Suite 12⁵ x 15⁹

Vaulted Sitting Room 9⁵ x 10³

Foyer 14'-0" HIGH CLG.

Covered Entry

Dining Room 10⁹ x 12⁰ 14'-0" HIGH CLG.

Vaulted Great Room 15⁰ x 18⁰ 14'-0" HIGH CLG.

Kitchen

Vaulted Breakfast

Bedroom 2 11⁰ x 11⁶

Bath

Bedroom 3 11⁰ x 11⁴

Garage 19⁵ x 22³

OPT. STAIRS TO BSMT.

BL/ML

High Ceilings Add Volume

Price Code: B

■ This plan features:

— Three bedrooms

— Two full baths

■ A covered entry gives way to a 14-foot high ceiling in the Foyer

■ An arched opening greets you in the Great Room

■ The Master Suite has a tray ceiling, a vaulted Stitting Area and a private Bath

■ An optional basement, slab or crawl space foundation — please specify when ordering

MAIN FLOOR — 1,715 SQ. FT.
BASEMENT — 1,715 SQ. FT.
GARAGE — 450 SQ. FT.

TOTAL LIVING AREA: 1,715 SQ. FT.

BL/ML/ZIP

Arches are Appealing

Price Code: B

■ This plan features:

— Three bedrooms

— Two full baths

■ Welcoming front Porch enhanced by graceful columns and curved windows

■ Expansive Great Room accented by a corner fireplace and outdoor access

■ Open and convenient Kitchen with a work island, angled, peninsula counter/eating bar, and nearby Laundry and Garage entry

■ Secluded Master Bedroom with a luxurious Bath

MAIN FLOOR — 1,642 SQ. FT.
BASEMENT — 1,642 SQ. FT.
GARAGE — 420 SQ. FT.

TOTAL LIVING AREA:
1,642 SQ. FT.

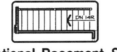

Optional Basement Stairs

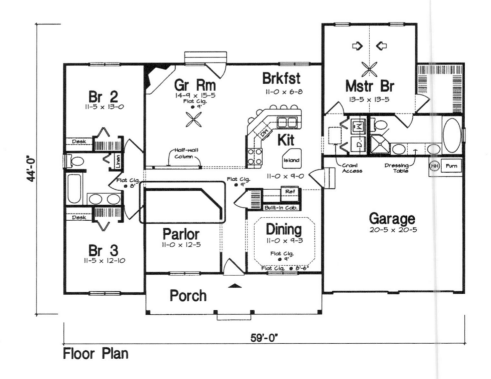

Floor Plan

To order your Blueprints, call 1-800-235-5700

© Frank Betz Associates

69'-0"

RAD. WDW.
RAD. WDW.
FPL.
VAULT
VAULT
Vaulted Family Room
18⁰ x 14⁰
PLANT SHELF ABOVE
ARCHED OPENING
PASS THRU
FRENCH DOOR
RADIUS WINDOW
VAULT

Sitting Room
11⁶ x 11⁹
W.i.c.
2-WAY FPL.
TRAY CLG.
Master Suite
16⁰ x 14¹⁰
K.S.
PLANT SHELF ABOVE
Vaulted M. Bath
LINEN
SHWR.

Breakfast
Kitchen
D.W.
SURFACE UNIT
REF.
OVEN
SERVING BAR

Vaulted Living Room
14⁴ x 18⁴

DESK
PANTRY
Pwdr.
COATS
Laundry
SINK
W. D.
Stor.

STAIRS UP
PLANT SHELF ABOVE
OPT. STAIRS TO BSMT.
Vaulted Foyer

W.H.
LINEN

Bedroom 3
11⁹ x 12⁰

Dining Room
12⁴ x 15⁴
15'-4" HIGH CLG.

VAULT
Bedroom 2
11⁶ x 13⁶
11'-4" HIGH CLG.
Bath
W.i.c.

MAIN FLOOR

Garage
20⁵ x 23³

W.i.c.
Bath
STAIRS DN.

Opt. Bonus Room
12⁵ x 23³

OPT. BONUS ROOM

BL/ML

Delightful Detailing

Price Code: F

■ This plan features:

— Three bedrooms

— Two full and one half baths

■ The vaulted ceiling extends from the Foyer into the Living Room

■ Dining Room is delineated by columns with a plant shelf above

■ Family Room has a vaulted ceiling, and a fireplace

■ The Master Suite is highlighted by a Sitting Room, a walk-in closet and a private Bath with a vaulted ceiling

■ An optional basement or a crawl space foundation — please specify when ordering

MAIN FLOOR — 2,622 SQ. FT.
BONUS ROOM — 478 SQ. FT.
BASEMENT — 2,622 SQ. FT.
GARAGE — 506 SQ. FT.

TOTAL LIVING AREA:
2,622 SQ. FT.

©1998 Donald A. Gardner Architects, Inc.

BL/ML

Country French Home

Price Code: F

■ This plan features:

— Three bedrooms

— Two full and one half baths

■ Unique Court leads to Porch and into Foyer opeing to curved Dining Area and Great Room defined by columns

■ An inviting fireplace nestled between shelves and a wall of glass with Deck access enhance the Great Room

■ Country Kitchen with cooktop island, curved Breakfast Area and easy access to Porch and Deck

■ Comfortable Master Bedroom offers tray ceiling, two walk-in closets and Master Bath with two vanities and a garden window tub

MAIN FLOOR — 2,250 SQ. FT.
GARAGE — 565 SQ. FT.

TOTAL LIVING AREA:
2,250 SQ. FT.

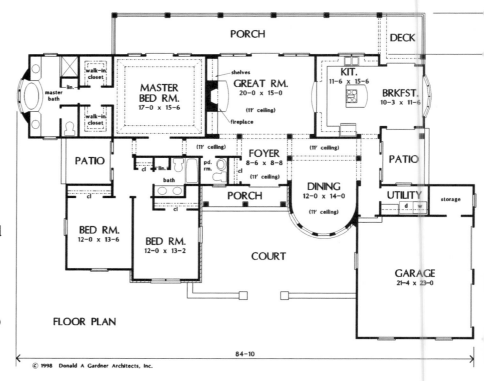

© 1998 Donald A Gardner Architects, Inc.

BL

Double Arches Add Elegance

Price Code: C

■ This plan features:
— Three bedrooms
— Two full baths
■ Double arches form the Entrance to this elegantly styled home
■ Two palladian windows add distinction to the elevation and give the home a timeless appeal
■ The Kitchen features an angled eating bar and opens to both the Breakfast Room and Living Room
■ The Master Suite includes a Master Bath with all the amenities, including a huge walk-in closet

MAIN FLOOR — 1,932 SQ. FT.
GARAGE — 552 SQ. FT.

TOTAL LIVING AREA:
1,932 SQ. FT.

COPYRIGHT LARRY E. BELK

MAIN FLOOR

BL

Southampton Style Cottage

Price Code: D

■ This plan features:
— Three bedrooms
— Two full baths
■ Stairs lead up to the covered entry Porch and into the Foyer
■ An arched opening leads into the Grand Room, which has a fireplace
■ Five French doors in various rooms open out onto the rear Lanai
■ Access the Dining Room from the Kitchen through an arched opening
■ The Kitchen has a walk-in Pantry located next to the Nook
■ The secondary Bedrooms share a Bath in their own wing of the home
■ On the opposite side of the home are a Study and the Master Suite
■ The space on the ground level can be finished into a Recreation Room

MAIN FLOOR — 2,068 SQ. FT.
LOWER FLOOR — 1,402 SQ. FT.
GARAGE — 560 SQ. FT.

TOTAL LIVING AREA:
2,068 SQ. FT.

MAIN FLOOR

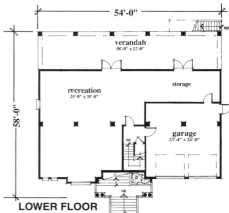

LOWER FLOOR

© 1994 Donald A. Gardner Architects, Inc.

BL/ML/ZIP/RRR

Perfect for Family Gatherings

Price Code: C

- This plan features:
- — Three bedrooms
- — Two full baths
- An open layout between the Great Room, Kitchen, and Breakfast Bay sharing a cathedral ceiling and a fireplace
- Master Bedroom with a soaring cathedral ceiling, direct access to the deck and a well appointed Bath with a large walk-in closet
- Additional Bedrooms sharing a full Bath in the hall
- Centrally located utility and storage spaces

MAIN FLOOR — 1,346 SQ. FT.
GARAGE AND STORAGE — 462 SQ. FT.

TOTAL LIVING AREA:
1,346 SQ. FT.

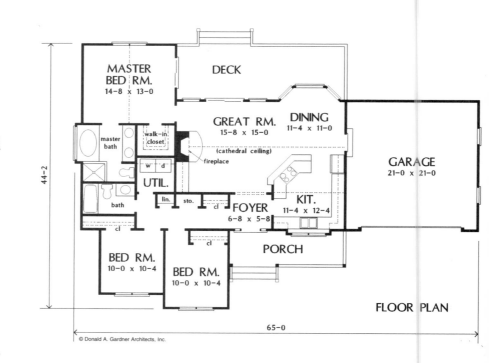

© Donald A. Gardner Architects, Inc.

FLOOR PLAN

©1998 Donald A. Gardner Architects, Inc.

B. NATHAN

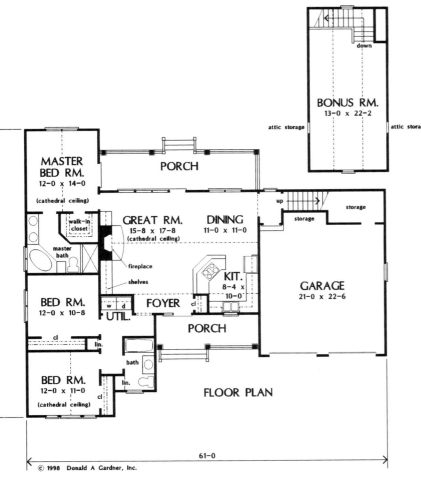

MASTER BED RM.
12-0 x 14-0
(cathedral ceiling)

PORCH

BONUS RM.
13-0 x 22-2

attic storage   attic storage

down

walk-in closet

GREAT RM.
15-8 x 17-8
(cathedral ceiling)

DINING
11-0 x 11-0

up

storage

storage

master bath

fireplace

shelves

KIT.
8-4 x 10-0

GARAGE
21-0 x 22-6

BED RM.
12-0 x 10-8

w d
UTIL.

FOYER

cl

PORCH

BED RM.
12-0 x 11-0
(cathedral ceiling)

cl

bath

lin.

lin.

cl

FLOOR PLAN

61-0

© 1998 Donald A Gardner, Inc.

BL/ML/RRR

Multiple Gables and Double Dormer

Price Code: C

■ This plan features:

— Three bedrooms

— Two full baths

■ Distinguished details inside and out make this modest home very appealing

■ Cathedral ceiling, cozy fireplace, built-in shelves and a wall of windows with Porch access enhance the Great Room, Dining Area and open Kitchen

■ Quiet corner Master Bedroom features a cathedral ceiling, walk-in closet and and plush Bath

■ Bonus Room over Garage provides options for growing family

MAIN FLOOR — 1,377 SQ. FT.
BONUS ROOM — 383 SQ. FT.
GARAGE & STORAGE — 597 SQ. FT.

TOTAL LIVING AREA:
1,377 SQ. FT.

PLAN NO. 98029

BL

For The Busy Family

Price Code: D

■ This plan features:

— Four Bedrooms

— Three full baths

■ Porch shelters entry into Gallery, Formal Dining Area, and Living Room with cozy fireplace between book shelves and a wall of windows

■ Open and efficient Kitchen easily serves Breakfast Alcove, Patio, and Dining Area

■ Two Bedrooms, one with two closets and a window seat, share a full Bath, while fourth Bedroom has separate Bath

■ No materials list is available for this plan

MAIN FLOOR — 2,233 SQ. FT.
GARAGE — 635 SQ. FT.

TOTAL LIVING AREA:
2,233 SQ. FT.

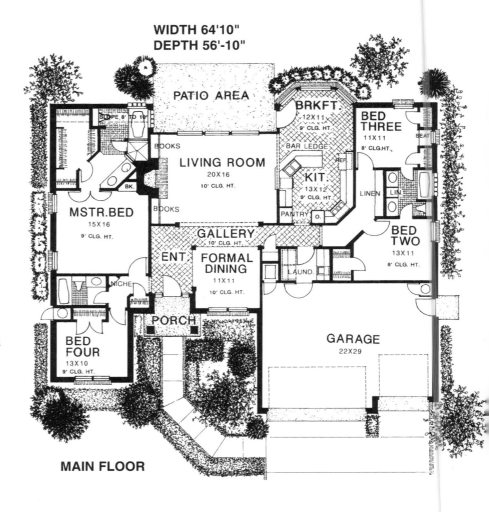

WIDTH 64'10"
DEPTH 56'-10"

MAIN FLOOR

To order your Blueprints, call 1-800-235-5700

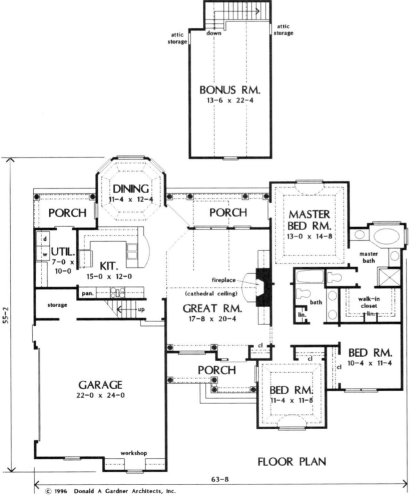

attic storage | down | attic storage

BONUS RM.
13-6 x 22-4

PORCH

DINING
11-4 x 12-4

PORCH

MASTER BED RM.
13-0 x 14-8

master bath

UTIL.
7-0 x 10-0

KIT.
15-0 x 12-0

pan.

storage

fireplace
(cathedral ceiling)

bath

walk-in closet

lin.

lin.

up

GREAT RM.
17-8 x 20-4

cl

cl

GARAGE
22-0 x 24-0

PORCH

BED RM.
10-4 x 11-4

cl

BED RM.
11-4 x 11-8

workshop

55-2

63-8

FLOOR PLAN

© 1996 Donald A Gardner Architects, Inc.

BL/ML/RRR

European Sophistication

Price Code: D

■ This plan features:

— Three bedrooms

— Two full baths

■ Keystone arches, gables, and stucco give the exterior European sophistication

■ Large Great Room with fireplace, and U-shaped Kitchen

■ Special ceiling treatments include a cathedral ceiling in the Great Room and tray ceilings in both the Master and front Bedrooms

■ Indulgent Master Bath with a separate toilet area and a garden tub, shower and dual vanity

MAIN FLOOR — 1,699 SQ. FT.
GARAGE — 637 SQ. FT.
BONUS — 386 SQ. FT.

TOTAL LIVING AREA:
1,699 SQ. FT.

BL/ML

Spacious Living Room

Price Code: E

- This plan features:
  — Four bedrooms
  — Three full and one half baths
- The spacious Living Room is topped by a decorative ceiling treatment and is enhanced by a corner fireplace
- The Kitchen boasts a built in desk and an angled counter/snack bar
- The secluded Master Suite has two walk-in closets and a five-piece Bath
- This plan is available with a basement or a crawl space foundation, please specify when ordering this plan

MAIN FLOOR — 2,483 SQ. FT.
GARAGE — 504 SQ. FT.

TOTAL LIVING AREA:
2,483 SQ. FT.

MAIN FLOOR

BL

Cabin in the Country

Price Code: A

- This plan features:
  — Two bedrooms
  — One full and one half baths
- A screened Porch for enjoyment of your outdoor surroundings
- A combination Living and Dining area with cozy fireplace for added warmth
- An efficiently laid out Kitchen with a built-in pantry
- Two large Bedrooms located at the rear of the home
- An optional slab or crawl space foundation — please specify when ordering

FIRST FLOOR — 928 SQ. FT.
SCREENED PORCH — 230 SQ. FT.
STORAGE — 14 SQ. FT.

TOTAL LIVING AREA:
928 SQ. FT.

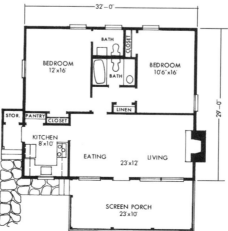

To order your Blueprints, call 1-800-235-5700

BL/ML

Outstanding Family Home

Price Code: D

■ This plan features:

— Three bedrooms

— Two full baths

■ Split bedroom layout, perfect floor plan for a family with older children

■ Great Room features a cozy fireplace, access to the rear Porch, and an open layout with the Nook and Kitchen

■ Extended counter in the Kitchen for snack bar, meals or snacks

■ Master Suite contains access to rear porch, a pampering Bath and walk-in closet

MAIN FLOOR — 2,162 SQ. FT.
GARAGE — 498 SQ. FT.

TOTAL LIVING AREA:
2,162 SQ. FT.

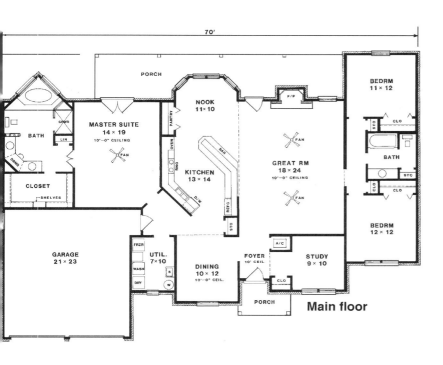

Main floor

BL/ML/ZIP/RRR

Skylight Brightens Master Bedroom

Price Code: B

■ This plan features:

— Three bedrooms

— Two full baths

■ A covered Porch entry

■ A Living Room enhanced by a vaulted beam ceiling and a fireplace

■ A Master Bedroom with a decorative ceiling and a skylight in the private Bath

■ An optional Deck accessible through sliding doors off the Master Bedroom

MAIN FLOOR — 1,686 SQ. FT.
BASEMENT — 1,676 SQ. FT.
GARAGE — 484 SQ. FT.

TOTAL LIVING AREA:
1,686 SQ. FT.

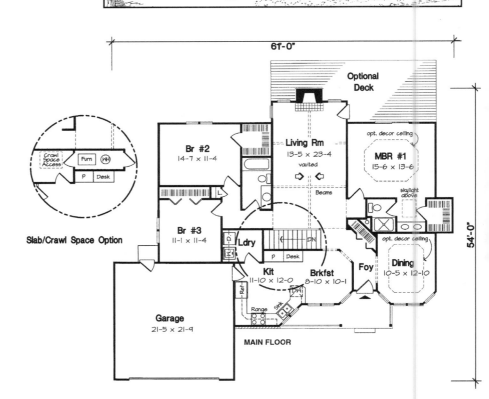

B. NATHAN

©1997 Donald A. Gardner Architects, Inc.

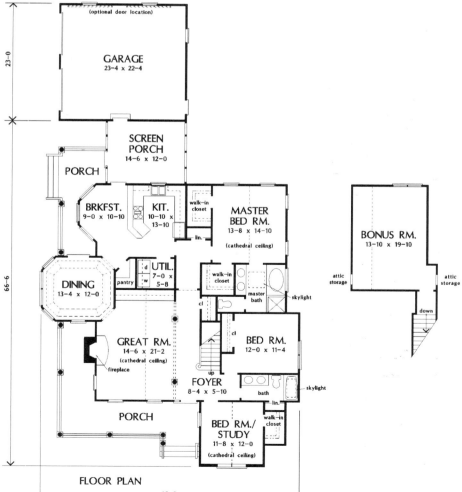

BL/RRR

For A Narrow Lot

Price Code: E

■ This plan features:

— Three bedrooms

— Two full baths

■ A wrap-around front Porch, triple gable and arched window add to this charming home

■ Columns, a vaulted ceiling and inviting fireplace accent the Great Room

■ Open Kitchen easily serves Dining Area, Breakfast Alcove and screen Porch

■ Master Bedroom offers walk-in closets and skylit Bath

■ No materials list is available for this plan

MAIN FLOOR — 1,918 SQ. FT.
BONUS ROOM — 307 SQ. FT.
GARAGE — 552 SQ. FT.

TOTAL LIVING AREA:
1,918 SQ. FT.

BL

Attractive Exterior

Price Code: D

■ This plan features:

— Three bedrooms

— Two full baths

■ In the gallery columns separate space into the Great Room and the Dining Room

■ The large Kitchen is a chef's dream with lots of counter space and a Pantry

■ The Master Bedroom is removed from traffic areas and contains a luxurious Master Bath

■ No materials list is available for this plan

MAIN FLOOR — 2,167 SQ. FT.
GARAGE — 690 SQ. FT.

TOTAL LIVING AREA:
2,167 SQ. FT.

MAIN FLOOR

To order your Blueprints, call 1-800-235-5700

Central Great Room Anchors the Home

Price Code: A

- This plan features:
— Three bedrooms
— Two full baths
- The Kitchen, Dining Room and Great Room share a large open space
- A graceful arch leads to the front Entry
- The Master Bath features separate tub and shower
- Plans include a Deck or Patio off the Great Room
- A large walk-in closet completes the Master Suite

MAIN FLOOR — 1,383 SQ. FT.
BASEMENT — 1,460 SQ. FT.
GARAGE — 416 SQ. FT.

TOTAL LIVING AREA:
1,383 SQ. FT

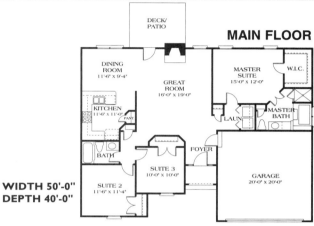

MAIN FLOOR

WIDTH 50'-0"
DEPTH 40'-0"

European Styling

Price Code: E

- This plan features:
— Three bedrooms
— Two full and one half baths
- The Kitchen features an island bar, double sink and a Pantry
- The home has two fireplaces, one in the Great Room the other in the Gathering Room
- The Master Suite features dual walk-in closets and a five-piece Bath
- This plan is available with a basement or a crawl space foundation, please specify when ordering

MAIN FLOOR — 2,290 SQ. FT.
BASEMENT — 2,290 SQ. FT.
BONUS — 304 SQ. FT.
GARAGE — 544 SQ. FT.

TOTAL LIVING AREA:
2,290 SQ. FT.

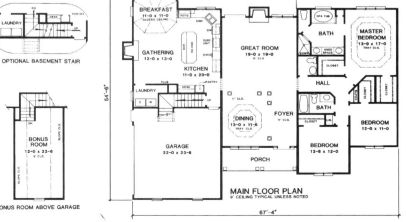

BL

European Styling

Price Code: C

- This plan features:
  — Three bedrooms
  — Two full and one half baths
- French doors in the Study open to a long view to the Kitchen.
- The Great Room leads to the covered Patio.
- The Master Bedroom has a sloped 10-foot high ceiling; all other rooms have 9 or 10-foot high ceilings.
- This home is designed with a slab foundation.

MAIN AREA — 1,902 SQ. FT.
GARAGE — 636 SQ. FT.

TOTAL LIVING AREA:
1,902 SQ. FT.

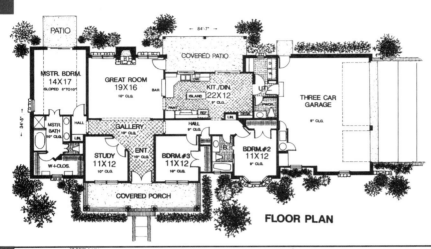

FLOOR PLAN

BL

Lavishly Appointed

Price Code: E

- This plan features:
  — Three bedrooms
  — Two full and one half bath
- The stone and stucco exterior with stucco details creates a great first impression.
- A 14-foot coffered ceiling graces the sumptuous Family Room.
- Upstairs, an optional Bedroom and Bath would be great for a future teenager.
- The fabulous Master suite features a vaulted ceiling and his and hers walk-in closets.
- This home was designed with a choice of crawlspace or basement foundation.

MAIN FLOOR — 2,403 SQ. FT
GARAGE — 488 SQ. FT.
UNFINISHED BASEMENT — 2,403 SQ. FT.
BONUS ROOM — 285 SQ. FT.

TOTAL LIVING AREA:
2,403 SQ. FT.

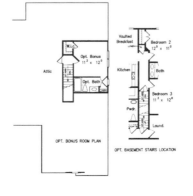

To order your Blueprints, call 1-800-235-5700

WIDTH 54'-0"
DEPTH 47'-6"

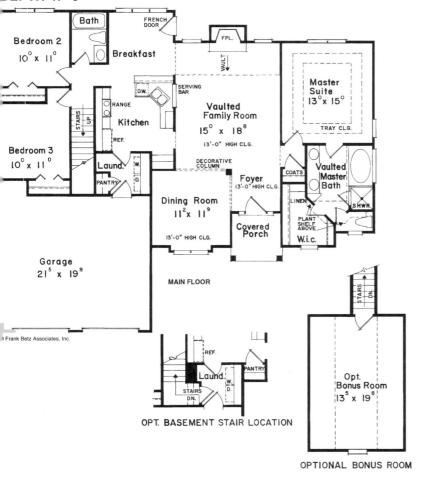

Frank Betz Associates, Inc.

BL

European Flair

Price Code: B

■ This plan features:

— Three bedrooms

— Two full baths

■ Fireplace serves as an attractive focal point for the vaulted Family Room

■ Master Suite topped by a tray ceiling over the Bedroom and a vaulted ceiling over the Master Bath

■ An optional basement or crawl space foundation — please specify when ordering

■ No materials list is available for this plan

MAIN FLOOR — 1,544 SQ. FT.
BONUS ROOM — 284 SQ. FT.
BASEMENT — 1,544 SQ. FT.
GARAGE — 440 SQ. FT.

TOTAL LIVING AREA:
1,544 SQ. FT.

BL/ZIP

Luxurious One-Floor Living

Price Code: I

■ This plan features:

— Four bedrooms

— Two full and one three-quarter baths

■ Decorative windows enhance front entrance of elegant home

■ Formal Living Room accented by fireplace

■ Breakfast bar, work island, and an abundance of storage and counter space featured in Kitchen

■ Spacious Master Bedroom with access to covered Patio

■ No materials list is available for this plan

MAIN FLOOR — 3,254 SQ. FT.
GARAGE — 588 SQ. FT.

TOTAL LIVING AREA:
3,254 SQ. FT.

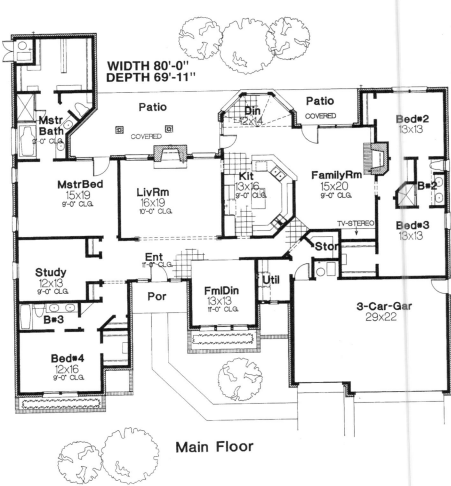

WIDTH 80'-0"
DEPTH 69'-11"

Main Floor

To order your Blueprints, call 1-800-235-5700

© 1998 Donald A. Gardner, Inc.

B. NATHAN

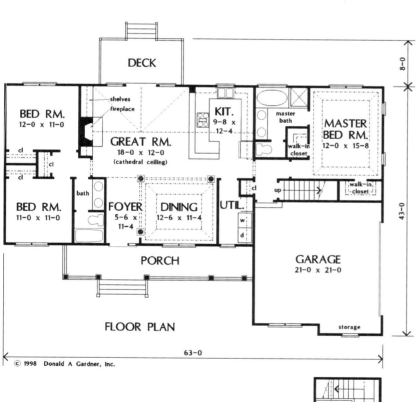

DECK

shelves
fireplace

BED RM.
12-0 x 11-0

cl

cl

cl

GREAT RM.
18-0 x 12-0
(cathedral ceiling)

KIT.
9-8 x
12-4

master
bath

MASTER
BED RM.
12-0 x 15-8

walk-in
closet

walk-in
closet

BED RM.
11-0 x 11-0

bath

FOYER
5-6 x
11-4

DINING
12-6 x 11-4

UTIL.

cl

up

w
d

PORCH

GARAGE
21-0 x 21-0

FLOOR PLAN

storage

8-0

43-0

63-0

© 1998 Donald A Gardner, Inc.

BONUS RM.
10-6 x 21-0

attic storage

attic storage

down

BL/ML/RRR

Economical Home

Price Code: D

■ This plan features:

— Three bedrooms

— Two full baths

■ Practical to build design offers gables, pediments and inviting front Porch

■ Tray ceiling and columns define Dining Area from Great Room

■ Great Room features a cathedral ceiling, fireplace with built-in shelves, Deck and Kitchen access

■ Corner Master Bedroom offers two walk-in closets and a double vanity Bath

■ Bonus room over Garage provides options for growing families

MAIN FLOOR — 1,544 SQ. FT.
BONUS ROOM — 320 SQ. FT.
GARAGE & STORAGE — 478 SQ. FT.

TOTAL LIVING AREA:
1,544 SQ. FT.

© 1998 Donald A. Gardner, Inc.

BL/ML/RRR

Stately Arched Entry

Price Code: F

■ This plan features:

— Three bedrooms

— Two full and one half baths

■ The stately arched entry Porch is supported by columns

■ The Dining Room has a tray ceiling and is defined by columns

■ The Great Room has a fireplace and accesses the rear Porch/Deck

■ The Kitchen is full of cabinet and counter space

■ The Master Bedroom has a bay window and a tray ceiling

■ The Master Bath features dual vanities and walk in closets

MAIN FLOOR — 2,024 SQ. FT.
BONUS — 423 SQ. FT.
GARAGE — 623 SQ. FT.

TOTAL LIVING AREA:
2,024 SQ. FT.

FLOOR PLAN

© 1998 Donald A Gardner, Inc.

BONUS RM.
16-4 x 23-0

To order your Blueprints, call 1-800-235-5700

uropean Flavor

Price Code: C

This plan features:

Three bedrooms

Two full baths

A covered Entry reveals a Foyer with a 14-foot ceiling

The Family Room has a vaulted ceiling

The Breakfast Area has a tray ceiling and a bay of windows

The privately located Master Suite has a tray ceiling

An optional basement or crawl space foundation — please specify when ordering

No materials list available for this plan

AIN FLOOR — 1,779 SQ. FT.
SEMENT — 1,818 SQ. FT.
RAGE — 499 SQ. FT.

TOTAL LIVING AREA:
1,779 SQ. FT.

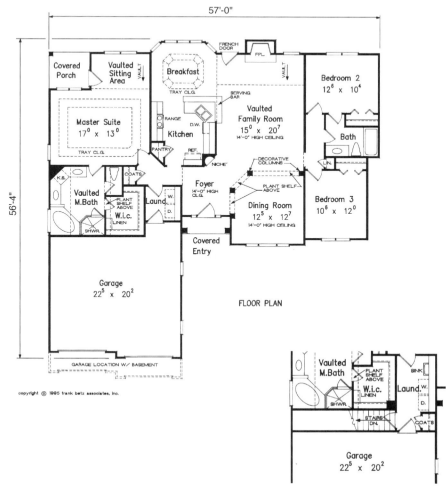

FLOOR PLAN

copyright © 1995 frank betz associates, inc.

OPT. BASEMENT STAIR LOCATION

BL

Adaptable Room

Price Code: D

■ This plan features:
— Four bedrooms
— Two full and one half baths
■ A front room conveniently located adjacent to the Foyer can be used as a home office or a Guest Room
■ Skylights brighten the rear covered Porch.
■ Each of the secondary Bedrooms has access to a separate vanity; the Bedrooms share a tub
■ This home is designed with basement, slab and crawlspace foundation options

MAIN AREA — 2,184 SQ. FT.
GARAGE — 462 SQ. FT.

TOTAL LIVING AREA:
2,184 SQ. FT.

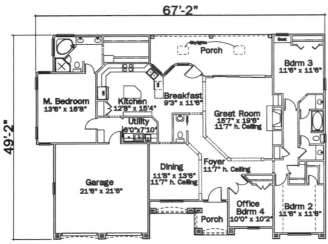

BL

Courtyard Entrance

Price Code: G

■ This plan features:
— Four bedrooms
— Three full and one half baths
■ This home has a sophisticated air created by the courtyard entrance
■ A large walk-in Pantry is located in the Breakfast area for ample Kitchen storage
■ The Master Bedroom has two walk-in closets and a luxurious Bath
■ The future Playroom on the second floor will keep children's happy noises and toys away from view and earshot

MAIN FLOOR — 2,911 SQ. FT.
GARAGE — 720 SQ. FT.

TOTAL LIVING AREA:
2,911 SQ. FT.

To order your Blueprints, call 1-800-235-5700

©1997 Donald A. Gardner Architects, Inc.

B. NATHAN.

(optional full bath)

BL/ML/RRR

Southwestern Style

Price Code: E

■ This plan features:

— Four bedrooms

— Two full and one half baths

■ Large circle-top windows, stucco, and a tile roof add to this home

■ The common space of the home is impressive with 12-foot ceilings and columns

■ The Kitchen is partially enclosed by 8-foot high walls

■ The Master Bedroom has a tray ceiling and a private Bath

■ An optional slab or a crawl space foundation — please specify when ordering

MAIN FLOOR — 1,954 SQ. FT.

TOTAL LIVING AREA:
1,954 SQ. FT.

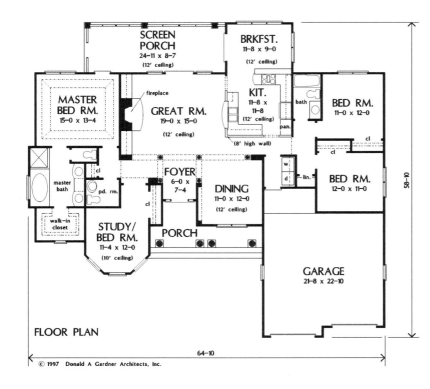

SCREEN PORCH
24-11 x 8-7
(12' ceiling)

BRKFST.
11-8 x 9-0
(12' ceiling)

MASTER BED RM.
15-0 x 13-4

fireplace

GREAT RM.
19-0 x 15-0
(12' ceiling)

KIT.
11-8 x 11-8
(12' ceiling)

bath

BED RM.
11-0 x 12-0

pan.

(8' high wall)

master bath

pd. rm.

cl

FOYER
6-0 x 7-4

DINING
11-0 x 12-0
(12' ceiling)

w.
d.

lin.

cl
cl

BED RM.
12-0 x 11-0

walk-in closet

cl

STUDY/ BED RM.
11-4 x 12-0
(10' ceiling)

PORCH

GARAGE
21-8 x 22-10

58-10

FLOOR PLAN

64-10

© 1997 Donald A Gardner Architects, Inc.

BL/ML

Easy to Build

Price Code: A

■ This plan features:

— Two bedrooms

— One full bath

■ Affordable Ranch with all the amenities

■ Covered entry leads into Foyer and Living and Dining rooms

■ Focal-point fireplace and bay window enhance the Living Room

■ Country-style Kitchen opens to Dining Room and Nook

■ Master Bedroom features a full Bath with whirlpool tub

■ Second Bedroom has an over-sized closet and access to full Bath

MAIN FLOOR — 1,313 SQ. FT.
GARAGE — 385 SQ. FT.

TOTAL LIVING AREA:
1,313 SQ. FT.

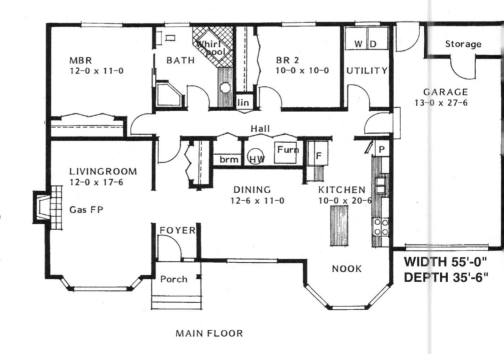

MAIN FLOOR

WIDTH 55'-0"
DEPTH 35'-6"

To order your Blueprints, call 1-800-235-5700

65'-0"

68'-8"

FLOOR PLAN

BL/ZIP

Lap of Luxury

Price Code: E

■ This plan features:

— Four bedrooms

— Three full baths

■ Entertaining in grand style in the formal Living Room, the Dining Room, or under the covered Patio in the backyard

■ Family Room crowned in a cathedral ceiling, enhanced by a center fireplace and built-in book shelves

■ Master Bedroom with a Sitting Area, huge walk-in closet, private Bath and access to a covered Lanai

■ No materials list is available for this plan

MAIN FLOOR — 2,445 SQ. FT.
GARAGE — 630 SQ. FT.

TOTAL LIVING AREA:
2,445 SQ. FT.

BL

Ranch of Distinction

Price Code: C

■ This plan features:

— Three bedrooms

— Two full and one half baths

■ The recessed entrance has an arched transom window over the door and a sidelight windows beside it

■ Once inside the Living Room boasts a high ceiling and a warm fireplace

■ The large Kitchen Area includes the open Dining Area with a rear bay that accessed the backyard

■ The Master and third Bedrooms both have bay windows

■ No materials list is available for this plan

MAIN FLOOR — 1,906 SQ. FT.
BASEMENT — 1,906 SQ. FT.

TOTAL LIVING AREA:
1,906 SQ. FT.

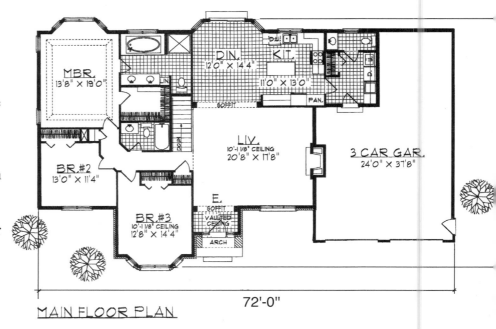

MBR.
13'8" X 19'0"

DIN.
12'0" X 14'4"

KIT.
11'0" X 13'0"

PAN.

SOFFIT

BR. #2
13'0" X 11'4"

LIV.
10'-1 1/8" CEILING
20'8" X 17'8"

3 CAR GAR.
24'0" X 37'8"

BR. #3
10'-1 1/8" CEILING
12'8" X 14'4"

E.
SOFFIT
VAULTED CEILING

ARCH

MAIN FLOOR PLAN

72'-0"

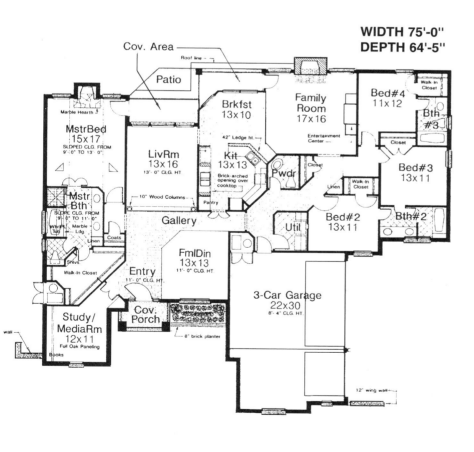

WIDTH 75'-0"
DEPTH 64'-5"

Cov. Area
Roof line
Patio
Brkfst 13x10
Family Room 17x16
Bed#4 11x12
Walk-In Closet
Bth #3
Marble Hearth
MstrBed 15x17
SLOPED CLG. FROM 9'-0" TO 13'-0"
LivRm 13x16
13'- 0" CLG. HT
42" Ledge ht.
Kit 13x13
Brick-arched opening over cooktop
Closet
Pwdr
Entertainment Center
Closet
Bed#3 13x11
Mstr Bth
SLOPE CLG. FROM 9'-0" TO 11'-0"
10" Wood Columns
Pantry
Gallery
Linen
Walk-In Closet
Bth#2
Whrlpl
Marble Ldg
Linen
Coats
Util
Bed#2 13x11
Shrvs.
FmlDin 13x13
11'- 0" CLG. HT
Walk-In Closet
Entry 11'-0" CLG. HT.
Study/ MediaRm 12x11
Full Oak Paneling
Books
wall
Cov. Porch
8" brick planter
3-Car Garage 22x30
8'- 4" CLG. HT.
12" wing wall

MAIN FLOOR

BL/ZIP

Especially Unique

Price Code: F

■ This plan features:

— Four bedrooms

— Three full and one half baths

■ From the 11-foot entry turn left into the Study/Media Room

■ The formal Dining Room is open to the Gallery, and the Living Room beyond

■ The Family Room has a built-in entertainment center, a fireplace and access to the rear Patio

■ The private Master Bedroom has a fireplace, a private Bath and a walk-in closet

■ No materials list is available for this plan

MAIN FLOOR — 2,748 SQ. FT.
GARAGE — 660 SQ. FT.

TOTAL LIVING AREA:
2,748 SQ. FT.

© 1997 Donald A. Gardner Architects, Inc.

BL/ML/RRR

Private Master Suite

Price Code: D

■ This plan features:

— Three bedrooms

— Two full baths

■ Working at the Kitchen island focuses your view to the Great Room with it's vaulted ceiling and a fireplace

■ Both the Dining Room and Master Bedroom are enhanced by tray ceilings

■ Skylights floods natural light into the Bonus space

■ The private Master Suite has its own bath and an expansive walk-in closet

MAIN FLOOR — 1,515 SQ. FT.
BONUS — 288 SQ. FT.
GARAGE — 476 SQ. FT.

TOTAL LIVING AREA:
1,515 SQ. FT.

© 1997 Donald A Gardner Architects, Inc.

To order your Blueprints, call 1-800-235-5700

BL/ML

Contemporary Good Looks

Price Code: A

- This plan features:
  - — Three bedrooms
  - — Two full baths
- A vaulted Great Room provides space for the whole family
- The covered Entry shelters guests at the door
- Dine-in breakfast bar graces the Kitchen counter
- The Master Suite benefits from a big walk-in closet
- A nice sized Laundry leads off of the Kitchen
- The Kitchen Pantry supplements already ample storage

MAIN FLOOR — 1,433 SQ. FT.
BASEMENT — 1,433 SQ. FT.
GARAGE — 456 SQ. FT.

TOTAL LIVING AREA: 1,433 SQ. FT

MAIN FLOOR

MAIN FLOOR W/O STAIRS

BL

Split-Bedroom Layout

Price Code: C

- This plan features:
  - — Four bedrooms
  - — Two full baths
- A built-in next to the Great-Room fireplace can store electronics
- The Dining Room, located to the left of the Foyer, features two windows that view the front
- The Garage has storage space for tools and gear
- This home is designed with crawlspace and slab foundation options

MAIN FLOOR — 1,940 SQ. FT.
GARAGE — 417 SQ. FT.

TOTAL LIVING AREA: 1,940 SQ. FT.

MAIN FLOOR

BL

Unique V-Shaped Home

Price Code: I

■ This plan features:

— Two bedrooms

— Three full baths

■ Four skylights brighten the Eating Nook in the Country Kitchen

■ A walk-in Pantry, range-top work island, built-in barbecue and a sink add to the amenities of the Kitchen

■ Master Suite with his and hers closets and adjacent dressing area

■ A Guest Suite with a private Sitting Area and full Bath

■ No materials list is available for this plan

MAIN FLOOR — 3,417 SQ. FT.
GARAGE — 795 SQ. FT.

TOTAL LIVING AREA:
3,417 SQ. FT.

WIDTH 128'-6"
DEPTH 79'-6"

MAIN FLOOR

To order your Blueprints, call 1-800-235-5700

BL/ZIP

French Country Styling

Price Code: I

- This plan features:
- — Four bedrooms
- — Two full, one three-quarter and one half baths
- Brick and stone blend masterfully for an impressive French Country exterior
- Separate Master Suite with expansive Bath and closet
- Study containing a built-in desk and bookcase
- Angled island Kitchen highlighted by walk-in pantry, and open to the Breakfast Bay
- No materials list is available for this plan

MAIN FLOOR — 3,352 SQ. FT.
GARAGE — 672 SQ. FT.

TOTAL LIVING AREA:
3,352 SQ. FT.

WIDTH 91'-0"
DEPTH 71'-9"

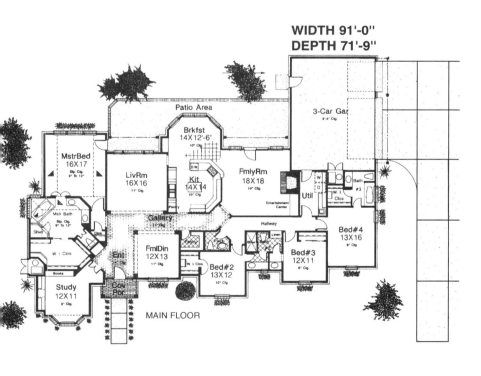

MAIN FLOOR

BL

Plenty of Room

Price Code: A

- This plan features:
  - — Three bedrooms
  - — Two full baths
- The large Living Room features a corner fireplace.
- The Master Bedroom, Dining Room and Living Room all feature an eleven-foot high vaulted ceiling and views to the backyard.
- Vaulted to eleven-feet is the Kitchen, with an open bar view of the fireplace in the Living Room.
- This home is designed with a slab foundation.

MAIN FLOOR — 1,199 SQ. FT.
GARAGE — 484 SQ. FT.

TOTAL LIVING AREA:
1,199 SQ. FT.

MAIN FLOOR

BL

Carefully Crafted Country

Price Code: A

- This plan features:
  - — Three bedrooms
  - — Two full baths
- Compact but complete, the Master Suite includes walk-in closet and 10 foot boxed ceiling.
- Set into the kitchen window, a cozy nook becomes just the place for an intimate meal.
- Enjoy summer afternoon relaxing in the shade of your own front Porch.
- The Laundry is convenient to the action-set into the hall between the two other Bedrooms.
- Consider the third Bedroom as a potential Home Office or Library.
- This plan comes with a choice of slab or crawl-space foundation.

MAIN FLOOR — 1,281 SQ. FT

TOTAL LIVING AREA:
1,281 SQ. FT.

MAIN FLOOR

To order your Blueprints, call 1-800-235-5700

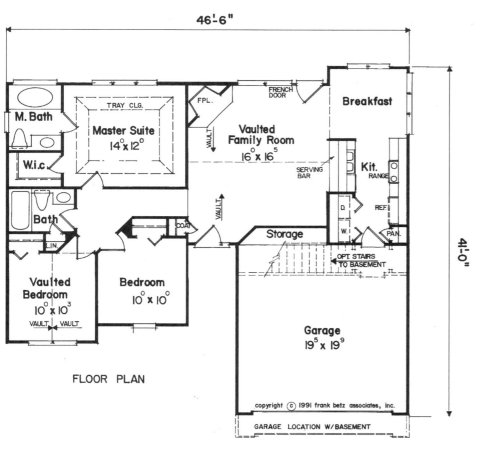

46'-6"

M. Bath

TRAY CLG.

Master Suite
14⁰ x 12⁰

W.i.c

FPL.

VAULT

FRENCH DOOR

Breakfast

Vaulted Family Room
16⁰ x 16⁵

SERVING BAR

Kit.
RANGE

D.

REF

W.

PAN.

Bath

LIN

COAT

VAULT

Storage

Vaulted Bedroom
10⁰ x 10³

VAULT   VAULT

Bedroom
10⁰ x 10⁰

OPT. STAIRS TO BASEMENT

41'-0"

Garage
19⁵ x 19⁹

FLOOR PLAN

copyright © 1991 frank betz associates, inc.

GARAGE LOCATION W/BASEMENT

BL

Decorative Ceilings

Price Code: A

■ This plan features:

— Three bedrooms

— Two full baths

■ The Family room has a vaulted ceiling, a corner fireplace, and a French door to the rear yard

■ The Breakfast Book is brightened by window on two of its walls

■ The Master Suite has a tray ceiling, a walk in closet and a private Bath

■ No materials list available for this plan

■ An optional basement, slab or crawl space foundation — please specify when ordering

MAIN FLOOR — 1,104 SQ. FT.
BASEMENT — 1,104 SQ. FT.
GARAGE — 400 SQ. FT.

TOTAL LIVING AREA:
1,104 SQ. FT.

© 1997 Donald A. Gardner Architects, Inc.

BL/ML/RRR

Casual Country Charmer

Price Code: E

- This plan features:
- — Three bedrooms
- — Two full baths
- Columns and arches frame the front Porch
- The open floor plan combines the Great Room, Kitchen and Dining Room
- The Kitchen offers a convenient breakfast bar for meals on the run
- The Master Suite features a private Bath oasis
- Secondary Bedrooms share a full Bath with a dual vanity

MAIN FLOOR — 1,770 SQ. FT.
BONUS — 401 SQ. FT.
GARAGE — 630 SQ. FT.

TOTAL LIVING AREA:
1,770 SQ. FT.

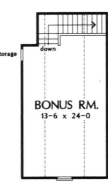

attic storage   down

BONUS RM.
13-6 x 24-0

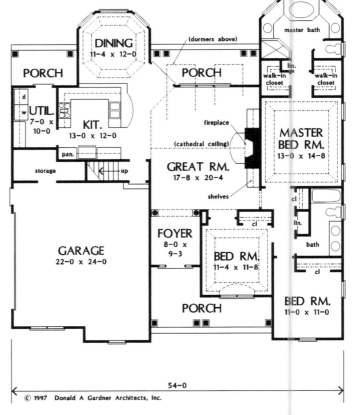

© 1997 Donald A Gardner Architects, Inc.

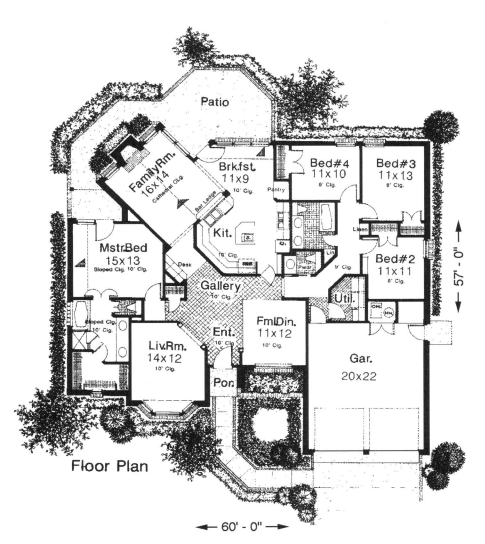

Floor Plan

← 60' - 0" →

57' - 0"

BL

Stunning Family Plan

Price Code: D

■ This plan features:

— Four bedrooms

— Two full and one half baths

■ Windows, brick, and columns combine to create an eye-catching elevation

■ A pair of columns greets you as you enter the Living Room

■ The formal Dining room is located just steps away from the Kitchen

■ Set away from the active areas the Master Bedroom is a quiet retreat

■ No materials list is available for this plan

MAIN FLOOR — 2,194 SQ. FT.
GARAGE — 462 SQ. FT.

TOTAL LIVING AREA :
2,194 SQ. FT.

BL/ML

One Floor Living

Price Code: A

■ This plan features:

— Three bedrooms

— Two full baths

■ A covered front Porch is supported by graceful columns

■ The Living Room features a cozy fireplace and a ceiling fan

■ The Kitchen is distinguished by an angled serving bar

■ The Dining Room is convenient to the Kitchen and the rear Porch

■ The Master Bedroom has a walk-in closet and a private Bath

■ A two-car Garage with storage space is located in the rear of the home

MAIN FLOOR — 1,247 SQ. FT.
GARAGE — 512 SQ. FT.

TOTAL LIVING AREA:
1,247 SQ. FT.

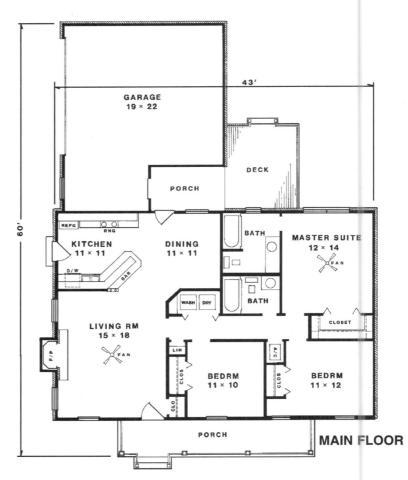

BL/ML

Lots of Cottage Charm

Price Code: A

- This plan features:
  — Three bedrooms
  — Two full baths
- A front Porch and rear Patio make the outdoors always available
- The Great Room fireplace greets visitors to the home
- Behind the Kitchen, the Laundry is ready to clean up after the kids
- The comfortable Dining Room is open to the Kitchen
- Because its bays are offset, the two-car Garage provides extra storage
- Separate shower and tub make the Master Bath more versatile

MAIN FLOOR — 1,417 SQ. FT.
GARAGE — 522 SQ. FT.

TOTAL LIVING AREA:
1,417 SQ. FT

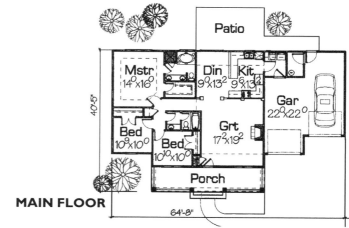

MAIN FLOOR

BL

Great-Room Accesses Grilling Porch

Price Code: C

- This plan features
  — Three bedrooms
  — Two full baths
- The bay window in the Breakfast Area brightens the adjacent Kitchen.
- A closet in the Garage stores tools and seasonal equipment.
- The Master Bedroom has a private Bath with a walk-in closet.
- This home is designed with basement, slab, and crawl space foundation options.

MAIN FLOOR — 1,787 SQ. FT
GARAGE — 417 SQ. FT

TOTAL LIVING AREA:
1,787 SQ. FT.

MAIN FLOOR

BL

Rambling Ranch

Price Code: C

- This plan features:
- — Three bedrooms
- — Two full baths
- The Living room is complemented by a vaulted ceiling, a corner fireplace, and a plant shelf
- The galley Kitchen is fully equipped and the entry to the Laundry room is at it's far end
- There are two secondary Bedrooms located in the front of the home, they share a full Bath
- This plan is available with a basement or a crawlspace foundation, please specify when ordering this plan

MAIN FLOOR — 1,042 SQ. FT.
BASEMENT — 1,042 SQ. FT.
GARAGE — 400 SQ. FT.

TOTAL LIVING AREA:
1,042 SQ. FT.

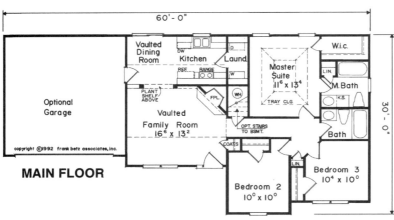

MAIN FLOOR

BL

Looks Like You've Arrived

Price Code: D

- This plan features:
- — Four bedrooms
- — Two full and one half baths
- The built-in Pantry and abundant storage and counter space add to the Kitchen's efficiency.
- Look up to the nearly 10-foot tall vaulted ceiling in the Master bedroom.
- The convenient Laundry features liberal built-ins.
- One full wing of this home is a suite of two Bedrooms connected by a Bath with separate vanities.
- This home was designed with a slab foundation.

MAIN FLOOR — 2,149 SQ. FT
GARAGE — 465 SQ. FT.

TOTAL LIVING AREA:
2,149 SQ. FT.

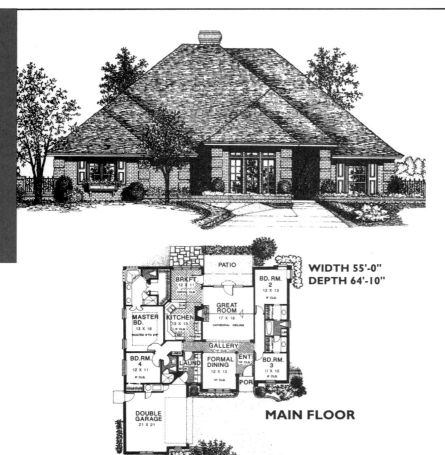

WIDTH 55'-0"
DEPTH 64'-10"

MAIN FLOOR

To order your Blueprints, call 1-800-235-5700

BL

Stately Columns Create A Classic

Price Code: A

■ This plan features:
— Two bedrooms
— Two full baths

■ Compact layout of this home is perfect for empty-nesters

■ The second Bedroom can also double as a Study or Home Office

■ Kitchen, Dining Room and Living Room combine in an open plan

■ For informal dining, a breakfast bar adjoins the Kitchen counter

■ Extra tall ceilings grace the Dining and Living Rooms

MAIN FLOOR — 1,172 SQ. FT.
GARAGE — 213 SQ. FT.

TOTAL LIVING AREA:
1,172 SQ. FT.

MAIN FLOOR

BL

Complete Efficiency

Price Code: A

■ This plan features:
— Three bedrooms
— Two full baths

■ Though only 30-ft. wide, this narrow-lot home includes a full double Garage.

■ A large Family Room, Kitchen and Dining Room are among the full-size spaces in this home.

■ An interior Laundry is centrally located between Kitchen and Bedrooms.

■ The rear-placed Master Suite is spacious and complete.

■ This home was designed with a slab foundation.

MAIN FLOOR — 1,284 SQ. FT.
GARAGE — 375 SQ. FT.

TOTAL LIVING AREA:
1,284 SQ. FT.

WIDTH 30'-0"
DEPTH 60'-10"

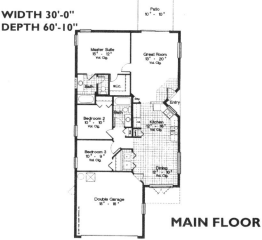

MAIN FLOOR

© 1987 Donald A. Gardner Architects, Inc.

BL/ML/RRR

Rustic Simplicity

Price Code: C

- ■ This plan features:
- — Three bedrooms
- — Two full and one half baths
- ■ The central living area is large and boasts a cathedral ceiling, exposed wood beams and a clerestory
- ■ A long screened Porch has a bank of skylights
- ■ The open Kitchen contains a convenient serving and eating counter
- ■ The generous Master Suite opens to the screened Porch and is enhanced by a walk-in closet and a whirlpool tub
- ■ Two more Bedrooms share a second full Bath

MAIN FLOOR — 1,426 SQ. FT.

TOTAL LIVING AREA:
1,426 SQ. FT.

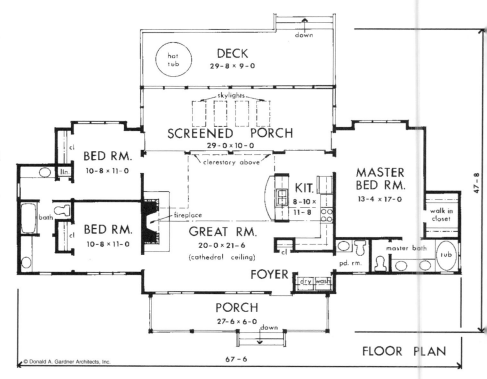

FLOOR PLAN

BL/ML/RRR

Prairie-Style Lines

Price Code: G

■ This plan features:
— Three bedrooms and one optional bedroom
— Two full and one three-quarter baths
■ Secluded Family Room/Breakfast Room has its own fireplace
■ The optional front Bedroom could also be a Home Office or Study
■ A luxurious Master Bath features his-and-her walk-in closets
■ An 11-foot ceiling creates a dramatic effect in the Living Room
■ Slightly staggered Garage doors create even more curb appeal

MAIN FLOOR — 2,441 SQ. FT.
GARAGE — 499 SQ. FT.

TOTAL LIVING AREA:
2,441 SQ. FT.

© 1998 Donald A. Gardner, Inc.

BL/ML

Perfect Use of Space

Price Code: B

■ This plan features:
— Three bedrooms
— Two full baths
■ A large Family Room with fireplace anchors this well-designed home
■ The Porch off the Family Room offers space for backyard barbecues
■ You'll fall in love with the Master Suite.
■ An unfinished basement offers a world of future growth options
■ This home was designed with a crawlspace or basement foundation options

MAIN FLOOR — 1,708 SQ. FT.
GARAGE — 544 SQ. FT.

TOTAL LIVING AREA:
1,708 SQ. FT

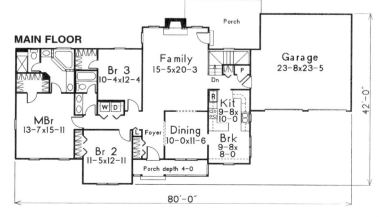

PLAN NO. 82003

BL

A Garage Designed for Golfers

Price Code: A

■ This plan features:
— Three bedrooms
— Two full baths
■ The Garage contains two full auto bays plus a golf cart Bay
■ Whirlpool and glassed-in shower round out the Master Bath
■ A covered Porch off the Breakfast Room provides an outdoor eating area
■ There's plenty of storage space throughout this home

MAIN FLOOR — 1,379 SQ. FT.
GARAGE — 493 SQ. FT.

TOTAL LIVING AREA:
1,379 SQ. FT.

MAIN FLOOR

PLAN NO. 69017

BL/ML

Fit for the Whole Family

Price Code: C

■ This plan features:
— Four bedrooms
— Two full baths
■ Use the front Bedroom as a Guest Room or turn it into your Home Office or Study.
■ The vaulted ceiling, walk-in closet and complete Bath spell Master Suite luxury.
■ A wrap-around counter and center island make the most of every square foot of kitchen space.
■ Got a riding lawnmower? Use the 55 sq. ft. of extra storage in the two-car Garage.
■ Watch the neighbors walk by from your covered front Porch or relax in privacy on the covered Patio.
■ This home comes with a basement foundation.

MAIN FLOOR — 1,791 SQ. FT
BASEMENT — 1,791 SQ. FT.
GARAGE — 406 SQ. FT.

TOTAL LIVING AREA:
1,791 SQ. FT.

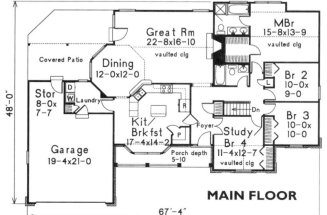

MAIN FLOOR

To order your Blueprints, call 1-800-235-5700

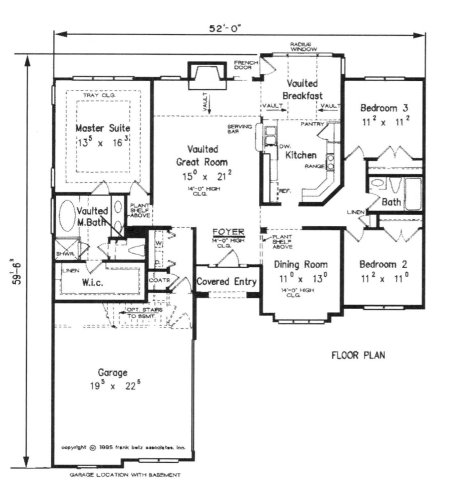

52'-0"

RADIUS WINDOW

FRENCH DOOR

Vaulted Breakfast

VAULT VAULT VAULT

TRAY CLG.

Master Suite
13⁵ x 16³

Vaulted Great Room
15⁰ x 21²
14'-0" HIGH CLG.

SERVING BAR

PANTRY

DW.
Kitchen
RANGE
REF.

Bedroom 3
11² x 11²

Bath

LINEN

Vaulted M.Bath

PLANT SHELF ABOVE

FOYER
14'-0" HIGH CLG.

PLANT SHELF ABOVE

SHWR.

W.

D.

LINEN

W.i.c.

COATS

Covered Entry

Dining Room
11⁰ x 13⁰
14'-0" HIGH CLG.

Bedroom 2
11² x 11⁰

OPT. STAIRS TO BSMT.

59'-6"

Garage
19⁵ x 22⁵

copyright © 1995 frank betz associates, inc.

FLOOR PLAN

GARAGE LOCATION WITH BASEMENT

BL/ML

Charming Stucco

Price Code: B

■ This plan features:

— Three bedrooms

— Two full baths

■ Attractive entrance with curved transom and side lights

■ A vaulted ceiling above the Great Room and Breakfast Room

■ Cozy fireplace with windows to either side in the Great Room

■ Tray ceiling crowning the Master Bedroom and a vaulted ceiling over the plush Master Bath

■ An optional basement or crawl space foundation — please specify when ordering

MAIN FLOOR — 1,696 SQ. FT.
GARAGE — 475 SQ. FT.
BASEMENT — 1,720 SQ. FT.

TOTAL LIVING AREA:
1,696 SQ. FT.

BL/ML/ZIP

Covered Porch with Columns

Price Code: C

■ This plan features:

— Three bedrooms

— Two full baths

■ Foyer with twelve-foot ceiling leads into the Family Room which has a focal-point fireplace

■ Living Room and Dining Room overlook the front Porch

■ Kitchen has a serving bar, Breakfast Area and a French door that opens to the backyard

■ An optional basement, slab or a crawl space foundation — please specify when ordering

MAIN FLOOR — 1,856 SQ. FT.
BASEMENT — 1,856 SQ. FT.
GARAGE — 429 SQ. FT.

TOTAL LIVING AREA:
1,856 SQ. FT.

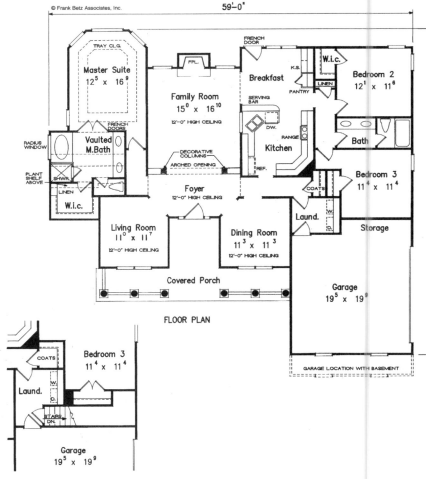

© Frank Betz Associates, Inc.

59'-0"

FLOOR PLAN

OPT. BASEMENT STAIR LOCATION

To order your Blueprints, call 1-800-235-5700

© design basics, inc.

MAIN FLOOR

58'-0"

56'-0"

BL/ML

Beautiful Arched Window

Price Code: C

■ This plan features:

—Three bedrooms

—Two full baths

■ Ten-foot ceilings top the Entry and the Great Room

■ Breakfast Room and Hearth Room are in an open layout and share a see-through fireplace

■ Split Bedroom plan assures homeowner's privacy in the Master Suite which includes a decorative ceiling, private Bath and large walk-in closet

■ Two additional Bedrooms at the opposite side of the home share a full, skylit Bath in the hall

MAIN FLOOR — 1,911 SQ. FT.
GARAGE — 481 SQ. FT.

TOTAL LIVING AREA:
1,911 SQ. FT.

BL

Open Spaces

Price Code: A

- ■ This plan features:
- — Three bedrooms
- — Two full baths
- ■ Open floor plan between the Family Room and the Dining Room
- ■ Vaulted ceilings adding volume and a fireplace in the Family Room
- ■ Three Bedrooms; the Master Suite with a five-piece private Bath
- ■ Convenient Laundry center located outside the Bedrooms

MAIN FLOOR — 1,135 SQ. FT.
GARAGE — 460 SQ. FT.

TOTAL LIVING AREA:
1,135 SQ. FT.

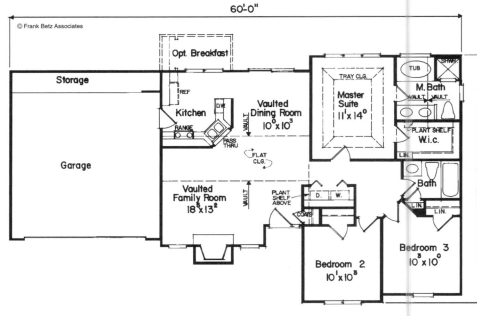

© Frank Betz Associates

60'-0"

Opt. Breakfast

Storage

Kitchen
REF
D.W.
RANGE
PASS THRU

Garage

Vaulted Dining Room 10⁰x10³

VAULT

FLAT CLG.

Vaulted Family Room 18⁸x13²

VAULT

PLANT SHELF ABOVE

COATS

D. W.

Master Suite 11'x14⁰
TRAY CLG.

TUB
M. Bath
VAULT VAULT
PLANT SHELF
W.i.c.
LIN.

Bath
LIN. LIN.

Bedroom 2 10'x10⁸

Bedroom 3 10⁸x10⁰

FLOOR PLAN

WHEELCHAIR BATH
(OPT.)

MAIN FLOOR

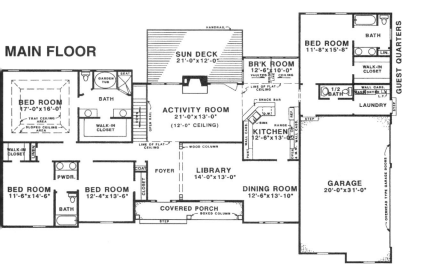

BL/ML

Stone and Siding

Price Code: F

■ This plan features:

— Four bedrooms

— Three full and one half baths

■ Attractive styling and a covered Porch create curb appeal

■ Formal Foyer giving access to the Bedroom wing, Library or Activity Room

■ A snack bar/peninsula counter highlights the Kitchen which also contains a built-in Pantry.

■ Master Suite topped by a tray ceiling and pampered by five-piece Bath

MAIN FLOOR — 2,690 SQ. FT.
BASEMENT — 2,690 SQ. FT.
GARAGE — 660 SQ. FT.
DECK — 252 SQ. FT.

TOTAL LIVING AREA:
2,690 SQ. FT.

BL/ML

Columned Keystone Arched Entry

Price Code: E

■ This plan features:

— Three bedrooms

— Two full baths

■ Keystone arches and arched transoms above the windows

■ Formal Dining Room and Study flank the Foyer

■ Fireplace in Great Room

■ Efficient Kitchen with a peninsula counter and bayed Nook

■ A step ceiling in the Master Suite and interesting master bath with a triangular area for the oval bath tub

■ The secondary Bedrooms share a full Bath in the hall.

MAIN FLOOR — 2,256 SQ. FT.
GARAGE — 514 SQ. FT.

TOTAL LIVING AREA:
2,256 SQ. FT.

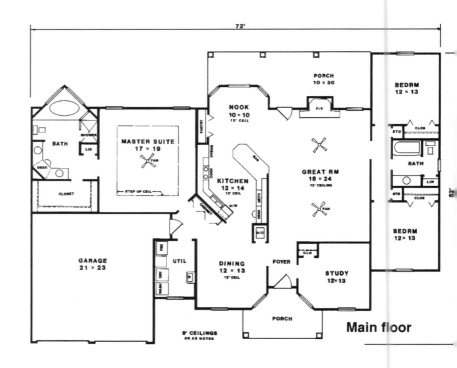

Main floor

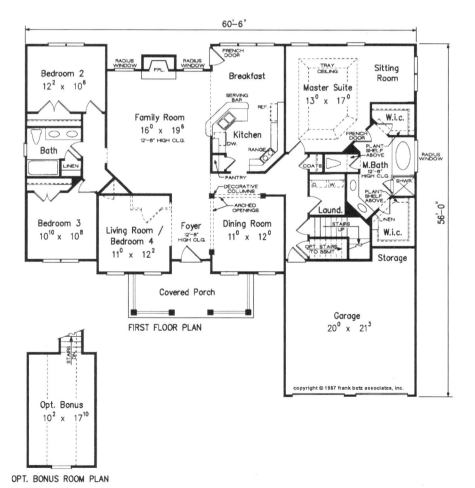

Bedroom 2
12² x 10⁶

RADIUS WINDOW   FPL   RADIUS WINDOW

FRENCH DOOR

Breakfast

SERVING BAR

REF.

Bath

LINEN

Family Room
16⁰ x 19⁶
12'-6" HIGH CLG.

Kitchen

DW.

RANGE

PANTRY

TRAY CEILING

Master Suite
13⁰ x 17⁰

Sitting Room

W.i.c.

FRENCH DOOR

PLANT SHELF ABOVE

COATS

M.Bath
12'-6" HIGH CLG.

SHWR

RADIUS WINDOW

Bedroom 3
10¹⁰ x 10⁸

DECORATIVE COLUMNS

ARCHED OPENINGS

Living Room / Bedroom 4
11⁰ x 12²

Foyer
12'-8" HIGH CLG.

Dining Room
11⁰ x 12⁰

D.   W.

Laund.

STAIRS UP

PLANT SHELF ABOVE

LINEN

W.i.c.

OPT. STAIRS TO BSMT.

Storage

Covered Porch

FIRST FLOOR PLAN

Garage
20⁰ x 21³

60'-6"

56'-0"

copyright © 1987 frank betz associates, inc.

STAIRS   DN

Opt. Bonus
10² x 17¹⁰

OPT. BONUS ROOM PLAN

BL

Stately Front Porch with Columns

Price Code: D

■ This plan features:

— Three bedrooms

— Two full baths

■ Tray ceiling crowning Master Bedroom highlighted by a Sitting Room

■ Arched openings accented by columns accessing the formal Dining Room

■ An optional basement or crawl space foundation — please specify when ordering

■ No materials list is available for this plan

MAIN FLOOR — 2,056 SQ. FT.
GARAGE — 454 SQ. FT.
BONUS — 208 SQ. FT.
BASEMENT — 2,056 SQ. FT.

TOTAL LIVING AREA:
2,056 SQ. FT.

BL/ML/ZIP

Backyard Views

Price Code: B

■ This plan features:

— Three bedrooms

— Two full baths

■ Front Porch accesses open Foyer, and spacious Dining Room and Great Room with sloped ceilings

■ Corner fireplace, windows and atrium door to Patio enhance Great Room

■ Convenient Kitchen with a pantry and a peninsula serving counter

■ Luxurious Bath, walk-in closet and backyard view offered in Master Bedroom

MAIN FLOOR — 1,746 SQ. FT.
GARAGE — 480 SQ. FT.
BASEMENT — 1,697 SQ. FT.

TOTAL LIVING AREA:
1,746 SQ. FT.

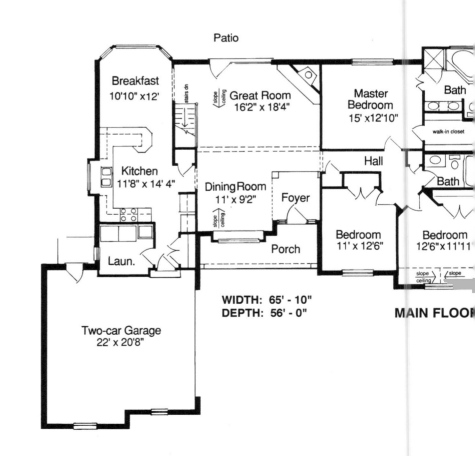

Patio

Breakfast
10'10" x 12'

stairs dn

slope ceiling

Great Room
16'2" x 18'4"

Master Bedroom
15' x 12'10"

Bath

walk-in closet

Kitchen
11'8" x 14' 4"

Dining Room
11' x 9'2"

Foyer

Hall

Bath

slope ceiling

Bedroom
11' x 12'6"

Bedroom
12'6"x 11'11"

Laun.

Porch

slope ceiling

slope

WIDTH: 65' - 10"
DEPTH: 56' - 0"

MAIN FLOOR

Two-car Garage
22' x 20'8"

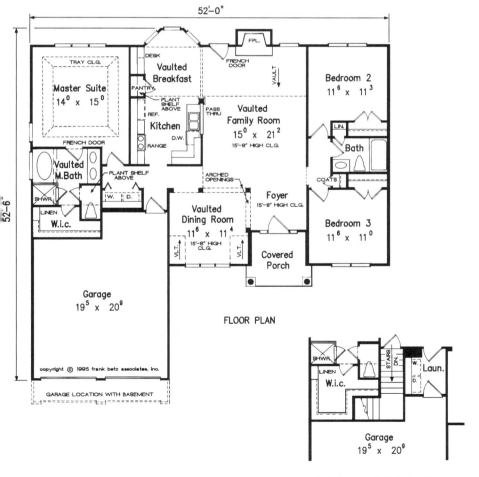

52'-0"

TRAY CLG.

Master Suite
14⁰ x 15⁰

FRENCH DOOR

Vaulted
M.Bath

SHWR.

LINEN

W.i.c.

DESK

Vaulted
Breakfast

PANTRY

REF.

Kitchen

PLANT
SHELF
ABOVE

RANGE

D.W.

PLANT SHELF
ABOVE

W. D.

FPL.

FRENCH
DOOR

VAULT

Vaulted
Family Room
15⁰ x 21²
15'-8" HIGH CLG.

PASS
THRU

ARCHED
OPENINGS

Vaulted
Dining Room
11⁶ x 11⁴
15'-8" HIGH
CLG.

VLT.

VLT.

Covered
Porch

Bedroom 2
11⁶ x 11³

LIN.

Bath

COATS

Foyer
15'-8" HIGH CLG.

Bedroom 3
11⁶ x 11⁰

52'-6"

Garage
19⁵ x 20⁹

copyright © 1995 frank betz associates, inc.

GARAGE LOCATION WITH BASEMENT

FLOOR PLAN

SHWR.

LINEN

W.i.c.

STAIRS

DN.

W.
D.

Laun.

Garage
19⁵ x 20⁹

Opt. Basement Stair Location

BL

Attention to Details

Price Code: B

■ This plan features:

— Three bedrooms

— Two full baths

■ Foyer, Family Room and Dining Room have 15'8" ceilings

■ Split Bedroom floor plan, affording additional privacy to the Master Suite

■ Master Suite enhanced by a tray ceiling, a five-piece Master Bath and a walk-in closet

■ An optional basement or crawl space foundation — please specify when ordering

■ No materials list is available for this plan

MAIN FLOOR — 1,575 SQ. FT
BASEMENT — 1,612 SQ. FT.
GARAGE — 456 SQ. FT.

TOTAL LIVING AREA:
1,575 SQ. FT.

BL/ML/ZIP

Hip Roof Ranch

Price Code: B

■ This plan features:

— Three bedrooms

— Two full baths

■ Cozy front Porch leads into Entry with vaulted ceiling and sidelights

■ Open Living Room enhanced by a cathedral ceiling, a wall of windows and corner fireplace

■ Large and efficient Kitchen with an extended counter and a bright Dining Area with access to screen Porch

■ Convenient Utility Area with access to Garage and Storage Area

MAIN FLOOR — 1,540 SQ. FT.
BASEMENT — 1,540 SQ. FT.

TOTAL LIVING AREA:
1,540 SQ. FT.

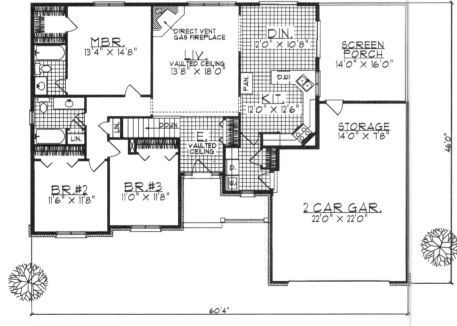

MAIN FLOOR

To order your Blueprints, call 1-800-235-5700

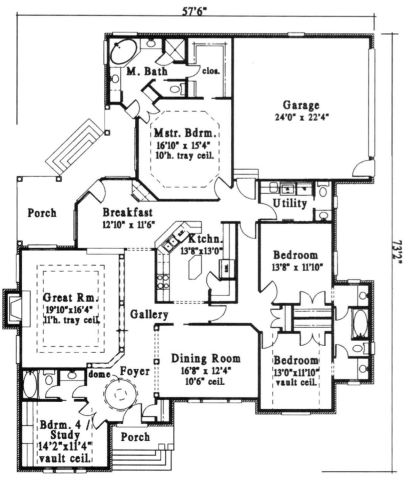

Main Level Floor Plan

BL

Tailored for a View to the Side

Price Code: F

■ This plan features:

— Three/Four bedrooms

— Three full and one half baths

■ Entry Foyer highlighted by a ceiling dome and French doors leading to the private Study

■ Elegant formal Dining Room with a high ceiling, columns and arched entrance

■ Sunken Great Room with a high tray ceiling, arched openings with columns and a fireplace

■ An island and walk-in Pantry add to the Kitchen's efficiency

■ No materials list is available for this plan

MAIN FLOOR — 2,579 SQ. FT.
GARAGE — 536 SQ. FT.

TOTAL LIVING AREA: 2,579 SQ. FT.

MAIN FLOOR

BL/ML

An Inset Garage

Price Code: B

■ This plan features:
— Three bedrooms
— Two full baths
■ Colonnaded front Porch speaks of traditional elegance
■ The compact Master Suite is secluded from the rest of the house
■ Dining Room and Great Room are joined by a central fireplace
■ Off the rear of the Great Room, a Patio or Deck are possibilities
■ The oversized Master Bedroom is available with a try ceiling
■ Ample storage is a convenience throughout

MAIN FLOOR — 1,589 SQ. FT.
GARAGE — 410 SQ. FT.

TOTAL LIVING AREA:
1,589 SQ. FT

MAIN FLOOR

BL/ML

Setting the Standard

Price Code: D

■ This plan features:
— Four bedrooms
— Two full baths
■ A row of clerestory windows in the dormer bathes the Great Room in natural light.
■ Enjoy the Study or use it as a Guest Room or Nursery.
■ This liberally laid-out Kitchen has it all, including a nearby Laundry.
■ A corner fireplace in the Great Room offers a cozy view in all directions.
■ Just off the Master Suite, the small Porch offers intimate relaxation.
■ This home was designed with a basement foundation.

MAIN FLOOR — 2,029 SQ. FT
GARAGE — 431 SQ. FT.

TOTAL LIVING AREA:
2,029 SQ. FT

To order your Blueprints, call 1-800-235-5700

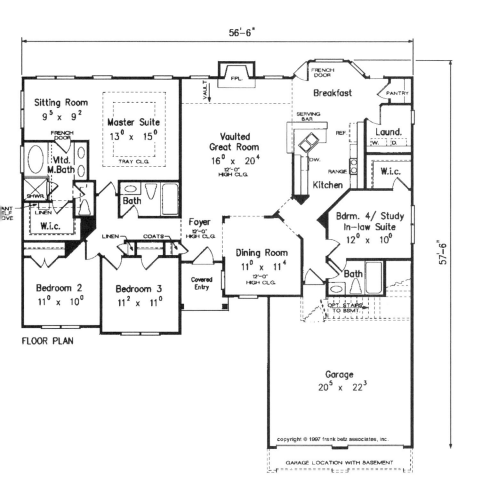

56'-6"

57'-6"

Sitting Room
9⁵ x 9²

Master Suite
13⁰ x 15⁰
TRAY CLG.

Vltd. M.Bath

W.i.c.

Bath

LINEN

Bedroom 2
11⁰ x 10⁰

Bedroom 3
11² x 11⁰

LINEN   COATS

Foyer
12'-0"
HIGH CLG.

Covered Entry

FPL.   VAULT

Breakfast   PANTRY

FRENCH DOOR

SERVING BAR

REF.   Laund.
W.   D.

DW.

RANGE   W.i.c.

Kitchen

Vaulted Great Room
16⁰ x 20⁴
12'-0" HIGH CLG.

Dining Room
11⁰ x 11⁴
12'-0" HIGH CLG.

Bdrm. 4/ Study In-law Suite
12⁰ x 10⁰

Bath

OPT. STAIRS TO BSMT.

Garage
20⁵ x 22³

copyright © 1997 frank betz associates, inc.

FLOOR PLAN

GARAGE LOCATION WITH BASEMENT

BL/ML

Exquisite Master Suite

Price Code: C

■ This plan features:

— Four Bedrooms

— Three full baths

■ Formal Foyer with a convenient coat closet

■ Vaulted ceiling over the Great Room highlighted by a fireplace flanked by windows

■ Cozy Breakfast Bay with French door to rear yard

■ Master Suite pampered by private Sitting Room and luxurious Master Bath

■ An optional basement or crawl space foundation — please specify when ordering

MAIN FLOOR — 1,915 SQ. FT.
GARAGE — 489 SQ. FT.
BASEMENT — 1,932 SQ. FT.

TOTAL LIVING AREA:
1,915 SQ. FT.

BL/ML/ZIP

No Wasted Space

Price Code: A

■ This plan features:

— Three bedrooms

— Two full baths

■ A centrally located Great Room with a cathedral ceiling, exposed wood beams, and large areas of fixed glass

■ The Living and Dining areas separated by a massive stone fireplace

■ A secluded Master Suite with a walk-in closet and private Master Bath

■ An efficient Kitchen with a convenient Laundry Area

■ An optional basement, slab or crawl space foundation — please specify when ordering

MAIN AREA — 1,454 SQ. FT.

TOTAL LIVING AREA:
1,454 SQ. FT.

© 1990 Donald A. Gardner Architects, Inc.

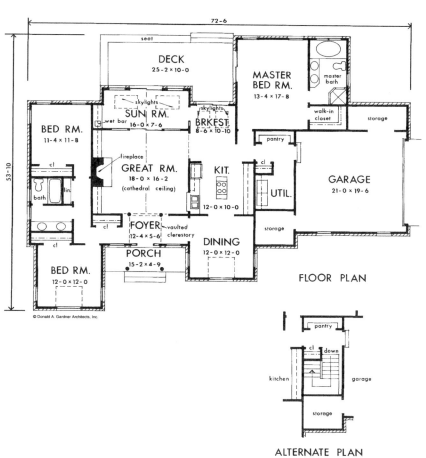

FLOOR PLAN

ALTERNATE PLAN
FOR BASEMENT

BL/ML/RRR

French Influenced One-Story

Price Code: F

- ■ This plan features:
- — Three bedrooms
- — Two full baths
- ■ Elegant details and arched windows, round columns and rich brick veneer
- ■ Arched clerestory window in the foyer introduces natural light to a large Great Room with cathedral ceiling and built-in cabinets
- ■ Kitchen with cooking island
- ■ Large Master Bedroom with Deck access

MAIN FLOOR — 2,045 SQ. FT.
GARAGE & STORAGE — 563 SQ. FT.

TOTAL LIVING AREA: 2,045 SQ. FT.

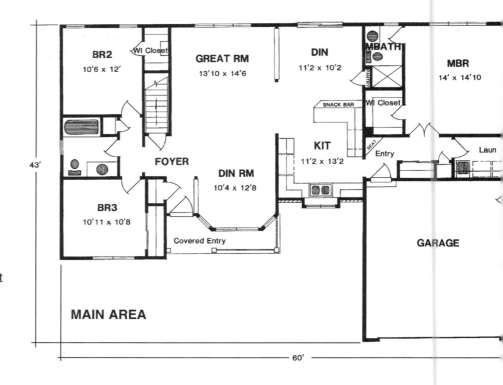

BL/ML

Small, But Not Lacking

Price Code: B

■ This plan features:

— Three bedrooms

— One full and one three-quarter baths

■ Great Room adjoins the Dining Room for ease in entertaining

■ Kitchen highlighted by a peninsula counter/snackbar extending work space and offering convenience in serving informal meals or snacks

■ Split-bedroom plan allows for privacy in the Master Bedroom with a Bath and a walk-in closet

■ Garage entry convenient to the Kitchen

MAIN AREA — 1,546 SQ. FT.
BASEMENT — 1,530 SQ. FT.
GARAGE — 440 SQ. FT.

TOTAL LIVING AREA:
1,546 SQ. FT.

224

To order your Blueprints, call 1-800-235-5700

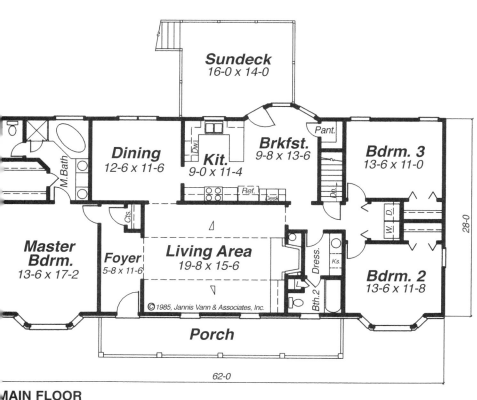

Sundeck
16-0 x 14-0

Dining
12-6 x 11-6

Kit.
9-0 x 11-4

Brkfst.
9-8 x 13-6

Pant.

Bdrm. 3
13-6 x 11-0

M.Bath

Dw

Ref.

Desk

Dn.

W D.

Master Bdrm.
13-6 x 17-2

Cts.

Foyer
5-8 x 11-6

Living Area
19-8 x 15-6

© 1985, Jannis Vann & Associates, Inc.

Dress.

Bth.2

Ks.

Bdrm. 2
13-6 x 11-8

28-0

Porch

62-0

MAIN FLOOR

BL/ML/ZIP

Bay Windows and a Terrific Front Porch

Price Code: C

- This plan features:
- — Three bedrooms
- — Two full baths
- A Country-style front Porch
- An expansive Living Area that includes a fireplace
- A Master Suite with a private Master Bath and a walk-in closet
- An efficient Kitchen serving the sunny Breakfast Area and the Dining Room with equal ease
- A built-in Pantry and Sun Deck access add to the appeal of the Breakfast Area

MAIN FLOOR — 1,778 SQ. FT.
BASEMENT — 1,008 SQ. FT.
GARAGE — 728 SQ. FT.

TOTAL LIVING AREA:
1,778 SQ. FT.

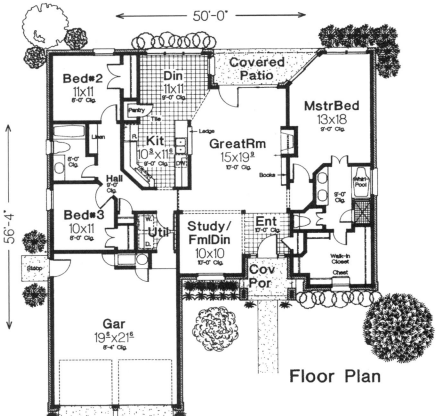

Floor Plan

BL

Brilliance in Brick an Fieldstone

Price Code: B

■ This plan features:

— Three bedrooms

— Two full baths

■ Hub of home is Great Room opening to Study/Formal Dini Area, covered Patio and Dining/Kitchen

■ An efficient Kitchen features a Pantry, serving ledge and brigh Dining Area

■ Master Bedroom wing offers access to covered Patio, a hug walk-in closet and a whirlpool Bath

■ No materials list is available f this plan

MAIN FLOOR — 1,640 SQ. FT.
GARAGE — 408 SQ. FT.

TOTAL LIVING AREA:
1,640 SQ. FT.

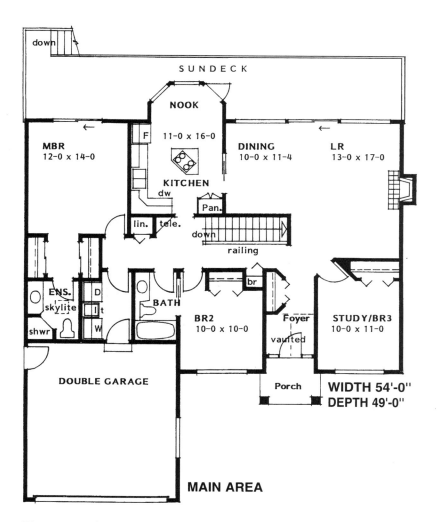

down

SUNDECK

NOOK
11-0 x 16-0

MBR
12-0 x 14-0

F

KITCHEN
dw

DINING
10-0 x 11-4

LR
13-0 x 17-0

lin. tele.

Pan.

down

railing

ENS.
skylite

D

BATH

br

shwr

t

W

BR2
10-0 x 10-0

Foyer
vaulted

STUDY/BR3
10-0 x 11-0

DOUBLE GARAGE

Porch

WIDTH 54'-0"
DEPTH 49'-0"

MAIN AREA

BL/ML

Comfort and Style

Price Code: A

■ This plan features:

— Three bedrooms

— One full and one three quarter baths

■ A walk-out basement providing additional space for family activities

■ A Master Suite complete with private Bath and skylight

■ A large Kitchen including an eating Nook

■ A Sun Deck that is easily accessible from the Master Suite, Nook and the Living/Dining Area

MAIN AREA — 1,423 SQ. FT.
BASEMENT — 1,423 SQ. FT.
GARAGE — 399 SQ. FT.

TOTAL LIVING AREA:
1,423 SQ. FT.

PLAN NO. 93222

BL/ML/ZIP/RRR

For an Established Neighborhood

Price Code: A

- This plan features:
- — Three bedrooms
- — Two full baths

- A covered entrance sheltering and welcoming visitors

- A Living Room enhanced by natural light streaming in from the large front window

- A bayed formal Dining Room with direct access to the Sun Deck and the Living Room

- An informal Breakfast Room with direct access to the Sun Deck

MAIN AREA — 1,276 SQ. FT.
FINISHED STAIRCASE — 16 SQ. FT.
BASEMENT — 392 SQ. FT.
GARAGE — 728 SQ. FT.

TOTAL LIVING AREA:
1,292 SQ. FT.

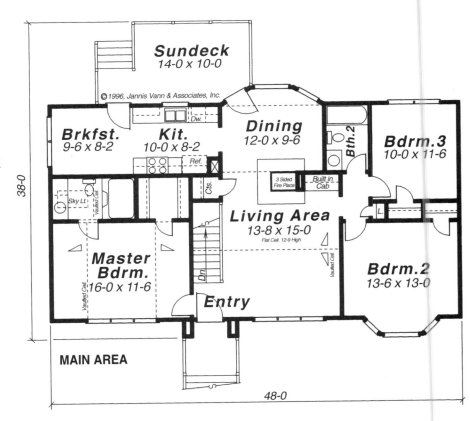

© 1996, Jannis Vann & Associates, Inc.

Sundeck
14-0 x 10-0

Brkfst.
9-6 x 8-2

Kit.
10-0 x 8-2

Dining
12-0 x 9-6

Bth.2

Bdrm.3
10-0 x 11-6

Dw.

Ref.

Sky Lt.

3 Sided Fire Place

Built in Cab

Living Area
13-8 x 15-0
Flat Ceil. 12-9 High

Master Bdrm.
16-0 x 11-6

Cts.

Dn

Bdrm.2
13-6 x 13-0

Entry

38-0

48-0

MAIN AREA

To order your Blueprints, call 1-800-235-5700

BL/ML/ZIP/RRR

Triple Tandem Garage

Price Code: C

■ This plan features:

— Three bedrooms

— Two full baths

■ A large Foyer leads to the bright and spacious Living Room

■ The open Kitchen has a central work island

■ The handy Laundry Room has a Pantry and Garage access

■ The Master Suite has a bay window in the Sitting Area, French doors and a private Master Bath

■ A triple tandem garage with space for a third car, boat or just extra space

MAIN FLOOR — 1,761 SQ. FT.
BASEMENT — 1,761 SQ. FT.
GARAGE — 658 SQ. FT.

TOTAL LIVING AREA:
1,761 SQ. FT.

MAIN FLOOR

MASTER BEDROOM
13'8"x16'4"

LIVING ROOM
15'6"x18'4"

NOOK
10'x11'9"

KITCHEN
10'6"x11'9"

11'x20'

FOYER

DINING ROOM
11'6"x12'4"

3 CAR GARAGE
22'x22'

BEDROOM #2
12'4"x11'9"

BEDROOM #3
13'x10'9"

BL

A Stylish, Open Concept Home

Price Code: A

■ This plan features:

— Three bedrooms

— Two full baths

■ An angled Entry creates the illusion of space

■ Two columns frame the snack bar and separate the Kitchen from the Living Room

■ The Dining Area accommodates both formal and informal occasions

■ The Master Bath has a dual vanity, linen closet and whirlpool tub/shower combination

MAIN FLOOR — 1,282 SQ. FT.
GARAGE — 501 SQ. FT.

TOTAL LIVING AREA:
1,282 SQ. FT.

WIDTH 48–10

DEPTH 52–6

OPTIONAL BAY WINDOW

FP

LIN

MASTER BATH

DINING
9–8 X 9–6
10 FT CLG

LIVING ROOM
16–0 X 17–6
10 FT CLG

BEDRM 3
10–0 X 10–0

SLOPE

MASTER BEDRM
11–0 X 14–0
10 FT CLG

10 FT CLG
KITCHEN
13–4 X 9–6

ARCH

FOYER

ARCH

BATH 2

LIN

BEDRM 2
10–0 X 12–0

STORAGE

PORCH

MAIN FLOOR

GARAGE

© Larry E. Belk

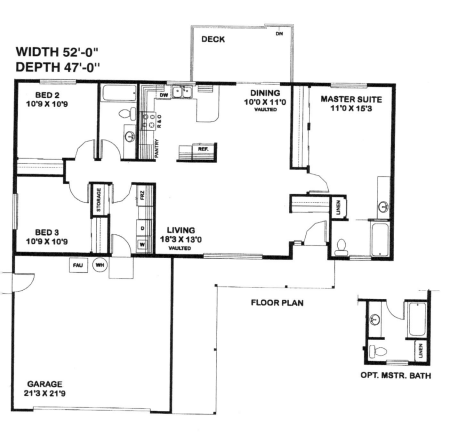

WIDTH 52'-0"
DEPTH 47'-0"

BED 2
10'9 X 10'9

DECK

DN

DINING
10'0 X 11'0
VAULTED

MASTER SUITE
11'0 X 15'3

DW

PANTRY

R & O

REF.

STORAGE

FRZ

LINEN

BED 3
10'9 X 10'9

D

W

LIVING
18'3 X 13'0
VAULTED

FAU

WH

FLOOR PLAN

GARAGE
21'3 X 21'9

LINEN

OPT. MSTR. BATH

BL/ML

L-Shaped Front Porch

Price Code: A

■ This plan features:

— Three bedrooms

— Two full baths

■ Attractive wood siding and a large L-shaped covered Porch

■ Generous Living Room with a vaulted ceiling

■ Large two-car Garage with access through Utility Room

■ Kitchen highlighted by a built-in Pantry and a garden window

■ Vaulted ceiling adds volume to the Dining Room

■ Master Suite in isolated location enhanced by abundant closet space, separate vanity and linen storage

MAIN FLOOR — 1,280 SQ. FT.

TOTAL LIVING AREA:
1,280 SQ. FT.

Making the Most of Living Spaces

Price Code: C

- This plan features:
— Four bedrooms
— Two full baths
- The L-shaped Living/Dining Areas create a private nook for quiet entertaining.
- The Kitchen is surrounded by Breakfast Area and Family Room.
- The secluded Master Suite comes with a soaking tub and private toilet/shower space for efficiency.
- Perfect for growing families, the secondary Bedrooms are grouped around Bath and Laundry.
- A traditional, formal elevation adds stature to the home's street appeal.
- This home is designed with a slab foundation.

MAIN FLOOR — 1,906 SQ. FT.
GARAGE — 444 SQ. FT.

TOTAL LIVING AREA:
1,906 SQ. FT.

WIDTH 58'-2"
DEPTH 59'-10"

MAIN FLOOR

What A Backyard View!

Price Code: B

- This plan features:
— Three bedrooms
— Two full baths
- This magnificent home includes a wall of windows in the back and two covered Porches.
- A three-car Garage provides all the storage you need for the tools to maintain your estate.
- Enjoy family meals in the vaulted-ceiling Dining Room.
- Efficiency and style mark the Kitchen and Breakfast Area.
- This home was designed with a slab, crawlspace or basement foundation options.

MAIN FLOOR — 1,721 SQ. FT
GARAGE — 626 SQ. FT.

TOTAL LIVING AREA:
1,906 SQ. FT.

To order your Blueprints, call 1-800-235-5700

tyle and Convenience

Price Code: A

This plan features:

Three bedrooms

Two full and one half baths

Vaulted ceiling in Foyer continues into Family Room which is highlighted by a fireplace

Formal Dining Room extents Family Room and adjoins the Kitchen

Kitchen has a pantry, a pass-thru to Family Room and Breakfast Area

A decorative tray ceiling, a lavish Bath and a walk-in closet accent the Master Suite

An optional basement or crawl space foundation — please specify when ordering

AIN FLOOR — 1,373 SQ. FT.

SEMENT — 1,386 SQ. FT.

TOTAL LIVING AREA:
1,373 SQ. FT.

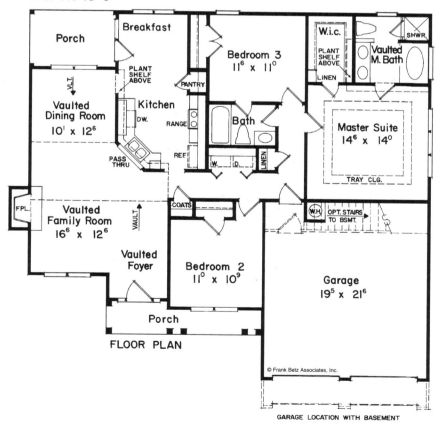

WIDTH 50'4"
DEPTH 45'-0"

FLOOR PLAN

© Frank Betz Associates, Inc.

GARAGE LOCATION WITH BASEMENT

To order your Blueprints, call 1-800-235-5700

BL/ZIP

Packed with Options

Price Code: D

■ This plan features:

— Three bedrooms

— Three full baths

■ The Great Room has a rear wall fireplace that is set between windows

■ Both Dining Areas are located steps away from the Kitchen

■ The Study has a sloped ceiling and a front bay of windows

■ The Master Bedroom has a private Bath and a galley-like walk-in closet

■ No materials list is available for this plan

MAIN FLOOR — 2,081 SQ. FT.
GARAGE — 422 SQ. FT.

TOTAL LIVING AREA:
2,081 SQ. FT.

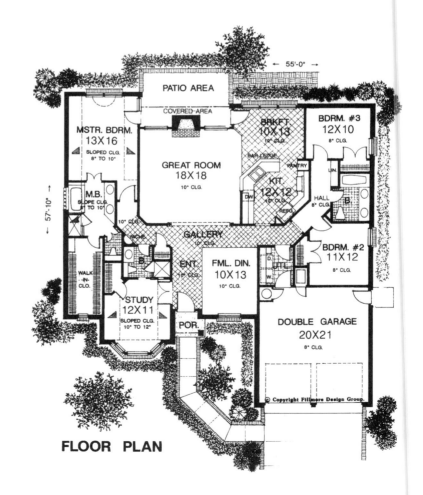

FLOOR PLAN

© Copyright Fillmore Design Group.

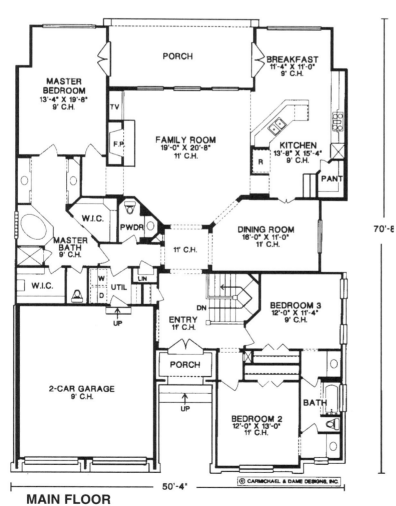

MAIN FLOOR

50'-4"

© CARMICHAEL & DAME DESIGNS, INC.

BL/ML/RRR

Classic Brick Exterior

Price Code: E

■ This plan features:

— Three bedrooms

— Two full and one half baths

■ An eleven-foot ceiling adorning the Foyer

■ Private access to the full Bath from the secondary Bedrooms

■ Central Family Room accented by a fireplace and a built in entertainment center

■ Secluded Master Suite highlighted by a lavish Master Bath

■ An angled peninsula counter/snack bar in the Kitchen extending work space

MAIN FLOOR — 2,404 SQ. FT.
GARAGE — 493 SQ. FT.

TOTAL LIVING AREA:
2,404 SQ. FT.

PLAN NO. 97151

BL

Beautiful and Functional

Price Code: D

■ This plan features:

— Three bedrooms

— Two full baths

■ Gracious, keystone arch entry opens to formal Dining Room and Great Room beyond

■ Spacious Great Room features fireplace surrounded by windows topped by a cathedral ceiling

■ Kitchen/Nook layout ideal for busy household with easy access to Deck, Dining Room, Laundry and Garage

■ No materials list is available for this plan

MAIN FLOOR — 2,007 SQ. FT.
GARAGE — 748 SQ. FT.

TOTAL LIVING AREA:
2,007 SQ. FT.

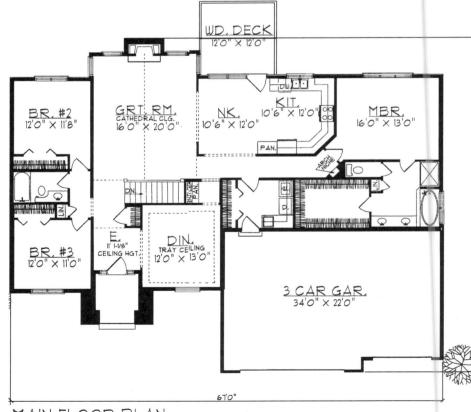

MAIN FLOOR PLAN

BL

Features of a Larger Home

Price Code: B

■ This plan features:
— Three bedrooms
— Two full baths

■ The Master Suite is topped in a tray ceiling and includes a walk-in closet and a vaulted ceiling over the Master Bath.

■ The Kitchen flows easily into the Breakfast Area and the formal Dining Room is just a few short steps away.

■ A French door leads to the Patio area, expanding living space to the outdoors.

■ The Family Room is at the heart of the home and is open to the Dining Room for ease in entertaining and is enhanced by a high ceiling and a fireplace.

MAIN FLOOR — 1,531 SQ. FT.
BASEMENT — 1,527 SQ. FT.
GARAGE — 441 SQ. FT.

TOTAL LIVING AREA:
1,531 SQ. FT.

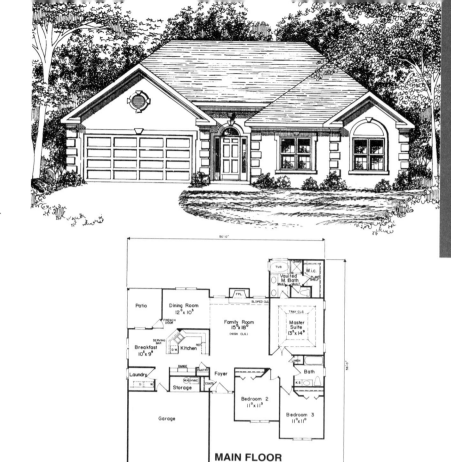

MAIN FLOOR

BL

Open Spaces

Price Code: A

■ This plan features:
— Three bedrooms
— Two full baths

■ An open layout between the Living Room, Dining Room and Kitchen creating and illusion of spaciousness

■ A peninsula counter/eating bar for a quick meal separating the Kitchen from the Living Room

■ A vaulted ceiling in the Living Room adding volume to the room

■ A Laundry center located near the bedrooms for efficiency

■ No material list available for this plan

MAIN FLOOR — 1,120 SQ. FT.
GARAGE — 288 SQ. FT.

TOTAL LIVING AREA:
1,120 SQ. FT.

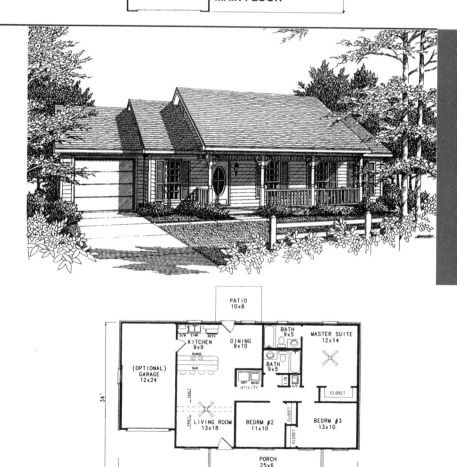

MAIN FLOOR

To order your Blueprints, call 1-800-235-5700

BL

Single-Level Three Bedroom

Price Code: A

- This plan features:
— Three bedrooms
— Two full baths
- A great first impression is given from the moment you step into the Foyer which is topped by a vaulted ceiling.
- The Family Room has a corner fireplace and is also topped by a vaulted ceiling.
- The Kitchen flows into the Breakfast Room and features a convenient pass through to the Family Room.
- A convenient Laundry center is located in the Breakfast Room.
- The Master Suite includes a tray ceiling over the Bedroom and a vaulted ceiling over the Bath.

MAIN FLOOR — 1,169 SQ. FT.
BASEMENT — 1,194 SQ. FT.
GARAGE — 400 SQ. FT.

TOTAL LIVING AREA:
1,169 SQ. FT.

FLOOR PLAN

©1998 Donald A. Gardner, Inc.

BL/ML

Warmth and Charm

Price Code: C

- This plan features:
— Three bedrooms
— Two full baths
- Multiple gables, an arched picture window, and a gracious front Porch with a metal roof lavish warmth and charm on this updated Country farmhouse.
- Upstairs, one Bedroom has its own Bath while two more Bedrooms and a Bonus Room share a spacious hall Bath.

MAIN FLOOR — 1,460 SQ. FT.
GARAGE & STORAGE — 490 SQ. FT.

TOTAL LIVING AREA:
2,363 SQ. FT.

FIRST FLOOR PLAN

© 1998 Donald A Gardner, Inc.

To order your Blueprints, call 1-800-235-5700

ML/RRR

zy *Front Porch*

Price Code: A

his plan features:

- ree bedrooms
- o full baths
- rrific Great Room with twelve-foot ceiling d fireplace flanked by windows
- tchen/Breakfast Room with ample counter ace and storage
- undry Room doubles as a Mudroom
- e Master bedroom includes a private, double nity Bath and a walk-in closet
- e two additional Bedrooms are in close prox- ity to the full Bath in the hall.

N FLOOR — 1,433 SQ. FT.

AGE — 504 SQ. FT.

TOTAL LIVING AREA:
1,433 SQ. FT.

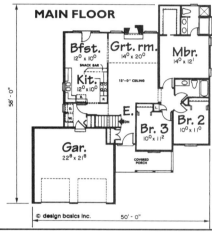

MAIN FLOOR

© design basics inc.

ML

ur *Bedroom*

Price Code: B

is plan features:

- ur bedrooms
- o full baths
- vaulted ceiling of the Foyer with convenient at closet
- vaulted ceiling crowning the Family Room th a French door to the rear yard and a cozy eplace
- ficient Kitchen located between the formal and ormal dining areas for ease in serving
- ay ceiling topping the Master Bedroom and a ulted ceiling crowning the Master Bath
- condary Bedrooms located near the full Bath the hall with a window seat accenting one droom and a vaulted ceiling highlighting other
- optional basement, slab or crawl space foun- tion — please specify when ordering

N FLOOR — 1,688 SQ. FT.

EMENT — 1,702 SQ. FT.

AGE — 402 SQ. FT.

TOTAL LIVING AREA:
1,688 SQ. FT.

MAIN FLOOR

© Donald A. Gardner Architects, Inc.

B. NATHAN

BL/ML

Stunning Stone and Stucco

Price Code: E

■ This plan features:

— Three bedrooms

— Two full baths

■ Expansive Great Room offers a cathedral ceiling, fireplace nestled between book shelves and access to Deck, Dining Area and screen Porch

■ Efficient Kitchen with curved serving counter and Pantry easily accesses Breakfast and Dining Areas, and Utility and Garage

■ Comfortable Master Bedroom suite with Deck access, walk-in closet and plush Bath

MAIN FLOOR — 1,933 SQ. FT.
GARAGE — 526 SQ. FT.

TOTAL LIVING AREA:
1,933 SQ. FT.

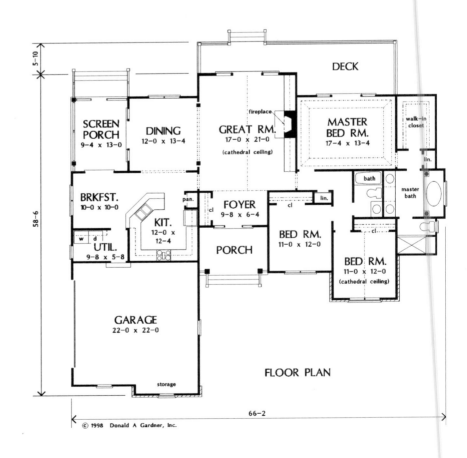

FLOOR PLAN

© 1998 Donald A Gardner, Inc.

240

To order your Blueprints, call 1-800-235-5700

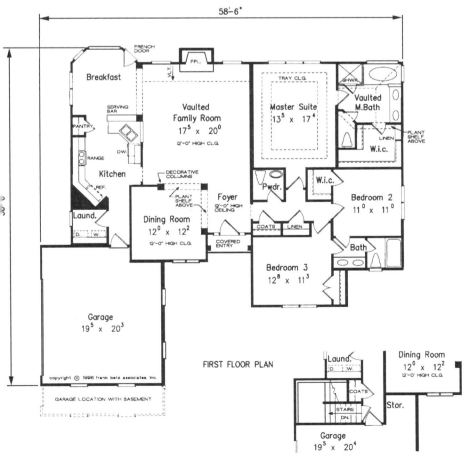

FIRST FLOOR PLAN

OPT. BASEMENT STAIR LOCATION

BL

Attention to Detail

Price Code: C

■ This plan features:
— Three bedrooms
— Two full and one half baths

■ A twelve-foot ceiling, large window and decorative columns highlight the elegant Dining Room

■ Vaulted ceiling tops the Family Room, which is further accented by a fireplace

■ An optional basement or crawl space foundation — please specify when ordering

■ No material list is available for this plan

FIRST FLOOR — 1,861 SQ. FT.
GARAGE — 450 SQ. FT.
BASEMENT — 1,898 SQ. FT.

TOTAL LIVING AREA:
1,861 SQ. FT.

PLAN NO. 97620

BL

Eye-Catching Dining Room

Price Code: A

- This plan features:
— Three bedrooms
— Two full baths
- Two-story window allows for streaming sunlight to enter the Dining Room
- Crowning vaulted ceiling over the Great Room
- Tray ceiling highlighting the Master Bedroom and a vaulted ceiling over the Master Bath
- French door from the Breakfast Room leading to the rear yard
- Laundry Center located at the end of the Breakfast Room
- An optional basement or crawl space foundation — please specify when ordering

MAIN FLOOR — 1,271 SQ. FT.
GARAGE — 400 SQ. FT.

TOTAL LIVING AREA:
1,271 SQ. FT.

56'-6"
33'-10"

FLOOR PLAN

Master Suite 11¹⁰ x 14⁰ — TRAY CLG.
Vaulted M. Bath
PLANT SHELF ABOVE
W.i.c.
LINEN
Bath
LIN.
Vaulted Great Room 15⁶ x 15⁶
RADIUS WINDOW — FPL. — RADIUS WINDOW
Kitchen
DW
RANGE — REF
W.H.
FRENCH DOOR
W D
Breakfast
PANTRY
OPT. STAIRS TO BASEMENT
PLANT SHELF ABOVE
Foyer (13'-0" HIGH CLG.)
COATS
Bedroom 3 10² x 10¹⁰
Dining Room 10³ x 12⁰ (13'-0" HIGH CLG.)
Bedroom 2 10⁰ x 11⁰
Garage
copyright © 1993 frank betz associates, inc.

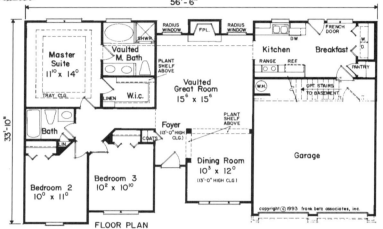

PLAN NO. 93049

BL/ML

Dignified Traditional

Price Code: C

- This plan features:
— Four bedrooms
— Two full and one half baths
- Dramatic columns defining the elegant Dining Room and framing the entrance to the large, spacious Great Room
- A breakfast bar and work island in the gourmet Kitchen which also includes an abundance of counter and cabinet space
- All bedrooms conveniently grouped at the opposite side of the home
- A Master Suite with an enormous walk-in closet and a luxuriant Master Bath
- Bedrooms two and three also have walk-in closets and share a full bath with a double vanity

MAIN FLOOR — 2,292 SQ. FT.
GARAGE — 526 SQ. FT.

TOTAL LIVING AREA:
2,292 SQ. FT.

WIDTH 80-7
DEPTH 50-6

MSTR BATH
MASTER BEDROOM 14-0 X 15-0 10 FT CLG
BEDROOM 4 /STUDY 11-4 X 10-0 8 FT CLG
PWDR
BATH 2
FOYER 10 FT CLG
GREAT ROOM 16-10 X 16-10 12 FT CLG
FP
BRKFST RM 12-6 X 10-6 10 FT CLG
KITCHEN 12-6 X 16-10
UTILITY 11-8 X 5-6
DINING ROOM 14-8 X 13-4 12 FT CLG
BEDROOM 3 12-4 X 11-8 8 FT CLG
BEDROOM 2 11-2 X 12-2 8 FT CLG
PORCH
GARAGE
STORAGE

To order your Blueprints, call 1-800-235-5700

/ML

Decorative Ceiling Treatments

Price Code: C

- This plan features:
  — Three bedrooms
  — Two full baths
- Covered front Porch creating curb appeal and extending living space
- A tray ceiling crowning the Great Room which includes a corner fireplace and access to the rear Deck
- Dining Area open to the Kitchen with angled snack bar for meals on the go
- Split Bedroom floor plan assuring the Master Suite of privacy.
- A tray ceiling topping the Master Bedroom which has direct access to a whirlpool Master Bath

MAIN FLOOR — 1765 SQ. FT.
GARAGE — 440 SQ. FT.

TOTAL LIVING AREA:
1,765 SQ. FT.

MAIN FLOOR

Eye-Catching Elevation

Price Code: D

- This plan features:
  — Four bedrooms
  — Two full baths
- Expansive Great Room with a vaulted ceiling and a fireplace with windows to either side
- Arched openings accented by columns accessing the formal Dining Room
- Efficient Kitchen with built-in Pantry, serving bar and double sinks
- Tray ceiling topping the Master Bedroom and a vaulted ceiling over the luxurious Master Bath
- Super walk-in closet in Master Suite with a plant shelf
- No materials list is available for this plan

MAIN FLOOR — 2,032 SQ. FT.
BASEMENT — 1,471 SQ. FT.
GARAGE — 561 SQ. FT.

TOTAL LIVING AREA:
2,032 SQ. FT.

FLOOR PLAN

BL/ML

Stone and Siding

Price Code: B

■ This plan features:

— Three bedrooms

— Two full baths

■ An arched opening with decorative columns

■ Ample cabinet and counter space with a built-in Pantry and serving bar in the Kitchen

■ French door to the outdoors or an optional bay window in the Breakfast Room

■ A vaulted ceiling crowning the Great Room, highlighted by a fireplace

■ Master Suite has a tray ceiling and a plush Master Bath

MAIN FLOOR — 1,571 SQ. FT.
BONUS — 334 SQ. FT.
BASEMENT — 1,642 SQ. FT.
GARAGE — 483 SQ. FT.

TOTAL LIVING AREA:
1,517 SQ. FT.

MAIN FLOOR

OPT. BONUS ROOM PLAN

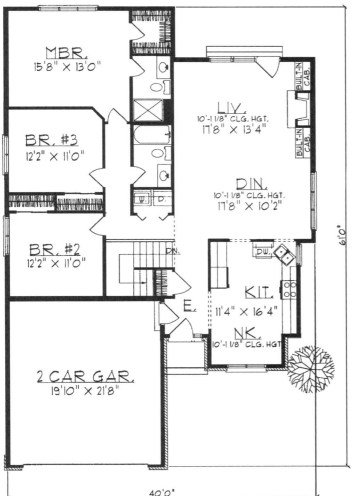

MAIN FLOOR

MBR.
15'8" × 13'0"

BR. #3
12'2" × 11'0"

BR. #2
12'2" × 11'0"

2 CAR GAR.
19'10" × 21'8"

LIV.
10'-1 1/8" CLG. HGT.
17'8" × 13'4"

DIN.
10'-1 1/8" CLG. HGT.
17'8" × 10'2"

KIT.
11'4" × 16'4"

NK.
10'-1 1/8" CLG. HGT.

BUILT-IN CAB.

40'0"

61'0"

BL

Cute Starter Home

Price Code: B

■ This plan features:

— Three bedrooms

— Two full baths

■ Spacious Living/Dining room allows comfortable gatherings with multiple windows and outdoor access

■ Open Kitchen/Nook easily accesses Dining area, Laundry closet and Garage

■ Corner Master Bedroom boasts full view of rear yard, walk-in closet and private Bath

■ No materials list is available for this plan

MAIN FLOOR — 1,557 SQ. FT.
BASEMENT — 1,557 SQ. FT.
GARAGE — 400 SQ. FT.

TOTAL LIVING AREA:
1,557 SQ. FT.

BL

Outstanding Arched Window

Price Code: E

■ This plan features:

— Three bedrooms

— Two full and one half baths

■ Expansive Family Room accented by a fireplace and active dormer with radius window

■ Luxurious Master Suite highlighted by a tray ceiling, private Sitting Room and Master Bath

■ Efficient Kitchen including double oven and work island

■ An optional basement, crawl space or slab foundation — please specify when ordering

■ No materials list is available for this plan

MAIN FLOOR — 2,322 SQ. FT.
BASEMENT — 2,322 SQ. FT.
GARAGE — 453 SQ. FT.

TOTAL LIVING AREA:
2,322 SQ. FT.

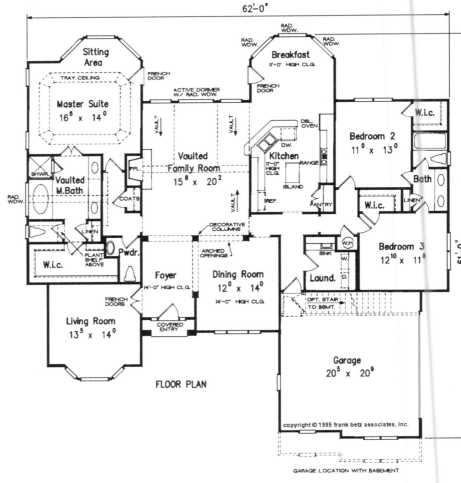

FLOOR PLAN

copyright © 1995 frank betz associates, inc.

GARAGE LOCATION WITH BASEMENT

To order your Blueprints, call 1-800-235-5700

Exterior Elevations

Scaled drawings of the front, rear and sides of the home. Information pertaining to the exterior finish materials, roof pitches and exterior height dimensions.

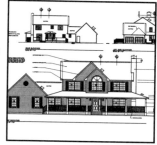

Cabinet Plans

These plans, or in some cases elevations, will detail the layout of the kitchen and bathroom cabinets at a larger scale. Available for most plans.

Typical Wall Section

This section will address insulation, roof components, and interior and exterior wall finishes. Your plans will be designed with either 2x4 or 2x6 exterior walls, but most professional contractors can easily adapt the plans to the wall thickness you require.

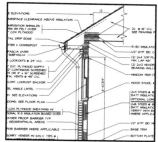

Fireplace Details

If the home you have chosen includes a fireplace, the fireplace detail will show typical methods to construct the firebox, hearth and flue chase for masonry units, or a wood frame chase for a zero-clearance unit. Available for most plans.

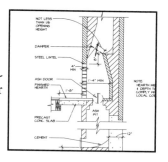

Foundation Plan

These plans will accurately dimension the footprint of your home including load bearing points and beam placement if applicable. The foundation style will vary from plan to plan.

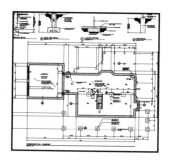

Roof Plan

The information necessary to construct the roof will be included with your home plans. Some plans will reference roof trusses, while many others contain schematic framing plans. These framing plans will indicate the lumber sizes necessary for the rafters and ridgeboards based on the designated roof loads.

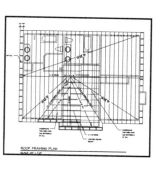

Typical Cross Section

A cut-away cross-section through the entire home shows your building contractor the exact correlation of construction components at all levels of the house. It will help to clarify the load bearing points from the roof all the way down to the basement. Available for most plans.

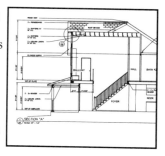

Detailed Floor Plans

The floor plans of your home accurately dimension the positioning of all walls, doors, windows, stairs and permanent fixtures. They will show you the relationship and dimensions of rooms, closets and traffic patterns. The schematic of the electrical layout may be included in the plan.

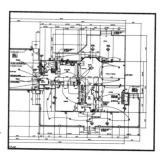

Stair Details

If stairs are an element of the design you have chosen, the plans will show the necessary information to build these, either through a stair cross section, or on the floor plans.

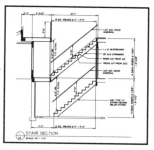

Reversed Plans Can Make Your Dream Home Just Right!

You could have exactly the home you want by flipping it end-for-end. Simply order your plans "reversed." We'll send you one full set of mirror-image plans (with the writing backwards) as a master guide for you and your builder.

The remaining sets of your order will come as shown in this book so the dimensions and specifications are easily read on the job site...but most plans in our collection come stamped "reversed" so there is no confusion.

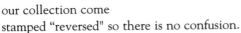
As Shown   Reversed

We can only send reversed plans with multiple-set orders. There is a $50 charge for this service.

Some plans in our collection are available in Right Reading Reverse. Right Reading Reverse plans will show your home in reverse, with the writing on the plan being readable. This easy-to-read format will save you valuable time and money. Please contact our Customer Service Department to check for Right Reading Reverse availability. There is a $135 charge for Right Reading Reverse. **RRR**

Remember To Order Your Materials List

Available at a modest additional charge, the Materials List gives the quantity, dimensions, and specifications for the major materials needed to build your home. You will get faster, more accurate bids from your contractors and building suppliers — and avoid paying for unused materials and waste. Materials Lists are available for all home plans except as otherwise indicated, but can only be ordered with a set of home plans. Due to differences in regional requirements and homeowner or builder preferences, electrical, plumbing and heating/air conditioning equipment specifications are not designed specifically for each plan. **ML**

What Garlinghouse Offers

Home Plan Blueprint Package

By purchasing a multiple set package of blueprints or a vellum from Garlinghouse, you not only receive the physical blueprint documents necessary for construction, but you are also granted a license to build one, and only one, home. You can also make simple modifications, including minor non-structural changes and material substitutions to our design, as long as these changes are made directly on the blueprints purchased from Garlinghouse and no additional copies are made.

Home Plan Vellums

By purchasing vellums for one of our home plans, you receive the same construction drawings found in the blueprints, but printed on vellum paper. Vellums can be erased and are perfect for making design changes. They are also semi-transparent making them easy to duplicate. But most importantly, the purchase of home plan vellums comes with a broader license that allows you to make changes to the design (ie, create a hand drawn or CAD derivative work), to make copies of the plan and to build one home from the plan.

License To Build Additional Homes

With the purchase of a blueprint package or vellums you automatically receive a license to build one home and only one home, respectively. If you want to build more homes than you are licensed to build through your purchase of a plan, then additional licenses may be purchased at reasonable costs from Garlinghouse. Inquire for more information.

Modify Your Favorite Design, Made Easy

#1 Modifying Your Garlinghouse Home Plan

Simple modifications to your dream home, including minor non-structural changes and material substitutions, can be made between you and your builder by marking the changes directly on your blueprints. However, if you are considering making significant changes to your chosen design, we recommend that you use the services of The Garlinghouse Design Staff. We will help take your ideas and turn them into a reality, just the way you want. Here's our procedure!

When you place your Vellum order, you may also request a free Garlinghouse Modification Kit. In this kit, you will receive a red marking pencil, furniture cut-out sheet, ruler, a self addressed mailing label and a form for specifying any additional notes or drawings that will help us understand your design ideas. Mark your desired changes directly on the Vellum drawings. NOTE: Please use only a **red pencil** to mark your desired changes on the Vellum. Then, return the red-lined Vellum set in the original box to us.

Important: Please roll the Vellums for shipping, *do not fold.*

We also offer modification estimates. We will provide you with an estimate to draft your changes based on your specific modifications before you purchase the vellums, for a $50 fee. After you receive your estimate, if you decide to have us do the changes, the $50 estimate fee will be deducted from the cost of your modifications. If, however, you choose to use a different service, the $50 estimate fee is non-refundable. (Note: Personal checks cannot be accepted for the estimate.)

Within 5 days of receipt of your plans, you will be contacted by a member of the design staff with an estimate for the design services to draw those changes. A 50% deposit is required before we begin making the actual modifications to your plans.

Once the design changes have been completed to your vellum plan, a representative will call to inform you that your modified Vellum plan is complete and will be shipped as soon as the final payment has been made. For additional information call us at 1-860-659-5667. Please refer to the Modification Pricing Guide for estimated modification costs.

#2 Reproducible Vellums for Local Modification Ease

If you decide not to use Garlinghouse for your modifications, we recommend that you follow our same procedure of purchasing Vellums. You then have the option of using the services of the original designer of the plan, a local professional designer or architect to make the modifications.

With a Vellum copy of our plans, a design professional can alter the drawings just the way you want, then you can print as many copies of the modified plans as you need to build your house. And, since you have already started with our complete detailed plans, the cost of those expensive professional services will be significantly less than starting from scratch. Refer to the price schedule for Vellum costs.

Important Exchange policy: Reproducible Vellum copies of our home plans are copyright protected and only sold under the terms of a license agreement that you will receive with your order. Should you not agree to the terms, then the Vellums may be exchanged. A 20% exchange fee will be charged. For any additional information, please call us at 1-860-659-5667.

"How to obtain a construction cost calculation based on labor rates and building material costs in your Zip Code area!"

What will your dream home cost? ZIP QUOTE has the answer!

Why? Do you wish you could quickly find out the building cost for your new home without waiting for a contractor to compile hundreds of bids? Would you like to have a benchmark to compare your contractor(s) bids against? Well, Now You Can!! with Zip-Quote Home Cost Calculator. Zip-Quote is only available for zip code areas within the United States.

How? Our Zip-Quote Home Cost Calculator will enable you to obtain the calculated building cost to construct your new home, based on labor rates and building material costs within your zip code area, without the normal delays or hassles usually associated with the bidding process. Zip-Quote can be purchased in two separate formats, an itemized or a bottom line format.

"How does Zip-Quote actually work?" When you call to order, you must choose from the options available, for your specific home, in order for us to process your order. Once we receive your Zip-Quote order, we process your specific home plan building materials list through our Home Cost Calculator which contains up-to-date rates for all residential labor trades and building material costs in your zip code area. "The result?" A calculated cost to build your dream home in your zip code area. This calculation will help you (as a consumer or a builder) evaluate your building budget.

All database information for our calculations is furnished by Marshall & Swift, L.P. For over 60 years, Marshall & Swift L.P. has been a leading provider of cost data to professionals in all aspects of the construction and remodeling industries.

Option 1 The **Itemized Zip-Quote** is a detailed building material list. Each building material list line item will separately state the labor cost, material cost and equipment cost (if applicable) for the use of that building material in the construction process. This building materials list will be summarized by the individual building categories and will have additional columns where you can enter data from your contractor's estimates for a cost comparison between the different suppliers and contractors who will actually quote you their products and services.

Option 2 The **Bottom Line Zip-Quote** is a one line summarized total cost for the home plan of your choice. This cost calculation is also based on the labor cost, material cost and equipment cost (if applicable) within your local zip code area. Bottom Line Zip-Quote is available for most plans. Please call for availability.

Cost The price of your Itemized Zip-Quote is based upon the pricing schedule of the plan you have selected, in addition to the price of the materials list. Please refer to the pricing schedule on our order form. The price of your initial Bottom Line Zip-Quote is $29.95. Each additional Bottom Line Zip-Quote ordered in conjunction with the initial order is only $14.95. Bottom Line Zip-Quote may be purchased separately and does NOT have to be purchased in conjunction with a home plan order.

FYI An Itemized Zip-Quote Home Cost Calculation can ONLY be purchased in conjunction with a Home Plan order. The Itemized Zip-Quote can not be purchased separately. If you find within 60 days of your order date that you will be unable to build this home, then you may exchange the plans and the materials list towards the price of a new set of plans (see order info pages for plan exchange policy). The Itemized Zip-Quote and the Bottom Line Zip-Quote are NOT returnable. The price of the initial Bottom Line Zip-Quote order can be credited towards the purchase of an Itemized Zip-Quote order, only if available. Additional Bottom Line Zip-Quote orders within the same order can not be credited. Please call our Customer Service Department for more information.

An Itemized Zip-Quote is available for plans where you see this symbol. **ZIP**

A Bottom-line Zip-Quote is available for all plans under 4,000 sq. ft. or where you see this symbol. **BL** Please call for current availability.

Some More Information The Itemized and Bottom Line Zip-Quotes give you approximated costs for constructing the particular house in your area. These costs are not exact and are only intended to be used as a preliminary estimate to help determine the affordability of a new home and/or as a guide to evaluate the general competitiveness of actual price quotes obtained through local suppliers and contractors. However, Zip-Quote cost figures should never be relied upon as the only source of information in either case. **Land, landscaping, sewer systems, site work, contractor overhead and profit, and other expenses are not included in our building cost figures. Excluding land and landscaping, you may incur an additional 20% to 40% in costs from the original estimate.** Garlinghouse and Marshall & Swift L.P. can not guarantee any level of data accuracy or correctness in a Zip-Quote and disclaim all liability for loss with respect to the same, in excess of the original purchase price of the Zip-Quote product. All Zip-Quote calculations are based upon the actual blueprints and do not reflect any differences or options that may be shown on the published house renderings, floor plans or photographs.

the Garlinghouse company

Order Form

BEST PLAN VALUE IN THE INDUSTRY!

Order Code No. **H1SL8**

Plan prices guaranteed until 5/02 After this date call for updated pricing

_____ foundation

____ Set(s) of blueprints for plan #_____	$_____
____ Vellum & Modification kit for plan #_____	$_____
____ Additional set(s) @ $50 each for plan #_____	$_____
____ Mirror Image Reverse @ $50 each	$_____
____ Right Reading Reverse @ $135 each	$_____
____ Materials list for plan #_____	$_____
____ Detail Plans @ $19.95 each	
❏ Construction ❏ Plumbing ❏ Electrical	$_____
____ Bottom line ZIP Quote @ $29.95 for plan #_____	$_____
____ Additional Bottom Line Zip Quote	
@ $14.95 for plan(s) #_____	$_____
Zip Code where building _____	
____ Itemized ZIP Quote for plan(s) #_____	$_____
Shipping (free standard shipping in Continental U.S.)	$_____
Subtotal	$_____
Sales Tax (CT residents add 6% sales tax) (Not required for other states)	$_____

TOTAL AMOUNT ENCLOSED $_____

Send your check, money order or credit card information to:
(No C.O.D.'s Please)

Please submit all United States & Other Nations orders to:
Garlinghouse Company
174 Oakwood Drive
Glastonbury, CT. 06033
CALL: (800) 235-5700   FAX: (860) 659-5692

Please Submit all Canadian plan orders to:
Garlinghouse Company
102 Ellis Street
Penticton, BC V2A 4L5
CALL: (800) 361-7526   FAX: (250) 493-7526

DDRESS INFORMATION:

AME: _____

TREET: _____

TY: _____

ATE: _____ ZIP: _____

YTIME PHONE: _____

MAIL ADDRESS: _____

Credit Card Information

Charge To: ❏ Visa   ❏ Mastercard

Card # | | | | | | | | | | | | | | | | |

Signature _____ Exp. _____ / _____

ment must be made in U.S. funds. Foreign Mail Orders: Certified bank checks in U.S. funds only

Privacy Statement
(please read)

Dear Valued Garlinghouse Customer,

Your privacy is extremely important to us. We'd like to take a little of your time to explain our privacy policy.

As a service to you, we would like to provide your name to companies such as the following:

- Building material manufacturers that we are affiliated with. In these cases, our affiliates would like to keep you current with their product line and specials.
- Building material retailers that would like to offer you competitive prices to help you save money.
- Financing companies that would like to offer you competitive mortgage rates.

In addition, as our valued customer, we would like to send you newsletters to assist your building experience. *We* would appreciate your feedback with a customer service survey to improve our operations.

You have total control over the use of your contact information. You can let us know exactly how you want to be contacted. Please check all boxes that apply. Thank you.

☐ Don't mail
☐ Don't call
☐ Don't email
☐ Only send Garlinghouse newsletters and customer service surveys

In closing, we hope this shows Garlinghouse's commitment to providing superior customer service and protection of your privacy. We thank-you for your time and consideration.

Sincerely,

Partner & COO   Partner & CEO

BEFORE ORDERING PLEASE READ ALL ORDERING INFORMATION

For Our USA Customers:
Order Toll Free — 1-800-235-5700
Monday-Friday 8:00 a.m. to 8:00 p.m. Eastern Time
or FAX your Credit Card order to 1-860-659-5692
All foreign residents call 1-860-659-5667

For Our Canadian Customers:
Order Toll Free — 1-800-361-7526
Monday-Friday 8:00 a.m. to 5:00 p.m. Pacific Time
or FAX your Credit Card order to 1-250-493-7526
Customer Service: 1-250-493-0942

Please have ready: 1. Your credit card number   2. The plan number   3. The order code number ⇨ **H1SL8**

Garlinghouse 2001 Blueprint Price Code Schedule

	1 Set	4 Sets	8 Sets	Vellums	ML	Itemized ZIP Quote
A	$345	$385	$435	$525	$60	$50
B	$375	$415	$465	$555	$60	$50
C	$410	$450	$500	$590	$60	$50
D	$450	$490	$540	$630	$60	$50
E	$495	$535	$585	$675	$70	$60
F	$545	$585	$635	$725	$70	$60
G	$595	$635	$685	$775	$70	$60
H	$640	$680	$730	$820	$70	$60
I	$685	$725	$775	$865	$80	$70
J	$725	$765	$815	$905	$80	$70
K	$765	$805	$855	$945	$80	$70
L	$800	$840	$890	$980	$80	$70

Shipping — (Plans 1-59999)	1-3 Sets	4-6 Sets	7+ & Vellum
Standard Delivery (UPS 2-Day)	$25.00	$30.00	$35.00
Overnight Delivery	$35.00	$40.00	$45.00

Shipping — (Plans 60000-99999)	1-3 Sets	4-6 Sets	7+ & Vellum
Ground Delivery (7-10 Days)	$15.00	$20.00	$25.00
Express Delivery (3-5 Days)	$20.00	$25.00	$30.00

International Shipping & Handling	1-3 Sets	4-6 Sets	7+ & Vellum
Regular Delivery Canada (7-10 Days)	$25.00	$30.00	$35.00
Express Delivery Canada (5-6 Days)	$40.00	$45.00	$50.00
Overseas Delivery Airmail (2-3 Weeks)	$50.00	$60.00	$65.00

Additional sets with original order $50

IMPORTANT INFORMATION TO READ BEFORE YOU PLACE YOUR ORDER

How Many Sets Of Plans Will You Need?

The Standard 8-Set Construction Package

Our experience shows that you'll speed every step of construction and avoid costly building errors by ordering enough sets to go around. Each tradesperson wants a set — the general contractor and all subcontractors; foundation, electrical, plumbing, heating/air conditioning and framers. Don't forget your lending institution, building department and, of course, a set for yourself. * Recommended For Construction *

The Minimum 4-Set Construction Package

If you're comfortable with arduous follow-up, this package can save you a few dollars by giving you the option of passing down plan sets as work progresses. You might have enough copies to go around if work goes exactly as scheduled and no plans are lost or damaged by subcontractors. But for only $ more, the 8-set package eliminates these worries. *Recommended For Bidding *

The Single Study Set

We offer this set so you can study the blueprints to plan your dream home in detail. They are stamped "study set only-not for construction", and you canno build a home from them. In pursuant to copyright laws, it is illegal to reproduce any blueprint.

Our Reorder and Exchange Policies:

If you find after your initial purchase that you require additional sets of plans you may purchase them from us at special reorder prices (please call for pricing details) provided that you reorder within 6 months of your original order date. There is a $28 reorder processing fee that is charged on all reorders. For more information on reordering plans please contact our Customer Service Department. Your plans are custom printed especially for you once you place your order. For that reason we canne accept any returns. If for some reason you find that the plan you have purchased from us does not meet your needs, then you may exchange that plan for any other plan in our collection. We allow you sixty days from your original invoice date to make an exchange. At the time of the exchange you will be charged a processing fee of 20% the total amount of your original order plus the difference in price between the plans (if applicable) plus the cost to ship the new plans to you. Call our Customer Service Department for more information. Please Note: Reproducible vellums can only be exchanged if they are unopened.

Important Shipping Information

Please refer to the shipping charts on the order form for service availability for your specific plan number. Our delivery service must have a street address or Rural Route Box number — never a post office box. (PLEASE NOTE: Supplying a P.O. Box number only will delay the shipping of your order.) Use a work address if no one is home during the day. Orders being shipped to APO or FPO must go via First Class Mail. Please include the proper postage.

For our International Customers, only Certified bank checks and money orders are accepted and must be payable in U.S. currency. For speed, we ship international orders Air Parcel Post. Please refer to the chart for the correct shipping cost.

Important Canadian Shipping Information

To our friends in Canada, we have a plan design affiliate in Penticton, BC. This relationship will help you avoid the delays and charges associated with shipments from the United States. Moreover, our affiliate is familiar with the building requirements in your community and country. We prefer payments in U.S. Curren If you, however, are sending Canadian funds please add 45% to the prices of the plans and shipping fees.

An Important Note About Building Code Requirements:

All plans are drawn to conform to one or more of the industry's major national building standards. However, due to the variety of local building regulations, you plan may need to be modified to comply with local requirements — snow loads, energy loads, seismic zones, etc. Do check them fully and consult your local building officials.

A few states require that all building plans used be drawn by an architect registered in that state. While having your plans reviewed and stamped by such an architect may be prudent, laws requiring non-conforming plans like ours to be completely redrawn forces you to unnecessarily pay very large fees. If your state ha such a law, we strongly recommend you contact your state representative to protest.

The rendering, floor plans, and technical information contained within this publication are not guaranteed to be totally accurate. Consequently, no information from this publication should be used either as a guide to constructing a home or for estimating the cost of building a home. Complete blueprints must be purchase for such purposes.

Index

Option Key

| BL | Bottom-line Zip Quote | ML | Materials List Available | ZIP | Itemized Zip Quote | RRR | Right Reading Reverse | DUP | Duplex Plan |

Plan	Pg.	Price	Option	Plan	Pg.	Price	Option	Plan	Pg.	Price	Option	Plan	Pg.	Price	Option	Plan	Pg.	Price	Option
9850	60	E	BL/ML/ZIP/RRR	90689	66	A	BL/ML	94986	48	B	BL/ML	98004	158	D	BL/ML/RRR	99802	69	D	BL/ML/ZIP/RRR
10507	52	D	BL/ML/ZIP	90865	190	A	BL/ML	96405	6	E	BL/ML/RRR	98007	163	G	BL/ML/RRR	99803	2	E	BL/ML/ZIP/RRR
10674	59	B	BL/ML/ZIP	90990	227	A	BL/ML	96413	26	G	BL/ML/ZIP/RRR	98008	138	E	BL/ML/RRR	99804	76	E	BL/ML/ZIP/RRR
10760	89	B	BL/ML/ZIP/RRR	91107	198	A	BL	96417	108	D	BL/ML/ZIP/RRR	98009	189	E	BL/ML/RRR	99805	8	E	BL/ML/ZIP/RRR
10839	4	B	BL/ML/ZIP/RRR	91346	67	D	BL/ML/RRR	96418	102	C	BL/ML/ZIP/RRR	98010	157	L	BL/ML/RRR	99806	82	C	BL/ML/RRR
20002	46	A	BL/ML	91797	106	A	BL/ML	96420	13	D	BL/ML/RRR	98011	186	F	BL/ML/RRR	99807	27	E	BL/ML/ZIP/RRR
20100	1	B	BL/ML/ZIP/RRR	91807	117	A	BL/ML	96421	223	F	BL/ML/RRR	98024	207	G	BL/ML/RRR	99808	12	E	BL/ML/ZIP/RRR
20161	28	A	BL/ML/ZIP/RRR	92156	38	F	BL/ML	96435	105	H	BL/ML/RRR	98026	160	C	BL/ML/RRR	99809	98	C	BL/ML/ZIP/RRR
20164	65	A	BL/ML/ZIP/RRR	92220	107	C	BL/ML/ZIP	96458	109	D	BL/ML/RRR	98027	185	D	BL/ML/RRR	99810	126	D	BL/ML/ZIP/RRR
20198	19	C	BL/ML/ZIP/RRR	92238	91	B	BL/ML	96463	110	D	BL/ML/RRR	98029	173	C	BL/ML/RRR	99811	115	D	BL/ML/ZIP/RRR
20220	93	B	BL/ML/ZIP	92240	151	F	BL	96468	30	E	BL/ML/RRR	98034	179	E	BL/RRR	99812	131	C	BL/ML/ZIP/RRR
22004	58	D	BL/ML/ZIP	92243	44	G	BL	96483	111	F	BL/ML/RRR	98076	45	G	BL/ML	99813	21	E	BL/ML/RRR
24304	34	A	BL/ML	92247	204	D	BL	96484	128	C	BL/ML/ZIP/RRR	98082	40	F	BL/ML	99815	156	E	BL/ML/ZIP/RRR
24700	24	A	BL/ML/ZIP	92265	153	K	BL	96488	17	D	BL/ML/RRR	98083	118	D	BL/ML	99826	172	C	BL/ML/ZIP/RRR
24701	22	B	BL/ML/ZIP	92273	184	I	BL/ZIP	96493	200	E	BL/ML/RRR	98095	170	F	BL/ML	99827	18	E	BL/ML/RRR
24708	29	B	BL/ML/ZIP	92275	164	F	BL	96496	77	G	BL/ML/RRR	98096	238	C	BL/ML	99830	162	C	BL/ML/ZIP/RRR
24714	135	C	BL/ML/ZIP	92404	136	E	BL/ML	96503	214	E	BL/ML	98097	240	E	BL/ML	99831	175	D	BL/ML/RRR
24717	168	B	BL/ML/ZIP	92430	143	A	BL	96504	177	D	BL/ML	98100	89	E	BL/ML	99835	194	D	BL/ML/RRR
24718	83	A	BL/ML/ZIP	92431	137	A	BL/ML	96505	75	D	BL/ML/ZIP	98108	36	I	BL/ML	99838	23	F	BL/ML/ZIP/RRR
24721	152	B	BL/ML/ZIP	92434	132	B	BL/ML	96506	33	B	BL/ML/ZIP	98128	62	E	BL/ML	99844	10	D	BL/ML/RRR
34003	166	A	BL/ML/ZIP/RRR	92501	57	F	BL/ML	96509	56	A	BL/ML	98146	103	D	BL/ML	99845	31	E	BL/ML/ZIP/RRR
34011	71	B	BL/ML/ZIP/RRR	92502	20	A	BL/ML	96511	202	A	BL/ML	98233	159	E	BL	99856	32	C	BL/ML/RRR
34029	178	B	BL/ML/ZIP/RRR	92523	79	A	BL/ML	96513	70	B	BL/ML/ZIP	98408	210	C	BL/ML/ZIP	99860	32	C	BL/ML/ZIP/RRR
34031	103	C	BL/ML/ZIP	92527	112	B	BL/ML	96519	113	A	BL	98411	233	A	BL/ML	99864	206	C	BL/ML/RRR
34043	15	B	BL/ML/ZIP/RRR	92528	149	A	BL/ML	96522	87	B	BL/ML	98415	35	A	BL/ML/RRR	99871	141	D	BL/ML/ZIP/RRR
34054	53	A	BL/ML/ZIP/RRR	92546	68	E	BL/ML	96525	85	C	BL/ML	98421	74	D	BL/ML	99878	28	E	BL/ML/ZIP/RRR
34150	50	A	BL/ML/ZIP/RRR	92550	29	F	BL/ML	96529	119	D	BL/ML/ZIP	98423	54	B	BL/ML/ZIP				
34154	127	A	BL/ML/ZIP/RRR	92552	146	C	BL/ML	96531	176	E	BL/ML	98424	92	D	BL/ML				
34353	77	A	BL/ML/ZIP	92557	99	A	BL/ML	96534	243	C	BL/ML	98425	72	C	BL/ML				
34976	41	C	BL/ML/ZIP/RRR	92625	100	B	BL/ML	96538	237	A	BL	98426	169	F	BL/ML				
35003	43	A	BL/ML/RRR	92630	39	C	BL/ZIP	96802	195	A	BL/ML	98427	94	D	BL/ML				
63018	61	G	BL	92649	121	B	BL/ML/ZIP	96811	47	C	BL	98430	81	C	BL/ML				
63021	122	I	BL	92655	216	B	BL/ML/ZIP	96902	123	C	BL	98432	97	B	BL/ML				
63136	151	D	BL	92657	25	L	BL/ZIP	96913	129	F	BL	98434	124	A	BL/ML				
63137	140	C	BL	93021	230	A	BL	96924	181	A	BL	98441	143	B	BL				
63140	205	A	BL	93033	71	E	BL	97135	132	D	BL	98456	167	B	BL/ML				
63141	232	C	BL	93049	242	E	BL	97137	137	A	BL	98460	183	B	BL				
63142	109	C	BL	93080	45	C	BL	97151	236	D	BL	98464	187	C	BL				
63143	104	C	BL	93095	63	E	BL/ML	97152	245	B	BL	98466	88	D	BL				
63144	97	C	BL	93098	171	C	BL	97224	139	A	BL	98468	199	A	BL				
65611	129	D	BL	93133	229	C	BL/ML/ZIP/RRR	97228	41	D	BL	98469	204	A	BL				
66000	159	H	BL	93143	64	C	BL	97244	182	E	BL	98479	217	B	BL				
66009	46	L	BL	93161	218	B	BL/ML/ZIP	97246	142	E	BL	98496	237	B	BL				
66013	118	I	BL	93165	125	A	BL	97253	84	C	BL	98497	238	A	BL				
69014	232	B	BL/ML	93190	55	D	BL/ML/ZIP	97254	144	B	BL	98498	212	A	BL				
69016	207	B	BL/ML	93222	228	A	BL/ML/ZIP/RRR	97259	147	A	BL	98501	201	D	BL				
69017	208	C	BL/ML	93261	225	C	BL/ML/ZIP	97274	150	A	BL/ML	98511	191	E	BL/ZIP				
69019	220	D	BL/ML	93279	104	A	BL/ML/ZIP	97296	92	A	BL	98512	180	D	BL				
82003	208	A	BL	93416	40	A	BL	97299	62	E	BL	98513	197	I	BL/ZIP				
82011	120	B	BL	93447	78	A	BL	97443	239	A	BL/ML/RRR	98521	174	D	BL				
82026	127	A	BL	93455	85	B	BL	97446	235	E	BL/ML/RRR	98522	161	B	BL				
82033	140	B	BL	93708	219	F	BL	97600	38	A	BL	98528	193	F	BL /ZIP				
82034	195	C	BL	93722	188	D	BL	97607	209	B	BL/ML	98554	86	D	BL				
82038	203	C	BL	94116	224	B	BL/ML	97615	244	B	BL/ML	98559	234	D	BL/ZIP				
82040	205	A	BL	94219	36	G	BL	97616	241	C	BL	98569	188	G	BL				
82042	198	A	BL	94220	80	I	BL/ML	97617	239	B	BL/ML	98580	226	B	BL				
84014	165	C	BL	94242	145	G	BL/ML	97618	221	C	BL/ML	98589	182	C	BL				
90007	49	C	BL/ML	94260	171	D	BL/ML	97619	243	D	BL	98747	231	A	BL/ML				
90412	222	A	BL/ML/ZIP	94307	116	A	BL	97620	242	A	BL	98912	37	A	BL/ML/ZIP				
90423	95	C	BL/ML/ZIP	94640	42	F	BL	97621	246	E	BL	99106	165	A	BL				
90433	176	A	BL/ML	94724	220	B	BL/ML	97622	215	D	BL	99113	192	C	BL				
90441	130	C	BL/ML/ZIP	94731	203	A	BL/ML	97703	148	C	BL	99167	122	B	BL				
90454	73	D	BL/ML	94810	213	F	BL/ML	97714	16	J	BL	99174	114	C	BL/RRR				
90461	88	E	BL/ML	94827	96	B	BL/ML	97837	74	F	BL	99284	86	D	BL/ML				
90467	181	E	BL/ML	94923	134	B	BL/ML	97857	120	E	BL	99365	61	A	BL/ML				
90476	90	C	BL/ML/ZIP	94966	211	C	BL/ML/RRR	97877	93	L	BL	99487	14	C	BL/ML				
90601	133	B	BL/ML	94971	114	D	BL/ML/RRR	98000	152	C	BL/ML/RRR	99639	51	A	BL/ML/ZIP				
90682	154	A	BL/ML/ZIP	94973	101	F	BL/ML/RRR	98003	155	F	BL/ML/RRR	99721	196	I	BL				

T O P   S E L L I N G
GARAGE PLANS

Save money by Doing-It-Yourself using our Easy-To-Follow plans. Whether you intend to build your own garage or contract it out to a building professional, the Garlinghouse garage plans provide you with everything you need to price out your project and get started. Put our 90+ years of experience to work for you. Order now!!

No. 06016C $86.00
Apartment Garage With One Bedroom

- 24' x 28' Overall Dimensions
- 544 Square Foot Apartment
- 12/12 Gable Roof with Dormers
- Slab or Stem Wall Foundation Options

No. 06015C $86.00
Apartment Garage With Two Bedrooms

- 26' x 28' Overall Dimensions
- 728 Square Foot Apartment
- 4/12 Pitch Gable Roof
- Slab or Stem Wall Foundation Options

No. 06012C $54.00
30' Deep Gable &/or Eave Jumbo Garages

- 4/12 Pitch Gable Roof
- Available Options for Extra Tall Walls, Garage & Personnel Doors, Foundation, Window, & Sidings
- Package contains 4 Different Sizes
  - 30' x 28'   • 30' x 32'   • 30' x 36'   • 30' x 40'

No. 06013C $68.00
Two-Car Garage With Mudroom/Breezeway

- Attaches to Any House
- 24' x 24' Eave Entry
- Available Options for Utility Room with Bath, Mudroom, Screened-In Breezeway, Roof, Foundation, Garage & Personnel Doors, Window, & Sidings

No. 06001C $48.00

12', 14' & 16' Wide-Gable 1-Car Garages

- Available Options for Roof, Foundation, Window, Door, & Sidings
- Package contains 8 Different Sizes
- 12' x 20' Mini-Garage • 14' x 22' • 16' x 20' • 16' x 24'
- 14' x 20'   • 14' x 24' • 16' x 22' º• 16' x 26'

No. 06003C $48.00

24' Wide-Gable 2-Car Garages

- Available Options for Side Shed, Roof, Foundation, Garage & Personnel Doors, Window, & Sidings
- Package contains 5 Different Sizes
- 24' x 22'   • 24' x 24'   • 24' x 26'
- 24' x 28'   • 24' x 32'

No. 06007C $60.00

Gable 2-Car Gambrel Roof Garages

- Interior Rear Stairs to Loft Workshop
- Front Loft Cargo Door With Pulley Lift
- Available Options for Foundation, Garage & Personnel Doors, Window, & Sidings
- Package contains 5 Different Sizes
- 22' x 26' • 22' x 28' • 24' x 28' • 24' x 30' • 24' x 32'

No. 06006C $48.00

22' & 24' Deep Eave 2 & 3-Car Garages

- Can Be Built Stand-Alone or Attached to House
- Available Options for Roof, Foundation, Garage & Personnel Doors, Window, & Sidings
- Package contains 6 Different Sizes
- 22' x 28'   • 22' x 32'   • 24' x 32'
- 22' x 30'   • 24' x 30'   • 24' x 36'

No. 06002C $48.00

20' & 22' Wide-Gable 2-Car Garages

- Available Options for Roof, Foundation, Garage & Personnel Doors, Window, & Sidings
- Package contains 7 Different Sizes
- 20' x 20'   • 20' x 24'   • 22' x 22'   • 22' x 28'
- 20' x 22'   • 20' x 28'   • 22' x 24'

No. 06008C $60.00

Eave 2 & 3-Car Clerestory Roof Garages

- Interior Side Stairs to Loft Workshop
- Available Options for Engine Lift, Foundation, Garage & Personnel Doors, Window, & Sidings
- Package contains 4 Different Sizes
- 24' x 26'   • 24' x 28'   • 24' x 32'   • 24' x 36'

Order Code No: **G1SL8**

Garage Order Form

Please send me 3 complete sets of the following GARAGE PLAN BLUEPRINTS:

Item no. & description	Price
	$ _____
Additional Sets	
(@ $10.00 EACH)	$ _____
Garage Vellum	
(@ $200.00 EACH)	$ _____
Shipping Charges: UPS-$3.75, First Class-$4.50	$ _____
Subtotal:	$ _____
Resident sales tax: KS-6.15%, CT-6% (NOT REQUIRED FOR OTHER STATES)	$ _____

Total Enclosed: $ _____

My Billing Address is:

Name: _____

Address: _____

City: _____

State: _____ Zip: _____

Daytime Phone No. (_____) _____

My Shipping Address is:

Name: _____

Address: _____
(UPS will not ship to P.O. Boxes)

City: _____

State: _____ Zip: _____

For Faster Service...Charge It!
U.S. & Canada Call
1(800)235-5700

All foreign residents call 1(860)659-5667

MASTERCARD, VISA

Card # | | | | | | | | | | | | | | | | | |

Signature _____ Exp. ___/___

If paying by credit card, to avoid delays:
billing address must be as it appears on credit card statement

or FAX us at (860) 659-5692

Here's What You Get

- Three complete sets of drawings for each plan order
- Detailed step-by-step instructions with easy-to-follow diagrams on how to build your garage (not available with apartment garages)
- For each garage style, a variety of size and garage door configuration options
- Variety of roof styles and/or pitch options for most garages
- Complete materials list
- Choice between three foundation options: Monolith Slab, Concrete Stem Wall or Concrete Block Stem V
- Full framing plans, elevations and cross-sectionals f each garage size and configuration

Garage Plan Blueprints

All blueprint garage plan orders contain three comple sets of drawings with instructions and are priced as list next to the illustration. **These blueprint garage pla can not be modified.** Additional sets of plans may obtained for $10.00 each with your original order. U shipping is used unless otherwise requested. Plea include the proper amount for shipping.

Garage Plan Vellums

By purchasing vellums for one of our garage plans, y receive one vellum set of the same construction drawir found in the blueprints, but printed on vellum pap Vellums can be erased and are perfect for making des changes. They are also semi-transparent making th easy to duplicate. But most importantly, the purchase garage plan vellums comes with a broader license t allows you to make changes to the design (ie, create hand drawn or CAD derivative work), to make copies the plan and to build one garage from the plan.

the **Garlinghouse** company

Send your order to:
(With check or money order payable in U.S. funds only)

The Garlinghouse Company
174 Oakwood Drive
Glastonbury, CT 06033

No C.O.D. orders accepted; U.S. funds only. UPS will not ship to Pos Office boxes, FPO boxes, APO boxes, Alaska or Hawaii. Canadian orders must be shipped First Class.
Prices subject to change without notice.